Cultural Contexts
for Ralph Ellison's
INVISIBLE MAN

A Bedford
Documentary Companion

- Race as metaphor, blackness as metaphor
- Existential novel
- African Diaspora → "give me your tired, your poor,

Cultural Contexts
for Ralph Ellison's
INVISIBLE MAN

A Bedford
Documentary Companion

Edited with an Introduction by

Eric J. Sundquist

University of California, Los Angeles

BEDFORD/ST. MARTIN'S
Boston ◆ New York

For Bedford/St. Martin's
President and Publisher: Charles H. Christensen
General Manager and Associate Publisher: Joan E. Feinberg
Managing Editor: Elizabeth M. Schaaf
Developmental Editor: Joan E. Feinberg
Editorial Assistant: Verity Winship
Production Editor: John Amburg
Production Assistant: Karen S. Baart
Copyeditor: Nancy Bell Scott
Text Design: Cate Rickard
Cover Design: Hannus Design Associates
Cover Photographs: Sharecropper, Dorothea Lange/Library of Congress; Louis Armstrong, Michael Ochs Archives, Venice, CA; Sid Grossman, *Harlem Street Scene,* 1939 (detail), Federal Arts Project, Museum of the City of New York, NY; Statue of Booker T. Washington, Tuskegee Institute Campus, Eric J. Sundquist, 1994.

Library of Congress Catalog Card Number: 94–71035

Manufactured in the United States of America.

5   4   3
j   i   h

For information, write: Bedford/St. Martin's
75 Arlington Street, Boston, MA 02116 (617–399–4000)

ISBN: 0–312–10081–7

Acknowledgments
W. T. Andrews, from *Negro Migration During the War,* by Emmett Jay Scott (Carnegie Endowment for International Peace. Division of Economics and History. Preliminary Economic Studies of the War. Edited by David Kinley, No. 16). New York: Oxford University Press, 1920. Reprinted by permission of the Carnegie Endowment for International Peace.

Acknowledgments and copyrights are continued at the back of the book on pages 256–258, which constitute an extension of the copyright page.

Preface

Published in 1952 to great acclaim at the outset of the civil rights movement, Ralph Ellison's *Invisible Man* is a novel in which artistic achievement and historical vision are in perfect balance. The book was immediately recognized as a literary classic that transcended America's racial dilemma and yet made it undeniably central to the nation's own story. In following the development of his anonymous hero through a sequence of historical events, Ellison used the techniques of literary modernism to recapitulate the course of modern African American history.

Few novels have the range of both literary and historical reference evident in *Invisible Man*. In this companion volume, central documents of African American history contextualize the major movements that Ellison weaves into his novel. The readings themselves and the headnotes that precede them, as well as the critical introduction, bibliography, and photographs, are intended to guide readers through Ellison's imaginative reconstruction of twentieth-century black American life. Although Ellison alludes to texts and events throughout the Western cultural tradition, *Cultural Contexts* focuses on African American traditions. Not only are these foremost in Ellison's narrative allegory and the experiences of the protagonist, but recent renewed critical interest in the historical interpretation of literature makes the reconstruction of this context of special value to teachers and students alike. Keyed to events in the novel, the documents include selections by African American leaders such as Booker T. Washington, W. E. B. Du Bois, and Marcus Garvey; excerpts from writers such as Langston Hughes, Richard Wright, and Alain Locke; songs, folktales, and other examples of black vernacular culture; and readings on African American migration, black labor in the industrial North, the role of communism in African American politics, and the end of legal segregation in the United States.

The selections are intended to provide concrete points of reference for those episodes in Ellison's novel that are clearly drawn from, or meant to reflect on, historical events or institutions. The volume is divided into three general sections, the first and third of which follow in a general chronological order the plot of the novel and the division of the narrator's experiences between the rural South and the urban North. The first section, "'The Scaffolding of a Nation': The Black Belt and Beyond," traces the novel's initial grounding of modern African American culture in the history and geography of the South. The second section, "'A Heap of Signifying': Vernacular Culture," reproduces various examples of the vernacular folk culture that plays such a strong role in the novel, in this case principally songs, folktales, and narratives composed in street language. The third section, "'The City within a City': Harlem, U.S.A.," focuses on the sequence of events that defined the urban North as the new cultural and political center of black life during the first half of the twentieth century. Each headnote gives historical background and sets the context for the individual selection, including cross-references to specific scenes in the novel and a list of further readings for students who wish to explore various topics in greater detail.

Invisible Man is unlikely to be exhausted by even the most detailed list of cultural documents, and the best such documents can do for us, in any case, is to provide something of a map of the author's vision. My intent is not to reduce the novel to a single mode of interpretation or to preclude other approaches to it. Rather, I seek to demonstrate the greatness of Ellison's historical imagination—his attempt both to rewrite modern black history in the life of a single protagonist and to preserve, in an extraordinary fusion, the social and cultural history of black America for future readers of his novel.

Acknowledgments

It is a pleasure to thank Joan Feinberg and Charles Christensen for their support of this volume. I would also like to thank John Amburg, Verity Winship, Karen Baart, Diane Bernard, and Nancy Bell Scott for their assistance with various aspects of the book's production. For invaluable suggestions about the volume's contents, as well as the introduction and headnotes, I am indebted to William Andrews, David Blight, William Cain, T. Susan Chang, Cheryl Greenberg, Wahneema Lubiano, Wilson Moses, Valerie Smith, and Brook Thomas. At an early stage I had the benefit of a research grant from the Robert Penn Warren Center for the Humanities at Vanderbilt University to support the research assistance of Lisa Siefker Long.

Contents

III. "The City within a City": Harlem, U.S.A. 147

Cultural Contexts
for Ralph Ellison's
INVISIBLE MAN

A Bedford
Documentary Companion

Introduction

Invisible Man: The Novel of Segregation

Published in 1952, on the eve of the civil rights movement that at long last initiated the dismantling of legalized racial segregation in the United States, *Invisible Man* is one of those rare novels whose historical importance and artistic greatness are perfectly matched. Through the first-person narrative of his anonymous protagonist, Ralph Ellison recapitulated the course of modern African American history and produced one of the most finely crafted and innovative novels of the twentieth century. *Invisible Man* was reviewed with immediate favor in many leading magazines and newspapers, won the National Book Award, remained on the best-seller list for sixteen weeks, and has since been reissued in numerous editions around the world in more than fifteen languages. Encyclopedic in scope, yet equally attentive to the protagonist's many psychological transformations, the book was immediately recognized as a literary classic that transcended America's racial dilemma and yet made that dilemma undeniably central to the nation's own story. In tracing the development of his protagonist through a sequence of historical events — black college life in the South, an encounter with veterans of World War I, migration to Harlem, northern factory work, involvement with a left-wing political group, and the advent of a writing career — Ellison combined the self-reflexive techniques of autobiography, the vernacular resources of ethnography, and the nuanced harmonies

of poetry. The narrator's own coming of age, realized through his
relentless disillusionment with the various goals denied him in a
world of racial prejudice, also represents the modern coming of age
of black America.

Even though *Invisible Man* has been judged by the great majority
of critics and teachers to be one of the finest works of modern fiction,
the source of its greatness has remained a subject of debate. It is frequently applauded for the universal appeal of its central themes —
the quest for identity in a chaotic world; the struggle between
hypocrisy and moral idealism; the abuse of political and economic
power. *Invisible Man* can, in fact, be read and appreciated without
detailed reference to African American history, but to do so is to miss
the true and lasting importance of the book. At the moment of its appearance, just two years before the landmark desegregation case of
Brown v. *Board of Education of Topeka*, the novel's focus on its
hero's anonymity and fluctuating identity had one embracing point of
reference — the laws and social customs that divided black Americans from white. Throughout the first half of the twentieth century,
African Americans in much of the nation, certainly in the South, either were excluded from schools, public places, business establishments, military service, voting booths, hospitals, and transportation
or were afforded far inferior separate services. Despite its obvious
contradiction of democratic ideals, America's own form of racial
apartheid — "separate but equal," as the law of segregation was mis-
leadingly described in the 1896 Supreme Court ruling of *Plessy* v.
Ferguson — governed the nation's racial life to such a degree that no
better metaphor than Ellison's could have been found to describe it.
In social practice and legal standing, African Americans were *invisible*
to a majority of white Americans and denied access to many of the
economic, political, and cultural institutions that whites controlled.

Although it would take more than a decade for its promises to
begin to be made real, the Supreme Court's reversal of the law of segregation is the watershed of modern American racial history. Composed at a time when the drift toward *Brown* v. *Board of Education*
in public policy and federal law was apparent, but when the end of
segregation could hardly have been predicted with any confidence,
Invisible Man draws a significant part of its power from the fact that
it is the novel of segregation par excellence. Other modern black
works might better record the rage of a racial underclass (as do
Richard Wright's *Native Son* and Ann Petry's *The Street*), or the recovery of African ancestry (as do Alex Haley's *Roots* and Paule Mar-

shall's *Praisesong for the Widow*), or the course of an individual encounter with and triumph over racism (as do the autobiographies of
Malcolm X and Maya Angelou), or the re-creation of the legacy of
slavery (as do Toni Morrison's *Beloved* and Charles Johnson's
Middle Passage). No book, however, sums up the psychological and
cultural effects of segregation in the United States more thoroughly
than Ellison's.

Out of the immorality of segregation Ellison composed a novel
that contained the contradiction of the nation's racial history by in-
sisting that the destinies of white and black America were, and always had been, indissolubly bound to one another. If one premise of
Invisible Man is the harsh reality of racial segregation, Ellison's
matching premise is the rich and complex historical vision through
which he records the redemptive cultural life of African America.
From the opening pages of his novel through its nightmarish conclusion, Ellison explores both the meaning of black invisibility in white
America and, in counterpoint, the vital culture of African Americans
that might have been circumscribed but was far from extinguished by
segregation. By adding a vital dimension of cultural resistance to the
work of many black writers and artists, segregation may, in fact,
have augmented the influence of African American language, music,
and art on the mainstream of American cultural life, making the nation itself increasingly southern, increasingly black.

Ellison was among the black writers for whom such resistance
often took the form of satire. He created a particularly apt tableau
for his argument about the corrosive effects of segregation in the protagonist's first New York job, at the Liberty Paints factory, where
vast quantities of paint "as white as George Washington's Sunday-
go-to-meetin' wig" are turned out under government contract, one
batch destined for a "national monument." Into the seemingly pure
white paint — "If It's Optic White, It's the Right White" — is stirred
a secret black substance that may be interpreted in several different
ways. To begin with, the Liberty Paints factory is a means for Ellison
to burlesque the federal government's longstanding endorsement of
state and local segregation. In addition, the episode allows Ellison to
offer a sly commentary on racial mixing, on passing for white, and on
the pressures for assimilation created by segregation: "KEEP AMERICA
PURE WITH LIBERTY PAINTS" (*Invisible Man* 196–202, 217).* At a

---

*All parenthetical references are keyed to the books listed in the bibliography at the
back of the volume, including *Invisible Man* (New York: Vintage Books, 1982).

more abstract level, however, the episode is metaphoric evidence of a thesis he stated on many occasions and in many different forms. Through the nation's history of racial prejudice and antagonism, Ellison contended, "the Negro entered the deepest recesses of the American psyche and became crucially involved in its consciousness, subconsciousness, and conscience. He became keeper of the nation's sense of democratic achievement, and the human scale by which would be measured its painfully slow advance toward true equality" (Ellison, "Perspective of Literature" 335). In many such moments in the novel, Ellison returns to a fact invisible to most white Americans at mid-century — that black culture had played a most profound, if frequently unacknowledged, part in American political life and culture.

As a representative African American as well as a representative artist, the novel's hero is a living embodiment of the collective story he tells. His anonymity allies him with older allegorical figures such as Everyman in John Bunyon's *Pilgrim's Progress.* Yet it ties him more specifically to the potent tradition of anonymity in African American letters — to the nameless (or pseudonymous) narrators of trickster folktales or slave narratives passed on orally, eventually to be written down and published; to the unknown, and no doubt collective, composers of the great black spirituals; and to particular fictive heroes such as the anonymous narrator of James Weldon Johnson's novel *The Autobiography of an Ex-Colored Man* (1912), a light-skinned African American who renounces his black identity and passes "invisibly" into white society. *Invisible Man* thus refers by implication to the key role played by anonymity, or namelessness, throughout African American history, from the destruction of African family identities in the slave trade through the legal strictures of the twentieth century. The protagonist's own painful search for an identity illustrates the figurative point made by the black novelist William Melvin Kelley in a 1963 essay very much indebted to Ellison. To be a "Negro" in mid-twentieth century America, said Kelley, "is to be a man waking up in a hospital bed with amnesia. He asks the doctor who he is, what is his name. The doctor tells him, but the name means nothing to the man. He will take the name anyway, simply because it is better to have a name, even one which holds no meaning, than to have no name at all" (Kelley 55).

Writing at a time before black nationalists of the 1960s and later years argued for casting off the slave names of the past in favor of African names — or, as in the case of the Nation of Islam, for canceling out the master's name altogether in a signature X emblematic of a lost African identity — Ellison in effect argued that African Americans must reclaim their own names and identities by first discarding those imposed on them by whites. Such a process of self-discovery requires acts of memory galvanized by imaginative invention. As he wrote in his well-known essay "Hidden Name and Complex Fate," our names "must become our masks and our shields and the containers of all those values and traditions which we learn and/or imagine as being the meaning of our familial past" (148). In spite of the kaleidoscopic set of roles that he is required to play, though, the unnamed protagonist of *Invisible Man* reaches the end of his tale without clearly having articulated an answer to the glaring question put to him, in a scene mixing trauma and hallucination, as he lies on the operating table following his accident at the paint factory:

WHAT . . . IS . . . YOUR . . . NAME?

WHO . . . ARE . . . YOU?

"When I discover who I am," the narrator thinks, on waking up from what seems his near lobotomy and castration, "I'll be free" (*Invisible Man* 240–43).

Whether or not the protagonist ever discovers who he is, *Invisible Man* itself offers nothing less than an archaeology of African American identity. This is, in fact, the novel's outstanding paradox: readers disturbed or offended by the protagonist's vacillation and manipulation have sometimes missed the fact that the novel, in contrast, offers an abundance of figures, events, and stories that constitute a century-long allegorical record of black culture and its search for effective leadership. To paradigms of the quest narrative drawn from world literature — from the *Odyssey* and the *Aeneid* to *Don Quixote* and *Moby-Dick* — *Invisible Man* thus adds fragments, echoes, and whole passages from black public history in order to restructure the struggle for freedom and racial equality in the United States according to classic literary models.

Many readers have agreed with the reviewer of a thirtieth-anniversary edition of the novel that no American book has a greater "claim to being that mythical, unattainable dream of American literature, 'the great American novel'" (Yardley 6). Having produced in his first novel a work frequently counted among the classics of modernism, however, Ellison died in 1994 without having published a second. In-

tervening years witnessed the appearance of a number of superb short
stories and the many scintillating essays on literature, music, art, and
the racial tensions of American society collected in *Shadow and Act*
(1964) and *Going to the Territory* (1986). But one is tempted to say
that in the magnificent achievement of *Invisible Man* Ellison at once
rearranged the whole of American and African American literature
through a multidimensional act of improvisation and left himself an
unanswerable challenge. Some readers familiar with the draft materials of his long-awaited second novel have gone so far as to suggest
that the unpublished book bears the same relation to *Invisible Man*
that James Joyce's *Ulysses* does to his earlier apprentice work, *A Portrait of the Artist as a Young Man*. Whether or not Ellison had within
him a second performance to match or surpass the first, *Invisible
Man* will remain the most comprehensive exposition of America's in-
eradicable moral dilemma — its foundation in a history of slavery
and lingering racism.

Ralph Ellison in Context

It is quite possible that Ralph Ellison would have been suspicious of
this volume, whose purpose is, through a selection of documentary
materials, to provide a cultural context in which *Invisible Man* may
be studied. Although he would never have denied that the protagonist's personal story also recapitulates African American history —
even though we are required to imagine it telescoped into a much
shorter period during the 1930s — Ellison might have disputed that
any set of documents focused on African American history could be
an adequate guide to *Invisible Man*. His recurrence to the founding
documents of the United States, the Declaration of Independence and
the Constitution, might well have dictated their inclusion here; likewise, his Marxist sympathies during his literary apprenticeship in the
1930s might suggest possible documents whose argument would
focus not on race but on class. Were the aim of the volume to demonstrate Ellison's intellectual borrowings and kinships, one might also
want to consult T. S. Eliot's "Tradition and the Individual Talent,"
or Sigmund Freud's *Totem and Taboo*, or Fyodor Dostoevsky's
Notes from Underground, or Jean-Paul Sartre's *No Exit*. Ellison was
deeply read in European, American, and African American literature
and intellectual history; that his own published essays and interviews
dwelled more often on the classic writers of the Western tradition is a

measure, in part, of the era in which he was formed as an artist. Yet even though Ellison's particular debts to the American literary mainstream of Herman Melville, Mark Twain, Henry James, Ernest Hemingway, and William Faulkner were insistently reiterated, the novel itself tells a specifically black story. As the narrator remarks, "I've illuminated the blackness of my invisibility — and vice versa" (*Invisible Man* 13). The brilliance of *Invisible Man* lies in its capacity to draw power from and contribute to canonical American culture, which until recently has been typically identified as "white," while at the same time articulating so perfectly the intellectual and social complexity of black America.

Few novels have the range of literary and historical reference evident in *Invisible Man*. In emphasizing African American cultural contexts, this volume contains readings that parallel the experiences of the novel's protagonist rather than Ellison's numerous sources of literary inspiration. Both the readings themselves and the headnotes that precede them, as well as the photographs that are keyed to important episodes in the novel, are intended to offer a partial historical account of African American life from the turn of the century through World War II and to guide readers through Ellison's imaginative reconstruction of that life. Although he was skeptical of any rigid ideological or historical explanations of reality, Ellison's borrowings from African American writers and African American history leave little doubt that he intended to illuminate the "blackness" of America from every conceivable angle of vision.

The novel also loosely illuminates the story of Ellison's life — less as autobiography per se than as a representative artistic life. Born in Oklahoma City in 1914 and named for Ralph Waldo Emerson, the great American essayist, Ralph Waldo Ellison graduated from Frederick Douglass High School. Between Emerson, a prime exponent of liberal individualism, and Douglass, the leading black abolitionist, one might locate the twin inspirations for Ellison's future intellectual life. In 1933 he entered Tuskegee Institute, the famous black college in Alabama founded by Booker T. Washington, to study classical music, although he had equal skill as a jazz and blues trumpet player. After three years of college, he went to New York in search of summer work; failing to earn sufficient money, he decided not to return to school in the fall but rather to pursue a career first in music (he barely missed an audition with Duke Ellington after the famous band-leader had to cancel) and then in sculpture (he studied with the

prominent African American artist Richmond Barthé for a year),
both of which failed to materialize. Working at various odd jobs, Ellison became acquainted with Langston Hughes, Richard Wright, and
other writers struggling to earn a living during the Great Depression.
Under Wright's close mentorship, and swayed by the brutal natural-
ism evident in Wright's collection of stories *Uncle Tom's Children*
(1938) and landmark novel *Native Son* (1940), Ellison began writing
short reviews and stories in 1937 for *New Masses* and other left-wing
magazines. From 1938 to 1942 he worked on the Federal Writers'
Project, a New Deal program that employed writers during the depression to write local histories and city guides, record urban and
rural folklore, and compile anthologies of oral narratives. By 1942,
he was editing the short-lived *Negro Quarterly* with Angelo Herndon, a black activist who had become the focus of a Communist
Party legal campaign when he was sentenced to death in Georgia for
labor organizing in the early 1930s (the fabricated charge, derived
from nineteenth-century slave codes, was "inciting insurrection").

Despite his sympathy with the goals of the Communist Party, however, Ellison never became an official member, and by the early
1940s he had begun to mark his intellectual distance from those
thinkers and writers who, in his view, sacrificed creativity to narrow
ideology. After serving in the merchant marine for two years during
World War II, Ellison won a Rosenwald Fellowship, which allowed
him time to work without interruption on shorter fiction, essays, and
the manuscript of *Invisible Man*, the opening chapter of which was
published as a short story in 1947. Following the novel's extraordinary success, Ellison dedicated himself to writing and lecturing. During the 1950s and 1960s he held brief teaching positions at Bard College, Rutgers University, and the University of Chicago; in 1970 he
was named Albert Schweitzer Professor of Humanities at New York
University. Among his numerous honors were election to the American Academy of Arts and Letters and, in 1969, receipt of the Medal
of Freedom, the highest civilian honor bestowed by the U.S. government. Ellison published a number of short excerpts from a long work
of fiction in progress and gained a deserved reputation as one of the
most distinguished essayists in American literary history; but his
long-awaited second novel, one draft of which was destroyed in a
fire, remained unpublished at the time of his death, as though his
own professional destiny and that of his protagonist were still bound
closely together.

The arc of the protagonist's life in the novel from high school graduation through the foreshadowing of his writing career follows that of Ellison to some degree, yet he is at best an alter ego, a persona, of Ralph Ellison, not an autobiographical double. More than that, the novel's protagonist is the persona of his age. Arriving in Harlem for the first time in 1936, Ellison too might well have felt that he had found "not a city of realities, but of dreams" (*Invisible Man* 159). Within the previous generation, Harlem had become the national center of African American culture and witnessed one of the greatest explosions of literary and artistic creativity in American history. Known as the Harlem Renaissance or the New Negro Renaissance, this flowering of black culture resulted in part from the combination of a large-scale migration of African Americans to the urban North and the post–World War I prosperity of the 1920s. By the time Ellison arrived, however, the so-called Jazz Age was over. The crash of the stock market in 1929 brought an end to much artistic activity in Harlem, especially to the degree that it had resulted from white patronage; and the depression hit Harlem quite hard, leading to massive unemployment, evictions, and heightened racial discrimination that sparked civil uprising and violence (characterized at the time as "riots") in 1935 and again in 1943.

As the selections in this volume indicate, the period of the 1930s through the 1940s was a time of great hardship and dimming dreams in Harlem. The hope aroused in the 1920s by the civic and religious appeal of the Jamaican black nationalist Marcus Garvey had been undermined by Garvey's deportation on charges of mail fraud. The concentration of extraordinary literary talent that had defined Harlem in the previous decade, including figures such as Hughes, Countee Cullen, Jessie Fauset, and Claude McKay, was dispersed by the depression. Some writers went to Europe, some to Russia, and some simply left Harlem. But it was also a period of exceptional advances in public art and documentary history, largely funded through depression-era federal programs. Significant African American fiction also continued to appear — Arna Bontemps's *Black Thunder* in 1936, Zora Neale Hurston's *Their Eyes Were Watching God* in 1937, Wright's *Uncle Tom's Children* in 1938 — and the modern history of Harlem itself began to be told in works such as James Weldon Johnson's *Black Manhattan* (1930), McKay's *Harlem: Negro Metropolis* (1940), and Roi Ottley's *New World A-Coming* (1943). Likewise, the painting of Romare Bearden and Jacob Lawrence flourished. Clubs and theaters, first the Lafayette and then the Apollo, remained showcases for the music of Cab Calloway, Duke Ellington, Billie Holiday, Count Basie, and others who led the way toward the bebop revolution of the early 1940s, which found Ellison regularly listening to the sessions of Charlie Parker and Dizzy Gillespie at the famous jazz club Minton's. There one could hear, as Ellison recalled in a passage with implications for his own art, "a continuing symposium on jazz, a summation of all the styles, personal and traditional . . . its resources of technique, ideas, harmonic structure, melodic phrasing and rhythmical possibilities explored more thoroughly than was ever possible before" (Ellison, "The Golden Age, Time Past" 210).

The action of *Invisible Man* appears to stop short of World War II, but the narrator's meditations in his underground cellar must be imagined to include this period, which served in part to crystallize the search for significant advances in black civil rights and economic opportunity. The campaign for what was called the "Double V" — victory abroad in the military, and victory at home against racism and discrimination — became a focal point for political organizing and a theme in many books and essays aimed at the overthrow of segregation. At the same time, legal victories that paved the way for *Brown* v. *Board of Education* were achieved one after another in the 1930s and 1940s, largely through the integrationist efforts of the National Association for the Advancement of Colored People (NAACP); World War II and its immediate aftermath produced an extensive national reexamination of the role of American democracy both abroad and within the United States; and the desegregation of the armed forces in 1948 ushered in a new age in the federal government's willingness to break down the barriers of segregation. In spirit and range of reference, *Invisible Man* encompasses this whole period of African American life, with Harlem at its center, as a microcosm of America itself. The novel's internal chronology might be framed by Alain Locke's famous anthology *The New Negro* (1925) at one end and Rayford Logan's World War II–era collection of political essays, *What the Negro Wants* (1944), at the other, by the world of Marcus Garvey and the same hipster's world frequented by "Detroit Red," a numbers runner and small-time drug dealer who, when he had later become better known as Malcolm X, renounced his days of conked hair and stylish zoot suits as a racist delusion.

The Groove of History:
Ellison and His Critics

Ellison's own training as a musician, as well as his several unsurpassed essays on jazz and the blues, has frequently provided readers a key to the stylistic virtuosity and improvisatory development of character and idea in *Invisible Man*. "Jazz, like the country which gave it birth," he wrote in a 1958 analysis of guitarist Charlie Christian, "is fecund in its inventiveness, swift and traumatic in its development and terribly wasteful of its resources." Some of the greatest jazz musicians have gone unrecorded or have witnessed their most original ideas pass immediately, and often anonymously, into the public domain. "Because jazz finds its very life in an endless improvisation upon traditional materials," Ellison added, the musician "must lose his identity even as he finds it" (Ellison, "The Charlie Christian Story" 234). The endless improvisation on traditional materials, as well as the invention of new melodic techniques, defines both the resilience of his hero in *Invisible Man* and Ellison's own attitude toward his novelistic craft.

It is therefore no mistake that Louis Armstrong is invoked in the Prologue of *Invisible Man* for his ability to make "poetry out of being invisible." Listening to Armstrong's rendition of "What Did I Do to Be So Black and Blue" while high on marijuana, the protagonist discovers that invisibility "gives one a slightly different sense of time, you're never quite on the beat. Sometimes you're ahead and sometimes you're behind. Instead of the swift and imperceptible flowing of time, you are aware of its nodes, those points where time stands still or from which it leaps ahead. And you slip into the breaks and look around" (*Invisible Man* 8). Among the many respects in which his novel might be compared to a jazz composition or performance, Ellison's sense of history as a form of subjective temporality — a constructed story, not a set of objective facts — is perhaps the most profound. His intricate individual variations, or riffs, on motifs or images, as well as the protagonist's self-evident improvisation of new identities in a spiraling serial of new circumstances, are lesser elements of the book's grander design, which narrates the course of modern African American life in the nameless protagonist's experiences. In telling the story of America from a black perspective, Ellison consciously faced the task of bringing those on the margins to the center, much as his protagonist, faced with the zoot-suited hipsters of Harlem, speaking a "jived-up transitional language full of country glamour" and wearing "costumes [that are] surreal variations of downtown styles," concludes: "They were outside the groove of history, and it was my job to get them in, all of them" (*Invisible Man* 441–43).

Attention to the influence of music on Ellison — especially to his contention that jazz may be the ultimate expression of the ironies of American democracy, most of all for black Americans — affords us a better way to understand his artistic intentions as well as his own reaction to critics of the novel. For despite its overwhelmingly favorable reviews and critical history, *Invisible Man* has hardly gone unchallenged. The novel's cultural heterogeneity was criticized from the outset by socialists who were offended by Ellison's renunciation of the communist sympathies he had shown in the 1930s and his proclamation of an ironic faith in democracy, views evident both in the novel itself and in his early published essays. Some critics focused on characters or scenes that appear to lend credence to racist stereotypes, while others brought all of these objections together. Writing in the black magazine *Freedom* in 1952, for example, fellow novelist John Oliver Killens excoriated Ellison for creating individual characters, such as Bledsoe, Rinehart, and Trueblood, whose actions threatened to underscore, rather than combat, racist interpretations of black social life as inherently pathological: "Mix a heavy portion of sex and a heavy, heavy portion of violence, a bit of sadism and a dose of redbaiting (Blame the Communists for everything bad) and you have the making of a bestseller today. . . . It is a vicious distortion of Negro life" (Cruse 235).

More recent objections to the novel, in our own era of more ideologically charged criticism, have centered on the broad categories of gender and race. Some readers have found the paucity of women characters a limitation; others have argued that the novel's depictions of female sexual objectification or violence against women, part of Ellison's critique of segregation and racism, are inadequately balanced by depictions of independent, self-assertive women (Tate). Likewise, Afrocentric critics have sometimes judged his skepticism about the retention of African cultural forms in America as a betrayal of race-centered values. "The African content of American Negro life is more fanciful than actual," Ellison once retorted. "As long as Negroes are confused as to how they relate to American culture, they will be confused about their relationship to places like Africa" (Isaacs 322). Not least because Ellison went out of his way to declare that his primary models were the great writers of the Western tradition — Homer, Dante, Cervantes, Melville, Twain, Dostoevsky, and Malraux — some readers also came to question his ability to speak effectively for a black audience. Especially to those African Americans of the 1960s who advocated a nationalist aesthetic focused more clearly on race consciousness or the cultivation of black cultural traditions, Ellison appeared to have sided with the enemy. The novelist Charles Johnson, for example, recalls asking for a copy of *Invisible Man* in a university black studies library in 1969, only to be told the library did not carry it — because Ralph Ellison was *not* a black writer (Remnick 36). Black Arts movement poet and critic Larry Neal succinctly asserted in 1968 that, for black youth of the day, the experiences of Ellison's protagonist lacked recognizable relevance: "We know who we are, and are not invisible, *at least not to each other. We are not Kafkaesque creatures stumbling through a white light of confusion and absurdity*" (Neal and Jones 652).

His own debates with his critics, however, have been the occasion for some of Ellison's most interesting definitions of the multiracial paradoxes of American culture. A case in point is his famous exchange not with a black nationalist but with a white liberal. Disturbed by what he imagined was Ellison's violation of the constraints placed on African American imagined life by the political and racial oppression of the early 1950s, New York critic Irving Howe, in his famous 1962 essay "Black Boys and Native Sons," chastised Ellison for not replicating the hard-edged, polemical style of Richard Wright and for indulging too readily in illusory freedom from "the ideological and emotional penalties suffered by Negroes in this country" (Howe 362). Aside from the imposed misreading of Ellison's novel required to make his argument, Howe's essay had the special virtue, as it happened, of provoking a bracing rejoinder from Ellison, "The World and the Jug." In this essay, one of many places where we can detect the influence of W. E. B. Du Bois's *The Souls of Black Folk* on Ellison, he elaborated on the African American's peculiar relationship to the nation's proclaimed ideology of freedom and equality, and described the ambiguous role of race in the creation of social identity:

> Howe makes of "Negroness" a metaphysical condition, one that is a state of irremediable agony which all but engulfs the mind. Happily,

the view from inside the skin is not so dark as it appears to be from
Howe's remote position, and therefore my view of "Negroness" is neither his nor that of the exponents of *negritude*. . . . Being a Negro
American has to do with the memory of slavery and the hope of emancipation and the betrayal by allies and the revenge and contempt inflicted by our former masters after the Reconstruction, and the myths,
both Northern and Southern, which are propagated in justification of
that betrayal. . . . It involves a rugged initiation into the mysteries and
rites of color which makes it possible for Negro Americans to suffer
the injustice which race and color are used to excuse without losing
sight of either the humanity of those who inflict that injustice or the
motives, rational or irrational, out of which they act. It imposes the uneasy burden and occasional joy of a complex double vision, a fluid,
ambivalent response to men and events which represents, at its finest, a
profoundly civilized adjustment to the cost of being human in this
modern world.

Most important, perhaps, being a Negro American involves a *willed*
(who wills to be a Negro? *I* do!) affirmation of self as against all outside pressures — an identification with the group as extended through
the individual self which rejects all possibilities of escape that do not
involve a basic resuscitation of the original American ideals of social
and political justice. (132)

To the extent that his inclusive vision of the writer's sources and
obligations crossed racial lines and sprang from his sense that the
grave flaws in America's democratic dream could be redeemed, Ellison, one might say, found himself in something of the same predicament he appreciated in Louis Armstrong. Armstrong's willingness to
use his vocal and instrumental art to reach a broad American audience provoked accusations among the purists of a younger bebop
generation of the 1940s and 1950s that he, arguably the greatest in-
novator in jazz history, had become a comic Uncle Tom (Ellison,
"The Golden Age, Time Past" 211). The Louis Armstrong to whom
one might best compare Ellison, though, was the one he himself elsewhere identified as a trickster, a figure capable of adapting to adverse
circumstances through inventive disguises and forceful displays of
wit. Like Armstrong, this Ralph Ellison is a figure whose putting on
of a deceptive mask is "motivated not so much by fear as by a profound rejection of the image created to usurp his identity," a figure
whose "clownish license and intoxicating powers" are a sign of kinship with other American tricksters such as Benjamin Franklin,
whom Ellison frequently cited as an adroit manipulator of the para-

doxes of democracy (Ellison, "Change the Joke and Slip the Yoke" 52–55). And it is the Ralph Ellison who found in Armstrong's music a suitable analogy for the complexities of T. S. Eliot's masterpiece of modernist poetry, *The Waste Land*, which Ellison first studied as a student at Tuskegee Institute and later often cited as an influence on *Invisible Man*: "Somehow [the poem's] rhythms were often closer to those of jazz than were those of the Negro poets, and . . . its range of allusion was as mixed and as varied as that of Louis Armstrong" (Ellison, "Hidden Name and Complex Fate" 159–60).

Like Armstrong, Ellison outdistanced his critics by mastering all traditions and by playing his instrument with greater virtuosity, sometimes even converting them to his own point of view. Writing just two years after his condemnation of Ellison, for instance, Larry Neal composed what remains perhaps the single best essay on *Invisible Man*, "Ellison's Zoot Suit," in which his favorable judgment of the novel's complex capacity to combine political critique and psychological exploration, and to suffuse an intricate, highly poetic fictive structure with layer upon layer of inherited black folk culture, is nearly unqualified. Renouncing his previous view that the novel did not properly accord with a philosophy of black nationalism, Neal embraced its historical complexity, its ironic attitude toward rigid ideologies of any kind, and its rich invocation of the African American vernacular tradition as an exemplary expression of black artistry. Neal's change of heart is a useful index of the novel's power to speak on many different levels. Just those readers who have resisted *Invisible Man* because of the protagonist's confusion or lack of strong racial identity, or because of Ellison's own antiseparatist aesthetic, have often found themselves ultimately drawn into the maelstrom of its historical vision and its subtle appropriation of many complex perspectives. As the haunting final line of the book puts it, "Who knows but that, on the lower frequencies, I speak for you?" (*Invisible Man* 581).

Beyond the Documentary Imagination

By the time of *Invisible Man*'s publication, Ellison's aesthetic theory was fully formed. The course of his development as a writer up to that point resembles his protagonist's at least to the extent that each works through a series of imprisonments, charting a course in African American history from the age of Booker T. Washington

through World War II and making a full circle from prologue to conclusion, without reaching any true conviction of freedom. The interplay between his protagonist's experience, Ellison's life, and the extensive record of historical events makes for a complex version of
what might best be seen as the author's attempt to extend the boundaries of the documentary imagination. The parallel between the illusions of the protagonist and the changing personal perspectives of
Ellison the author is never exact yet always informative — not least
because the evolution of his own point of view dictated a changing
interpretation of his own past experiences. Likewise, although Ellison
shares with a number of novelists of the 1930s and 1940s an interest
in photographic realism, he infused documentary fiction with a
heightened sense that the writer's distortion of, and improvisation on,
the observed world could bring out more effectively the moral and
psychological density of its internal meaning.

In 1945, well after he renounced his sympathies with the Communist Party, for example, Ellison saw a parallel between the constraints
of the party and those of Tuskegee Institute. He wrote to Wright that
the break "has allowed me to come alive to many of the things of
which I was becoming aware during my bitterly isolated college experience" (Fabre 208) — presumably in part the degree to which each
institution promised liberation but still replicated the racism of surrounding society, as Langston Hughes charged in the essay on black
colleges reprinted in this volume. Nonetheless, in his later remembrances of Tuskegee, after his embrace of the premises of American
democracy had become even more firm, Ellison even made a virtue of
segregation, pointing to the camaraderie and educational freedom
that he enjoyed in college. "I rode freight trains to Macon County,
Alabama, during the Scottsboro trial," he recalled, "because I desired
to study with the Negro conductor-composer William L. Dawson . . .
the greatest classical musician in that part of the country. I had no
need to attend a white university when the master I wished to study
with was available at Tuskegee. Besides, why should I have wished to
attend the white state-controlled university where the works of the
great writers might not have been so easily available?" ("The World
and the Jug" 135–36). Ellison, that is to say, recognized that the segregated college might ironically afford him a better education. Even if
its resources were more limited, he would never be denied access to
them because of the color of his skin.

Ellison's longtime friend and Tuskegee classmate Albert Murray, in his memoir *South to a Very Old Place* (1971), provided an astute, jazz-inflected picture of the young Ellison taking full advantage of the school to read widely, to play and study music, and to store up materials for a future novel. Murray's reminiscence provides an arresting portrait of the artist as a young man, who later "concocts marvelously outrageous anecdotes about a Bitch's Sabbath Juke joint, which, not unmindful of a book by Lewis Mumford, he calls the Golden Day" (among the many books of Mumford, a leading critic of the mid-century, is a study of classic American literature entitled *The Golden Day*); or who tenderly burlesques the looming, almost ancient presence of Booker T. Washington on the annual Founder's Day, as Murray himself recalled it: "what with the choir singing against the background of the stained-glass windows, what with the words being spoken as if recited from parchment scrolls, what with his monument outside among the academic cedars . . . he seemed to have belonged not to any specific generation at all but to all ages" (Murray, *South to a Very Old Place* 108, 120). And it was not Tuskegee alone that provided the young man's education. Ellison recalled also that during graduation week, when "the big-shot word artists were making their most impressive speeches," the local farm people would be having square dances, picnics, and baseball games. "I found their celebrations much more attractive than the official ceremonies," said Ellison, "and I would leave my seat in the orchestra and sneak out to watch them; and while my city background had cut me off from the lives they led and I had no desire to live the life of a sharecropper, I found their unrhetorical activities on the old football field the more meaningful" ("That Same Pain, That Same Pleasure" 19–20). In the curriculum that Murray shared with Ellison, Chaucer coexisted with Count Basie, and the "bitter isolation" of segregated education, or the capitulation to hypocrisy portrayed in his fictive version of the college president, Dr. Bledsoe, was countered by deeper and more lasting cultural lessons.

To read *Invisible Man* as an autobiographical confession would thus be a serious mistake. Certain parts of his novelistic protagonist's college experience may have resembled Ellison's own — for instance, the hero's indulgent re-creation of the music of the famed Tuskegee choir, which debuted at the opening of Radio City Music Hall in 1932 and toured Europe in 1934, or his wild rendition of the traditional Founder's Day speech contained in the sermonic oration of Homer Barbee. The chapters devoted to black college life are, however, a means for Ellison to anatomize, in grand comic form, the racial and class hierarchy, assimilative pressures, disdain for folk culture, and personal aggrandizement that *might* also be found at a black college founded by Washington. That the Founder is carefully distinguished from Washington hardly prevents one from recognizing that Ellison is probing not the great man's own life or achievement at Tuskegee but rather the sometimes humorous, sometimes agonizing accommodations to racism summed up in the famous statue of Washington in which the protagonist cannot tell "whether the veil is really being lifted, or lowered more firmly in place; whether [he is] witnessing a revelation or a more efficient blinding" (*Invisible Man* 36; see the illustration on p. 30 of this book).

Likewise, Ellison's flirtation with the Communist Party is not in any literal way rewritten in the protagonist's manipulation by the Brotherhood, and he stated repeatedly that the two groups are not equivalent. To imagine a strict symbolic relationship, he cautioned, would allow "the reader to escape confronting certain political patterns, patterns which still exist and of which our two major political parties are [also] guilty in their relationships" to African Americans (Ellison, "On Initiation Rites and Power" 59). Even so, his portrait of Richard Wright's eventual disillusion with the Communist Party — Wright had hoped that the Communists could offer a "viable solution" to the race problem, but instead "he discovered that they were blind" — remains an accurate description of Ellison's protagonist's own dealings with the party, and the novel's Brotherhood simply cannot be understood outside the framework of communism's appeal for African Americans and Ellison's own apprenticeship in writing for Marxist magazines (Ellison, "Remembering Richard Wright" 213). Communists in New York organized actively beginning in the 1920s, competing with Marcus Garvey, the NAACP, and others for the allegiance of blacks in Harlem; but the movement was given significant momentum when the Sixth Congress of the Communist International, meeting in Moscow in 1928, adopted a "Resolution on the Negro Question," which introduced the demand for black self-determination as a key concept in communist politics in the United States. Under the initial influence of Wright and others, Ellison distanced himself from the writers of the Harlem Renaissance, considered by 1930s activists too bourgeois and lacking in class consciousness, and his book reviews in particular are laden with the "scientific" discourse of historical materialism, a theory that explained social and cultural relations strictly in terms of the world's economic structure. Yet by the early 1940s Ellison, too, had become overtly suspicious of the party's international agenda and its manipulation of African Americans. For Ellison, as for other African Americans, the rigidity of party doctrine and its dangerous militancy posed a problem apparent in the case of the Oklahoma newspaper editor Roscoe Dunjee, whose antisegregation efforts Ellison commended in "Hidden Name and Complex Fate," and who once wrote: "Yonder stands the poor white with a bomb under his arm — yet love in his heart for me. What shall I do about it? Does that unsanitary looking human being hold within his grasp my rainbow of promise, and the power I sorely need? Is Communism the instrumentality through which I am to secure the racial opportunity which for years I have longed for and prayed?" (Ellison, "Hidden Name and Complex Fate" 154; Dunjee 714).

Both significant efforts of the Communist Party to combat American racism and its use of blacks for its own political ends are woven into the novel's Brotherhood, especially in the racial dynamics between its white and black leaders, and in the suspicion cast on it for its role in the race riot that concludes the novel's action. At the same time, however, Ellison also clearly drew on other sources and organizations devoted to racial politics and labor solidarity, such as the federated black trade union, the National Brotherhood Workers of America, organized in 1919, and its more powerful offshoot, the Brotherhood of Sleeping Car Porters, which dates from 1925. He most likely had in mind an independent communist organization of the post–World War I period known as the African Blood Brotherhood, which was antagonistic to the integrationist policies of the NAACP and to the black nationalism of Garvey's Universal Negro Improvement Association. But the African Blood Brotherhood also distanced itself from the Communist Party International, even though it espoused a utopian belief in the revolutionary doctrines that were characteristic of the party in the 1930s and so effectively mimicked by Ellison in *Invisible Man* (Naison 3–10; Spero and Harris 117–19, 394–97). One of the Brotherhood's own polemics in favor of unified radical action against the discrimination and violence of the post–World War I years includes an oath that reads: "I swear never to love any flag simply for its color, nor any country for its name. . . . I am a Patriot. I am not merely of a Race and a Country, but of the world. I am BROTHERHOOD" (J. Johnson 250–51). All of these institutional ideals are folded into the novel's Brotherhood, but Ellison, in the end, trusted none of them to show the way to the multiracial promised land of a Brotherhood poster, "The Rainbow of America's Future" (*Invisible Man* 385).

Ellison's unwillingness to be bound by any particular ideology, especially Marxism, is indirectly exemplified in the novel's perspective on Frederick Douglass as a model of black leadership. Even though Booker T. Washington, W. E. B. Du Bois (a co-founder of the NAACP), and other black leaders struggled to get out of his shadow, Douglass was venerated by most African Americans, publicly and privately, well into the twentieth century. His invocation in *Invisible Man* as a kind of patron saint of the Brotherhood — a prestige betrayed when Brother Tarp's portrait of him turns up missing before the organization, undermined by deceit, begins to splinter into factions — no doubt has several sources in Ellison's imagination, including his view that Washington's *Up from Slavery* had attempted to deliver "the *coup de grâce* to the memory of Frederick Douglass" (Ellison, "An American Dilemma" 308). But the most important, surely, is Angelo Herndon's essay "Frederick Douglass: Negro Leadership and War," which appeared alongside Ellison's editorial on blacks and World War II in *Negro Quarterly*. (See p. 233 in this book for Ellison's essay.) Herndon's essay found in Douglass's life — from slavery, to his condescending manipulation by white abolitionists, to his achievement of intellectual independence and a position of military influence on behalf of black soldiers during the Civil War — an analog for African American activism during World War II (Herndon 303–29). As Ellison saw, however, not only did Douglass have to fight against whites whose help was sometimes only a finer form of manipulation, something the novel's protagonist discovers in the Brotherhood, but Douglass's memory itself was likely to be defiled by self-aggrandizing black leaders who wished to assume his mantle or use his image for their own purposes. In *Invisible Man* the figure of Douglass thus harks back to the formative years of African American political activism and at the same time provides the more disturbing historical lesson that the exploitation of African Americans was not easily to be separated from their liberation. By focusing our attention on Douglass's portrait in the Brotherhood office, Ellison underscores that it is in the cultural representation of historical figures, events, and documents — their transformation into useful rhetorical weapons — that we can discover the nature of political power.

In his depiction of such institutions as the black college and the Brotherhood, then, Ellison's fictionalization is not equivalent to Tuskegee or the Communist Party, and yet it cannot be understood without reference to those institutions. The novel's *realism*, to put it another way, springs to a degree from the fact that *Invisible Man* filters a documentary content through a narrative compounded of practical politics, allegory, and surrealism. In this respect, Ellison's participation in the Federal Writers' Project — he was assigned to the Living Lore Unit in New York City — is of profound importance. Because the Federal Writers' Project focused its attention on an art of the people, the folk masses, it seemed to Ellison to offer a "resuscitation and transformation of that very vital artistic impulse that is abiding among Afro-Americans," an impulse nurtured in the rituals of slavery, passed down among the people, and given an "accelerated release" by the economic disaster of the depression (Ellison, "Remembering Richard Wright" 205). In both his collection of oral narratives and his numerous reviews for such journals as *New Masses*, Ellison, too, grounded his artistry in the daily lives of people on the street, those who had migrated from sharecropping in the southern Black Belt to the often failed promise of northern industrial work, and those who carried with them into the new environment of the urban North familial histories embodied in the folklore, black language, and music of the South. In particular, his ethnographic collecting for the Federal Writers' Project fine-tuned Ellison's ear for the street language represented with such precision in *Invisible Man*. He recalled straining to find a process of notation adequate to the oral narratives he recorded: "I couldn't quite get the tone of the sounds in but I could get some of the patterns and get an idea of what it was like" (O'Meally, *Craft of Ralph Ellison* 34). As much as the multiplicity of character types in the novel, it is through the multiplicity of their voices that Ellison was able to re-create Harlem's aural poetry, making his own technique, as he said of Romare Bearden's explosive juxtapositions on the painted canvas, "eloquent of the sharp breaks, leaps in consciousness, distortions, paradoxes, reversals, telescoping of time, and surreal blending of styles, values, hopes, and dreams which characterize much of Negro American history" (Ellison, "The Art of Romare Bearden" 237).

It is one of the principal achievements of *Invisible Man* to have shown that the black migration from the beginning of the twentieth century on through World War II was as much a cultural as a social

or economic phenomenon, a means of spreading African American
music and language across the nation and embedding it permanently
in the mainstream. Between the resonantly provocative blues narrative delivered by Jim Trueblood in rural Alabama and the ultra-hip
signifying — that is, the punning vernacular language games — of
Peter Wheatstraw on the streets of Harlem, Ellison captured linguisti-
cally the translation of black culture from South to North. A survey
of his writing of the late 1930s and early 1940s, in fact, would find
the recounting of the migration that took a large proportion of the
South's black population to northern urban centers such as New
York, Chicago, and Detroit to be a principal theme. Before his estrangement from Wright because of artistic differences, Ellison effu-
sively praised Wright's own brilliant study of the migration, *12 Million Black Voices* (a Federal Writers' Project volume illustrated by the
photographs of Dorothea Lange, Russell Lee, Jack Delano, and others; see p. 104 of this book); and his reviews of other novels devoted
to the migration characteristically either admired their adherence to
the dictates of social realism or derided their failed vision of class solidarity. By the same token, some of Ellison's writing on the left fore-
shadowed his own mature aesthetic theory. A review of William
Attaway's excellent 1942 migration and labor novel, *Blood on the
Forge*, thus shows the radical perspective that Ellison would soon
abandon even as it offers a preview of his own eventual treatment of
the same themes:

> There is no center of consciousness, lodged in a character or charac-
> ters, capable of comprehending the sequence of events. Possibly this
> would have called for an entirely new character. But at the same time it
> would have saved the work from finally disintegrating into a catalogue
> of meaningless casualties and despairs. Inclusion of such a conscious-
> ness would not have been a mere artistic device; it would have been in
> keeping with historical truth.
>   Conceptually, Attaway grasped the destruction of the folk, but
> missed its rebirth on a higher level. The writer did not see that while
> the folk individual was being liquidated in the crucible of steel, he was
> also undergoing fusion with new elements. Nor did Attaway see that
> the individual which emerged, blended of old and new, was better fit-
> ted for the problems of the industrial environment. (Ellison, "The
> Great Migration" 24).

One might simply turn the review back on itself. After his reaction
against what he came to consider the crude simplifications of much

proletarian fiction, Ellison rewrote the critique of Attaway as an exaggerated parody of the northern migration and of the black industrial worker's new condition and susceptibility to radical politics. In doing so he reconceived the strategies of documentary realism, turning historical fiction into more than a means of moral instruction and racial affirmation. *Invisible Man* includes those intentions, of course, but it becomes as well a fully imagined fictive form of national memory.

A Blueprint of
African American Culture

Accounts of the great migration or the racism encountered by African American soldiers in World War I or the vicissitudes of black industrial labor thus provide a crucial context for *Invisible Man* not because they mirror the novel but because they allow us to see the many dimensions of Ellison's reconfiguration of broad historical metaphors and narratives. Given the subtleties of the novel, however, one has to fear that any series of contextual readings will achieve illumination by reduction; no list of possibilities could be equal to the sheer range of events, personalities, and issues in African American history that Ellison brings into play, let alone comparable to the imaginative density of the novel itself. One can choose nearly at random pages of *Invisible Man* where a multitude of allusions, wordplays, and signifying inversions are at work. At times Ellison echoes other black writers' metaphoric constructs, as in the case of this passage from Du Bois's *Dusk of Dawn* (1940), which appears to anticipate the whole course of the protagonist's experience, from the opening pages of *Invisible Man* through the Liberty Paints episode through the concluding scenes of apocalyptic violence:

> It is difficult to let others see the full psychological meaning of caste segregation. It is as though one, looking out from a dark cave in a side of an impending mountain, sees the world passing and speaks to it; speaks courteously and persuasively, showing them how these entombed souls are hindered in their natural movement, expression, and development; and how their loosening from prison would be a matter not simply of courtesy, sympathy, and help to them, but aid to all the world. One talks on evenly and logically in this way, but notices that the passing throng does not even turn its head, or if it does, glances curiously and walks on. It gradually penetrates the minds of the prisoners

that the people passing do not hear; that some thick sheet of invisible but horribly tangible plate glass is between them and the world. They get excited; they talk louder; they gesticulate. Some of the passing stop in curiosity; these gesticulations seem so pointless; they laugh and pass on. They still either do not hear at all, or hear but dimly, and even what they hear, they do not understand. Then the people within may become hysterical. They may scream and hurl themselves against the barriers, hardly realizing in their bewilderment that they are screaming in a vacuum unheard and that their antics may actually seem funny to those outside looking in. They may even, here and there, break through in blood and disfigurement, and find themselves faced by a horrified, implacable, and quite overwhelming mob of people frightened for their own very existence. (Du Bois, *Dusk of Dawn* 130–31)

In contrast to his implied reference to such passages from other writers and the large-scale episodes of black history that are dramatized at length in *Invisible Man*, Ellison also frequently works small details into intensely wrought centers of meaning comparable to the icons that accumulate in the protagonist's briefcase — his high school diploma, the Jim Crow bank, Tod Clifton's paper Sambo doll, Brother Tarp's leg shackle, the hipster's sunglasses. Perhaps the object of most bitter pain is the Jim Crow coin bank, which the narrator tries futilely to discard, a reminder of the racist stereotypes with which blacks have had to live (*Invisible Man* 311–12; see the illustration on p. 131 of this book). The icon most charged with compressed meaning, however, is the broken link from Brother Tarp's leg shackle, which incorporates the ordeal of enslavement, the injustices of convict lease, and the hypocrisy of Dr. Bledsoe, who displays the leg iron not as a talisman of resistance but as an accommodating "symbol of progress." Tarp's shackle (wrenched open with a hatchet), not Bledsoe's (smooth and unmarked), is the true weapon; and, like other iconographic details, it conjoins material and cultural power: "it's got a heap of signifying wrapped up in it and it might help you remember what we're really fighting against" (*Invisible Man* 141, 388; see the illustration on p. 122 of this book).

Numerous scenes, moments, or phrases reverberate with this kind of energy. The array of musical allusions, for instance, constitutes a course in African American music. One could begin with Ellison's references to Dvořák's adaptation of "Swing Low, Sweet Chariot" in his symphony *From the New World* and hence to Du Bois's use of it in *The Souls of Black Folk*; to Louis Armstrong's version of Jelly Roll

Morton's "Funky Butt," a tune in turn about trumpeter Buddy
Bolden (Lomax 60, 276–77); to Mary Rambo's borrowing of Bessie
Smith's "Back Water Blues" or her unidentified allusion to Mahalia
Jackson's "Move On Up a Little Higher"; to the traditional funeral
dirge and mocking blues "Pick Poor Robin Clean," which Ellison
himself associated with the career of Charlie Parker, who was "poor
robin come to New York and here to be sacrificed to the need for en-
tertainment and for the creation of a new jazz style" (*Invisible Man*
193; "On Bird, Bird-Watching, and Jazz," 231–32). Other significant
details are fleeting but nonetheless telling. To read the inquisition
about Brer Rabbit, Buckeye the Rabbit, and "YOUR MOTHER" inflicted on the narrator in the hospital after his accident at the Liberty
Paints factory (*Invisible Man* 240–42), one must know something
about playing the dozens — the African American verbal toasts and
word games sometimes involving risqué denigration of mothers —
and about the derivation of some rabbit trickster tales from African
American folk rhymes of imprisonment, convict labor, and escape, as
in this example from the period of the novel's action:

> The rabbit run, the rabbit jumped,
> The rabbit skipped the river.
> O buckeye rabbit, hey! hey!
> (Odum and Johnson, *Negro Workaday Songs* 110)

To appreciate Ellison's comic depiction of Ras the Destroyer on
horseback in the concluding scenes of the novel, one should have a
sense not only of the political demise of Marcus Garvey but also of
the importance of the horsed rider in African sculpture and in such
key African American works as the piece by Ellison's mentor, Richmond Barthé, devoted to the Haitian revolutionary general Jean-
Jacques Dessalines on horseback (Cole 116–35; Huggins 166).

Many such details expand in several directions at once. Consider
the episode in which the protagonist, enraged by his sexual as well as
his racial exploitation, scrawls a lipstick epithet about her rape by
Santa Claus on the belly of the drunken Sybil. The scene is brought
into special relief when one recognizes the protagonist's joking allusion to D. W. Griffith's classic racist film about the rise of the Ku
Klux Klan, *The Birth of a Nation*, and juxtaposes his epithet to the
poignant and socially complex tradition of recorded blues, including
some by Peetie Wheatstraw, about Santa Claus (*Invisible Man* 522;
Oliver, *Screening* 26–43). Or take the scene in which the protagonist

confronts on the streets of Harlem the homeless figure, pushing a cart full of discarded blueprints and singing Jimmy Rushing's "Boogie Woogie Blues," who identifies himself as Peter Wheatstraw, the name of the same blues singer who styled himself the Devil's Son-in-Law (one version of his song of that name is included in this volume on p. 123). The blueprints invoke the long history of documents that have failed African Americans, from the Declaration of Independence to the Emancipation Proclamation to the Communist Manifesto to liberal exposés such as sociologist Gunnar Myrdal's massive study of racism, *An American Dilemma* (1944), which Ellison, in an acerbic review, called "the blueprint for a more effective exploitation of the South's natural, industrial and human resources" (Ellison, "An American Dilemma" 313). Most important, Wheatstraw's blueprints form a bridge from the down-home traditions evoked in his own black talk to the imperfect attempt by Richard Wright, in "Blueprint for Negro Writing" (1938), to translate black nationalist aspirations into Marxist terms. From Ellison's retrospective vantage point, the figure of Peter Wheatstraw, an archetype of the satanic wanderer met at the crossroads in countless blues, offered his hero all at once an initial lesson in remembering his roots, those things "long ago shut out of my mind," and an admonition that paper promises, whether created by whites or blacks, are not to be trusted by African Americans: "Here I got 'bout a hundred pounds of blueprints and I couldn't build nothing! . . . Plenty of these ain't never been used, you know" (*Invisible Man* 175).

The narrative as a whole thus resembles the charged scene of the Harlem eviction in which the protagonist enumerates the elderly couple's possessions — a catalog of personal and public African American history since the days of slavery that once again carries him back to his own lost heritage, "far-away-and-long-ago . . . linked verbal echoes, images, heard even when not listening at home" — before he explodes into the extemporaneous "dispossession" speech that brings him to the attention of the Brotherhood (*Invisible Man* 273; see the illustration on p. 211 of this book). Like Tarp's shackle, these possessions are no relics of bondage but the living evidence of kinship and culture maintained in the midst of, and as a response to, racism. They are at once a reminder of fearful suffering and a source of inspiration, of grounding in collective history.

The protagonist's own accumulated possessions, including the miscellaneous papers he burns to illuminate his darkness in the coal cellar, do not cohere into a clear record of his identity, and it would be easy enough to conclude that he ends his own narrative still in a state of dispossession. The same, however, cannot be said of Ellison or *Invisible Man*. Given its encyclopedic characteristics, the novel is unlikely to be exhausted by even the most elaborate historically contextualized interpretation. To investigate Ellison's many sources and analogs in modernist literature would provide different angles of vision on *Invisible Man*. The purpose of this volume, however, is to offer something of a blueprint for reading the novel as a reconstruction of African American history.

The volume is divided into three general parts, the first and third of which follow in a general chronological order the plot of *Invisible Man* and the division of the protagonist's experiences between the rural South and the urban North. Part One, "'The Scaffolding of a Nation': The Black Belt and Beyond," borrows its title from a phrase in Homer Barbee's sermon about the Founder (*Invisible Man* 124). The phrase refers both in the sermon and in this volume's context to the grounding of modern African American culture in the history of the Black Belt — that is, the geographical region of the South with a majority black population from the later days of slavery on into the twentieth century. Part Three, "'The City within a City': Harlem, U.S.A.," borrows its title from the phrase used to describe Harlem on the protagonist's first view of it (*Invisible Man* 159). Like "Harlem, U.S.A.," the phrase is a common colloquial expression designating the concentration (and segregation) of black cultural life of New York City in Harlem in the early twentieth century and its reputation as the unofficial capital of black America. Part Two, "'A Heap of Signifying': Vernacular Culture," takes its title from Brother Tarp's comments about his leg shackle, cited above, and refers to the central role played by vernacular folk culture in the novel, in this case principally songs, folktales, and narratives composed in street language. Within this part of the volume, the examples are arranged not in historical order but again in an order keyed to their appearance throughout the novel.

The selections are intended to provide concrete points of reference for those episodes in Ellison's novel that are clearly drawn from, or meant to reflect on, historical events or institutions. Our purpose is not to reduce the novel to one logical sequence or a single interpretive grid but rather to demonstrate the extraordinary wealth and vitality of Ellison's historical imagination, his capacity to rewrite African

American history in the experiences of a single hero and to recover for future readers those materials of black culture, from slavery through the end of legal segregation, that threatened to become lost from view. There is no doubt that *Invisible Man* is a complex and challenging novel. Written at a moment when the true promise of equality had only begun to be realized for African Americans, the novel envisions nothing less than undoing their cultural dispossession. A work that dramatically reordered the course of modern literature, *Invisible Man* did not turn away from painful issues of racial antagonism that have shaped black America. Instead, by confronting such issues in all their bewildering force, Ellison found a way both to probe and to celebrate the "blackness" of American culture.

The famous statue of Booker T. Washington at Tuskegee Institute depicts
Washington lifting a veil, symbolic of disadvantage or illiteracy, from the
face of a rising figure, perhaps a former slave. Ellison's protagonist wonders,
however, if Washington might not be lowering, rather than lifting, the veil
(*Invisible Man* 36).

Part One

"THE SCAFFOLDING OF A NATION"

The Black Belt and Beyond

Booker T. Washington

Atlanta Exposition Address

Booker T. Washington (1856–1915) was arguably the most influential and controversial African American leader of the early twentieth century. As the first principal of Tuskegee Institute, a school for blacks in Macon County, Alabama, founded in 1881, Washington developed an educational and economic philosophy based to a great extent on accommodation to the prevailing white supremacy of the post-Reconstruction South. His autobiography, *Up from Slavery* (1901), turned his own life story into a parable of self-help, and it has remained a key text in the tradition of African American autobiography. The book's most famous section, an 1895 speech presented at the Atlanta Cotton States and International Exposition which came to be known colloquially as the "Atlanta Compromise," exemplified Washington's view that African Americans should follow a program of family and community uplift, making themselves economically valuable to the South as a first step in defeating racial prejudice.

Born a slave on the eve of the Civil War, Washington worked in West Virginia coal mines and salt furnaces before making his way to Hampton Institute in Virginia, where he graduated in 1875. He briefly explored careers in law and the ministry before returning to teaching and accepting the appointment at Tuskegee. Coming of age in an era of increasingly rigid segregation, Washington maintained that higher education, social equality, and political rights must remain secondary goals for blacks until they acquired the agricultural and industrial skills that were central to Tuskegee's own curriculum. Although his speeches and writing were frequently masked in obsequiousness in order to gain a calculated advantage, such gains came at the cost of his declaring, for example, that "notwithstanding the cruel wrongs inflicted upon us, the black man got nearly as much out of slavery as the white man did." In contrast to the unrestrained demand for equal rights voiced throughout his life by the black abolitionist and early civil rights advocate Frederick Douglass, who died in 1895, the same year as the Atlanta speech, Washington stressed work skills, morality, and cleanliness — the "philosophy of the toothbrush," as he called it. Washington's success at Tuskegee, his extraordinary capacity as a speaker, and his cunning use of a network of black and white political connections — known to its detractors as the Tuskegee Machine — made him a man of great influence during the presidencies of Theodore Roosevelt and William Howard Taft. Even when he worked behind the scenes to combat racist policies, however, Washington remained identified with a politics of acquiescence to segregation and was usually at odds with leaders such as W. E. B. Du Bois and organizations such as the National Association for the Advancement of Colored People (NAACP), which was founded in 1909. Washington remained at Tuskegee until his death, but he also lectured widely, wrote or contributed to many books, and was instrumental in establishing such organizations as the National Negro Business League.

Washington is a key figure in *Invisible Man*. Ellison's protagonist alludes to the best-known passage of Washington's Atlanta speech at the outset of the first chapter and quotes from it in his graduation speech at the men's smoker (*Invisible Man* 15, 29). To the extent that the protagonist's college in *Invisible Man* is modeled on Tuskegee Institute, it is the version that Ellison himself knew as a student in the 1930s rather than the one presided over by Washington. But the college's unnamed Founder, although distinguished from the actual Booker T. Washington (*Invisible Man* 305–06), is an amalgamation of mythology and inventive hyperbole built in part of fragments from Washington's own life and legend. Washington was regularly referred to after his death as the Founder (see p. 48 of this book), and the statue of the Founder lifting a veil from the head of a kneeling former slave is derived directly from the famous statue of Washington erected after his death at Tuskegee (*Invisible Man* 36; see the illustration p. 30 of this book). Likewise, the college president, Dr. A. Herbert Bledsoe, is a man of a later era who may bear some resemblance to Washington's successor, Robert Russa Moton, whose philosophy and publications, such as *Finding a Way Out: An Autobiography* (1921) and *What the Negro Thinks* (1929), maintained the conservative tradition established by Tuskegee's founder. But Bledsoe's philosophy of self-aggrandizement also corresponds to one interpretation of Washington's style of wielding power to benefit both black institutions and himself, and he provides a paradigm against which to judge subsequent models of black leadership in the novel. The ambiguous presence of Washington as a role model reappears throughout *Invisible Man*, and by the novel's conclusion it is a delicate question whether the protagonist, dwelling in his Harlem underground, has not made a full, if utterly ironic, circle back to Bledsoe's advice to "learn where you are and get yourself power . . . then stay in the dark and use it" (*Invisible Man* 145).

FURTHER READING: August Meier, *Negro Thought in America, 1880–1915: Racial Ideologies in the Age of Booker T. Washington* (Ann Arbor: U of Michigan P, 1963); Rayford W. Logan, *The Betrayal of the Negro from Rutherford B. Hayes to Woodrow Wilson* (New York: Collier, 1965); Louis T. Harlan, *Booker T. Washington: The Making of a Black Leader, 1856–1901* (New York: Oxford UP, 1972), and *Booker T. Washington: The Wizard of Tuskegee, 1901–1915* (New York: Oxford UP, 1983); Hugh Hawkins, ed., *Booker T. Washington and His Critics,* 2nd ed. (Lexington, MA: Heath, 1974).

One-third of the population of the South is of the Negro race. No enterprise seeking the material, civil, or moral welfare of this section can disregard this element of our population and reach the highest success. I but convey to you, Mr. President and Directors, the sentiment of the masses of my race when I say that in no way have the value and manhood of the American Negro been more fittingly and generously recognized than by the managers of this magnificent Exposition at every stage of its progress. It is a recognition that will do more to cement the friendship of the two races than any occurrence since the dawn of our freedom.

Not only this, but the opportunity here afforded will awaken among us a new era of industrial progress. Ignorant and inexperienced, it is not strange that in the first years of our new life we began at the top instead of at the bottom; that a seat in Congress or the state legislature was more sought than real estate or industrial skill; that the political convention or stump speaking had more attractions than starting a dairy farm or truck garden.

A ship lost at sea for many days suddenly sighted a friendly vessel. From the mast of the unfortunate vessel was seen a signal, "Water, water; we die of thirst!" The answer from the friendly vessel at once came back, "Cast down your bucket where you are." A second time the signal, "Water, water; send us water!" ran up from the distressed vessel, and was answered, "Cast down your bucket where you are." And a third and fourth signal for water was answered, "Cast down your bucket where you are." The captain of the distressed vessel, at last heeding the injunction, cast down his bucket, and it came up full of fresh, sparkling water from the mouth of the Amazon River. To those of my race who depend on bettering their condition in a foreign land or who underestimate the importance of cultivating friendly relations with the Southern white man, who is their next-door neighbour, I would say: "Cast down your bucket where you are" — cast it down in making friends in every manly way of the people of all races by whom we are surrounded.

Cast it down in agriculture, mechanics, in commerce, in domestic service, and in the professions. And in this connection it is well to bear in mind that whatever other sins the South may be called to bear, when it comes to business, pure and simple, it is in the South that the Negro is given a man's chance in the commercial world, and in nothing is this Exposition more eloquent than in emphasizing this chance. Our greatest danger is that in the great leap from slavery to freedom we may overlook the fact that the masses of us are to live by the productions of our hands, and fail to keep in mind that we shall prosper in proportion as we learn to dignify and glorify common labour and put brains and skill into the common occupations of life; shall prosper in proportion as we learn to draw the line between the superficial and the substantial, the ornamental gewgaws of life and the useful. No race can prosper till it learns that there is as much dignity in tilling a field as in writing a poem. It is at the bottom of life we must begin, and not at the top. Nor should we permit our grievances to overshadow our opportunities.

To those of the white race who look to the incoming of those of foreign birth and strange tongue and habits for the prosperity of the South, were I permitted I would repeat what I say to my own race, "Cast down your bucket where you are." Cast it down among the eight millions of Negroes whose habits you know, whose fidelity and love you have tested in days when to have proved treacherous meant the ruin of your firesides. Cast down your bucket among these people who have, without strikes and labour wars, tilled your fields, cleared your forests, builded your railroads and cities, and brought forth treasures from the bowels of the earth, and helped make possible this magnificent representation of the progress of the South. Casting down your bucket among my people, helping and encouraging them as you are doing on these grounds, and to education of head, hand, and heart, you will find that they will buy your surplus land, make blossom the waste places in your fields, and run your factories. While doing this, you can be sure in the future, as in the past, that you and your families will be surrounded by the most patient, faithful, law-abiding, and unresentful people that the world has seen. As we have proved our loyalty to you in the past, in nursing your children, watching by the sick-bed of your mothers and fathers, and often following them with tear-dimmed eyes to their graves, so in the future, in our humble way, we shall stand by you with a devotion that no foreigner can approach, ready to lay down our lives, if need be, in defence of yours, interlacing our industrial, commercial, civil, and religious life with yours in a way that shall make the interests of both races one. In all things that are purely social we can be as separate as the fingers, yet one as the hand in all things essential to mutual progress.

There is no defence or security for any of us except in the highest intelligence and development of all. If anywhere there are efforts tending to curtail the fullest growth of the Negro, let these efforts be turned into stimulating, encouraging, and making him the most useful and intelligent citizen. Effort or means so invested will pay a thousand per cent interest. These efforts will be twice blessed — "blessing him that gives and him that takes."

There is no escape through law of man or God from the inevitable: —

> The laws of changeless justice bind
> Oppressor with oppressed;
> And close as sin and suffering joined
> We march to fate abreast.

Nearly sixteen millions of hands will aid you in pulling the load upward, or they will pull against you the load downward. We shall constitute one-third and more of the ignorance and crime of the South, or one-third its intelligence and progress; we shall contribute one-third to the business and industrial prosperity of the South, or we shall prove a veritable body of death, stagnating, depressing, retarding every effort to advance the body politic.

Gentlemen of the Exposition, as we present to you our humble effort at an exhibition of our progress, you must not expect overmuch. Starting thirty years ago with ownership here and there in a few quilts and pumpkins and chickens (gathered from miscellaneous sources), remember the path that has led from these to the inventions and production of agricultural implements, buggies, steam-engines, newspapers, books, statuary, carving, paintings, the management of drug-stores and banks, has not been trodden without contact with thorns and thistles. While we take pride in what we exhibit as a result of our independent efforts, we do not for a moment forget that our part in this exhibition would fall far short of your expectations but for the constant help that has come to our educational life, not only from the Southern states, but especially from Northern philanthropists, who have made their gifts a constant stream of blessing and encouragement.

The wisest among my race understand that the agitation of questions of social equality is the extremest folly, and that progress in the enjoyment of all the privileges that will come to us must be the result of severe and constant struggle rather than of artificial forcing. No race that has anything to contribute to the markets of the world is long in any degree ostracized. It is important and right that all privileges of the law be ours, but it is vastly more important that we be prepared for the exercises of these privileges. The opportunity to earn a dollar in a factory just now is worth infinitely more than the opportunity to spend a dollar in an opera-house.

In conclusion, may I repeat that nothing in thirty years has given us more hope and encouragement, and drawn us so near to you of the white race, as this opportunity offered by the Exposition; and here bending, as it were, over the altar that represents the results of the struggles of your race and mine, both starting practically empty-handed three decades ago, I pledge that in your effort to work out the great and intricate problem which God has laid at the doors of the South, you shall have at all times the patient, sympathetic help of my race; only let this be constantly in mind, that, while from representations in these buildings of the product of field, of forest, of mine, of factory, letters, and art, much good will come, yet far above and beyond material benefits will be that higher good, that, let us pray God, will come, in a blotting out of sectional differences and racial animosities and suspicions, in a determination to administer absolute justice, in a willing obedience among all classes to the mandates of law. This, this, coupled with our material prosperity, will bring into our beloved South a new heaven and a new earth.

W. E. B. Du Bois

Of Our Spiritual Strivings

Of Mr. Booker T. Washington

W. E. B. Du Bois (1868–1963) was best known during his lifetime as the director of publications for the NAACP, the editor of its journal *Crisis* from 1910 to 1932, an advocate of Pan-Africanism, and a prolific scholar of African American history and culture. His major work, *The Souls of Black Folk* (1903), is often singled out as the most influential book in their early reading by important black writers and activists. An unusual combination of historical essay, autobiography, and philosophical reflection, it has over the course of the century been recognized as a classic text in the history of American culture. The selections below are drawn from two of the most influential chapters of Du Bois's book — his argument about African American "double consciousness" and his critique of Booker T. Washington. Born in Great Barrington, Massachusetts, Du Bois was educated at Fisk University, the University of Berlin, and Harvard University, where he received his Ph.D. in 1895 for a dissertation on the history of the slave trade. His cosmopolitan interests and his advocacy of advanced higher education helped to make him a natural antagonist to Booker T. Washington, and his attack on Washington in *The Souls of Black Folk* was only one of many occasions on which Du Bois argued that black Americans must disavow accommodation and instead struggle for absolute political, economic, and educational equality. His great range of interests and tireless energy are evident in Du Bois's voluminous writings, which include brilliant sociological studies of both rural and urban black America, including *The Philadelphia Negro* (1899); novels such as *The Quest of the Silver Fleece* (1911) and *Dark Princess* (1928); studies of Africa and the African diaspora such as *The Negro* (1915) and *The World and Africa* (1946); and unusual combinations of autobiography, lyrical creative writing, and polemic such as *Darkwater* (1920) and *Dusk of Dawn* (1940).

The Souls of Black Folk comprises fourteen chapters that tell the story of African America, especially in the Black Belt of the South, while mounting an argument for equal rights and the integrity of black culture. By featuring a passage from an African American spiritual as a headnote to each chapter and matching it against a corresponding literary passage from the Euro-American tradition, Du Bois provided a textual illustration of what came to be known as his central insight into the life of African Americans — that they are marked by a "two-ness," a double consciousness of being both American and black (or "Negro," to cite the term that Du Bois often used positively and expansively to indicate the unity of black people throughout Africa, the Caribbean, and South and North America). The book's last chapter focuses on the cultural foundation of black America provided by the "sorrow songs." Washington, too, admired black spirituals and defended their role in Tuskegee's curriculum, but by featuring the legacy of Fisk University's Jubilee Singers, a famous choir whose concert tours raised a great deal of money for the school, Du Bois provided a theory of culture that bound together the experience of slavery and the contemporary fight for racial justice.

While his college life borrows from the history and surroundings of Tuskegee, the intellectual promise of Ellison's protagonist also suits him for membership in what Du Bois referred to as the Talented Tenth, the professionally educated segment of the black population that would lead the way toward equality. By the same token, his career, as his grandfather predicts, turns out to be a contradiction of such promises. In the first chapter of *The Souls of Black Folk*, Du Bois introduces the figure of the veil, which appears throughout his book and, in fact, throughout much of African American literature. In this resonant metaphor, as in the question of double consciousness and the quizzical opening of the chapter itself — "How does it feel to be a problem?" Du Bois asks — one can find elements of the multifaceted identity of Ellison's protagonist as well as images that can be traced from the novel's Prologue through its concluding scenes in Harlem.

FURTHER READING: Arnold Rampersad, *The Art and Imagination of W. E. B. Du Bois* (Cambridge, MA: Harvard UP 1976); William Toll, *The Resurgence of Race: Black Social Theory from Reconstruction to the Pan-African Conference* (Philadelphia: Temple UP 1979); William L. Andrews, ed., *Critical Essays on W. E. B. Du Bois* (Boston: Hall, 1985); Manning Marable, *W. E. B. Du Bois: Black Radical Democrat* (Boston: Twayne, 1986); David Levering Lewis, *W. E. B. Du Bois: The Biography of a Race, 1868–1919* (New York: Henry Holt, 1993).

Of Our Spiritual Strivings

Between me and the other world there is ever an unasked question: unasked by some through feelings of delicacy; by others through the difficulty of rightly framing it. All, nevertheless, flutter round it. They approach me in a half-hesitant sort of way, eye me curiously or compassionately, and then, instead of saying directly, How does it feel to be a problem? they say, I know an excellent colored man in my town; or, I fought at Mechanicsville; or, Do not these Southern outrages make your blood boil? At these I smile, or am interested, or reduce the boiling to a simmer, as the occasion may require. To the real question, How does it feel to be a problem? I answer seldom a word.

And yet, being a problem is a strange experience, — peculiar even for one who has never been anything else, save perhaps in babyhood and in Europe. It is in the early days of rollicking boyhood that the revelation first bursts upon one, all in a day, as it were. I remember well when the shadow swept across me. I was a little thing, away up in the hills of New England, where the dark Housatonic winds between Hoosac and Taghkanic to the sea. In a wee wooden schoolhouse, something put it into the boys' and girls' heads to buy gorgeous visiting-cards — ten cents a package — and exchange. The exchange was merry, till one girl, a tall newcomer, refused my card, — refused it peremptorily, with a glance. Then it dawned upon me with a certain suddenness that I was different from the others; or like, mayhap, in heart and life and longing, but shut out from their world by a vast veil. I had thereafter no desire to tear down that veil, to creep through; I held all beyond it in common contempt, and lived above it in a region of blue sky and great wandering shadows. That sky was bluest when I could beat my mates at examination-time, or beat them at a foot-race, or even beat their stringy heads. Alas, with the years all this fine contempt began to fade; for the worlds I longed for, and all their dazzling opportunities, were theirs, not mine. But they should not keep these prizes, I said; some, all, I would wrest from them. Just how I would do it I could never decide: by reading law, by healing the sick, by telling the wonderful tales that swam in my head, — some way. With other black boys the strife was not so fiercely sunny: their youth shrunk into tasteless sycophancy, or into silent hatred of the pale world about them and mocking distrust of everything white; or wasted itself in a bitter cry, Why did God make me an outcast and a stranger in mine own house? The shades of the prison-house closed round about us all: walls strait and stubborn to the whitest, but relentlessly narrow, tall, and unscalable to sons of night who must plod darkly on in resignation, or beat unavailing palms against the stone, or steadily, half hopelessly, watch the streak of blue above.

After the Egyptian and Indian, the Greek and Roman, the Teuton and Mongolian, the Negro is a sort of seventh son, born with a veil, and gifted with second-sight in this American world, — a world which yields him no true self-consciousness, but only lets him see himself through the revelation of the other world. It is a peculiar sensation, this double-consciousness, this sense of always looking at one's self through the eyes of others, of measuring one's soul by the tape of a world that looks on in amused contempt and pity. One ever feels his two-ness, — an American, a Negro; two souls, two thoughts, two unreconciled strivings; two warring ideals in one dark body, whose dogged strength alone keeps it from being torn asunder.

The history of the American Negro is the history of this strife — this longing to attain self-conscious manhood, to merge his double self into a better and truer self. In this merging he wishes neither of the older selves to be lost. He would not Africanize America, for America has too much to teach the world and Africa. He would not bleach his Negro soul in a flood of white Americanism, for he knows that Negro blood has a message for the world. He simply wishes to make it possible for a man to be both a Negro and an American, without being cursed and spit upon by his fellows, without having the doors of Opportunity closed roughly in his face. . . .

Of Mr. Booker T. Washington

Easily the most striking thing in the history of the American Negro since 1876 is the ascendancy of Mr. Booker T. Washington. It began at the time when war memories and ideals were rapidly passing; a day of astonishing commercial development was dawning; a sense of doubt and hesitation overtook the freedmen's sons, — then it was that his leading began. Mr. Washington came, with a simple definite programme, at the psychological moment when the nation was a little ashamed of having bestowed so much sentiment on Negroes, and was concentrating its energies on Dollars. His programme of industrial education, conciliation of the South, and submission and silence as to civil and political rights, was not wholly original; the Free Negroes from 1830 up to wartime had striven to build industrial schools, and the American Missionary Association had from the first taught various trades; and Price and others had sought a way of honorable alliance with the best of the Southerners. But Mr. Washington first indissolubly linked these things; he put enthusiasm, unlimited energy, and perfect faith into this programme, and changed it from a by-path into a veritable Way of Life. And the tale of the methods by which he did this is a fascinating study of human life.

It startled the nation to hear a Negro advocating such a programme after many decades of bitter complaint; it startled and won the applause of the South, it interested and won the admiration of the North; and after a confused murmur of protest, it silenced if it did not convert the Negroes themselves.

To gain the sympathy and coöperation of the various elements comprising the white South was Mr. Washington's first task; and this, at the time Tuskegee was founded, seemed, for a black man, well-nigh impossible. And yet ten years later it was done in the word spoken at Atlanta: "In all things purely social we can be as separate as the five fingers, and yet one as the hand in all things essential to mutual progress." This "Atlanta Compromise" is by all odds the most notable thing in Mr. Washington's career. The South interpreted it in different ways: the radicals received it as a complete surrender of the demand for civil and political equality; the conservatives, as a generously conceived working basis for mutual understanding. So both approved it, and to-day its author is certainly the most distinguished Southerner since Jefferson Davis, and the one with the largest personal following. . . .

Mr. Washington represents in Negro thought the old attitude of adjustment and submission; but adjustment at such a peculiar time as to make his programme unique. This is an age of unusual economic development, and Mr. Washington's programme naturally takes an economic cast, becoming a gospel of Work and Money to such an ex-

tent as apparently almost completely to overshadow the higher aims
of life. Moreover, this is an age when the more advanced races are
coming in closer contact with the less developed races, and the race-
feeling is therefore intensified; and Mr. Washington's programme
practically accepts the alleged inferiority of the Negro races. Again, in
our own land, the reaction from the sentiment of war time has given
impetus to race-prejudice against Negroes, and Mr. Washington
withdraws many of the high demands of Negroes as men and American citizens. In other periods of intensified prejudice all the Negro's
tendency to self-assertion has been called forth; at this period a policy
of submission is advocated. In the history of nearly all other races
and people the doctrine preached at such crises has been that manly
self-respect is worth more than lands and houses, and that a people
who voluntarily surrender such respect, or cease striving for it, are
not worth civilizing.

In answer to this, it has been claimed that the Negro can survive
only through submission. Mr. Washington distinctly asks that black
people give up, at least for the present, three things —

First, political power,
Second, insistence on civil rights,
Third, higher education of Negro youth, —

and concentrate all their energies on industrial education, the accumulation of wealth, and the conciliation of the South. This policy has
been courageously and insistently advocated for over fifteen years,
and has been triumphant for perhaps ten years. As a result of this tender of the palm-branch, what has been the return? In these years
there have occurred:

1. The disfranchisement of the Negro.
2. The legal creation of a distinct status of civil inferiority for the
   Negro.
3. The steady withdrawal of aid from institutions for the higher
   training of the Negro.

These movements are not, to be sure, direct results of Mr. Washington's teachings; but his propaganda has, without a shadow of
doubt, helped their speedier accomplishment. The question then
comes: Is it possible, and probable, that nine millions of men can
make effective progress in economic lines if they are deprived of political rights, made a servile caste, and allowed only the most meagre

chance for developing their exceptional men? If history and reason give any distinct answer to these questions, it is an emphatic *No.* . . .

In failing thus to state plainly and unequivocally the legitimate demands of their people, even at the cost of opposing an honored leader, the thinking classes of American Negroes would shirk a heavy responsibility, — a responsibility to themselves, a responsibility to the struggling masses, a responsibility to the darker races of men whose future depends so largely on this American experiment, but especially a responsibility to this nation, — this common Fatherland. It is wrong to encourage a man or a people in evil-doing; it is wrong to aid and abet a national crime simply because it is unpopular not to do so. The growing spirit of kindliness and reconciliation between the North and South after the frightful differences of a generation ago ought to be a source of deep congratulation to all, and especially to those whose mistreatment caused the war; but if that reconciliation is to be marked by the industrial slavery and civic death of those same black men, with permanent legislation into a position of inferiority, then those black men, if they are really men, are called upon by every consideration of patriotism and loyalty to oppose such a course by all civilized methods, even though such opposition involves disagreement with Mr. Booker T. Washington. We have no right to sit silently by while the inevitable seeds are sown for a harvest of disaster to our children, black and white.

First, it is the duty of black men to judge the South discriminatingly. The present generation of Southerners are not responsible for the past, and they should not be blindly hated or blamed for it. Furthermore, to no class is the indiscriminate endorsement of the recent course of the South toward Negroes more nauseating than to the best thought of the South. The South is not "solid"; it is a land in the ferment of social change, wherein forces of all kinds are fighting for supremacy; and to praise the ill the South is to-day perpetrating is just as wrong as to condemn the good. Discriminating and broad-minded criticism is what the South needs, — needs it for the sake of her own white sons and daughters, and for the insurance of robust, healthy mental and moral development.

To-day even the attitude of the Southern whites toward the blacks is not, as so many assume, in all cases the same; the ignorant Southerner hates the Negro, the workingmen fear his competition, the money-makers wish to use him as a laborer, some of the educated see a menace in his upward development, while others — usually the

sons of the masters — wish to help him to rise. National opinion has
enabled this last class to maintain the Negro common schools, and to
protect the Negro partially in property, life, and limb. Through the
pressure of the money-makers, the Negro is in danger of being reduced to semi-slavery, especially in the country districts; the workingmen, and those of the educated who fear the Negro, have united to
disfranchise him, and some have urged his deportation; while the passions of the ignorant are easily aroused to lynch and abuse any black
man. To praise this intricate whirl of thought and prejudice is nonsense; to inveigh indiscriminately against "the South" is unjust; but to
use the same breath in praising Governor Aycock, exposing Senator
Morgan, arguing with Mr. Thomas Nelson Page, and denouncing
Senator Ben Tillman, is not only sane, but the imperative duty of
thinking black men.

It would be unjust to Mr. Washington not to acknowledge that in
several instances he has opposed movements in the South which were
unjust to the Negro; he sent memorials to the Louisiana and Alabama
constitutional conventions, he has spoken against lynching, and in
other ways has openly or silently set his influence against sinister
schemes and unfortunate happenings. Notwithstanding this, it is
equally true to assert that on the whole the distinct impression left by
Mr. Washington's propaganda is, first, that the South is justified in
its present attitude toward the Negro because of the Negro's degradation; secondly, that the prime cause of the Negro's failure to rise
more quickly is his wrong education in the past; and, thirdly, that his
future rise depends primarily on his own efforts. Each of these propo-
sitions is a dangerous half-truth. The supplementary truths must
never be lost sight of: first, slavery and race-prejudice are potent if
not sufficient causes of the Negro's position; second, industrial and
common-school training were necessarily slow in planting because
they had to await the black teachers trained by higher institutions, —
it being extremely doubtful if any essentially different development
was possible, and certainly a Tuskegee was unthinkable before 1880;
and, third, while it is a great truth to say that the Negro must strive
and strive mightily to help himself, it is equally true that unless his
striving be not simply seconded, but rather aroused and encouraged,
by the initiative of the richer and wiser environing group, he cannot
hope for great success.

In his failure to realize and impress this last point, Mr. Washington is especially to be criticised. His doctrine has tended to make the

whites, North and South, shift the burden of the Negro problem to the Negro's shoulders and stand aside as critical and rather pessimistic spectators; when in fact the burden belongs to the nation, and the hands of none of us are clean if we bend not our energies to righting these great wrongs.

The South ought to be led, by candid and honest criticism, to assert her better self and do her full duty to the race she has cruelly wronged and is still wronging. The North — her copartner in guilt — cannot salve her conscience by plastering it with gold. We cannot settle this problem by diplomacy and suaveness, by "policy" alone. If worse come to worst, can the moral fibre of this country survive the slow throttling and murder of nine millions of men?

The black men of America have a duty to perform, a duty stern and delicate, — a forward movement to oppose a part of the work of their greatest leader. So far as Mr. Washington preaches Thrift, Patience, and Industrial Training for the masses, we must hold up his hands and strive with him, rejoicing in his honors and glorying in the strength of this Joshua called of God and of man to lead the headless host. But so far as Mr. Washington apologizes for injustice, North or South, does not rightly value the privilege and duty of voting, belittles the emasculating effects of caste distinctions, and opposes the higher training and ambition of our brighter minds, — so far as he, the South, or the Nation, does this, — we must unceasingly and firmly oppose them. By every civilized and peaceful method we must strive for the rights which the world accords to men, clinging unwaveringly to those great words which the sons of the Fathers would fain forget: "We hold these truths to be self-evident: That all men are created equal; that they are endowed by their Creator with certain unalienable rights; that among these are life, liberty, and the pursuit of happiness."

Anson Phelps Stokes

Founder's Day Address at Tuskegee, 1931

The Founder's Day Address delivered by Anson Phelps Stokes on the fiftieth anniversary of the founding of Tuskegee Institute in 1931 is a characteristic example of the genre and of the homage paid to Booker T. Washington on ceremonial occasions at Tuskegee. Washington was succeeded as president by Robert Russa Moton (1915–35) and Frederick D. Patterson (1935–53). Because he attended Tuskegee in the years 1933–35, Ellison would not have heard Stokes's address, but he is likely to have heard others much like it, including a chapel address by Moton that recalled Washington's deathbed advice to him to continue the traditions of Tuskegee (O'Meally, *Craft of Ralph Ellison* 12–16). Unlike the black and blind preacher Homer Barbee, who delivers the rousing memorial address on the Founder's life and deeds in *Invisible Man,* Stokes (1874–1958) was a white educator, clergyman, and philanthropist who served as secretary of Yale University and as a trustee of Tuskegee.

Tuskegee's own publications record numerous examples of the Founder's Day addresses that would have been familiar to students and provided inspiration for Barbee's magnificent oration. A further instance of the white dignitary's view of the Founder can be found in the more predictably paternalistic 1943 Founder's Day Address delivered by Governor Chauncey Sparks of Alabama and reproduced in Anne Kendrick Walker's *Tuskegee and the Black Belt* (xiii–xx). Equally revealing is Moton's autobiography, *Finding a Way Out,* in which he quotes Washington's praise of him at length. Moton compares Washington's death to that of Lincoln, much as Barbee's elaborate account of the journey of the Founder's coffin back home might be said to resemble the famous ritual journey of Lincoln's coffin from Washington to its final resting place in Illinois. Moton also reproduces his own inaugural speech at Tuskegee, the essence of which is a eulogy in praise of the Bookerite "spirit of cooperation between the coloured workers of the school and the white citizens outside of the school . . . a consecration for the relief of mankind everywhere, whether in Macon County, the State of Alabama, or in the

Nation" (Moton 194, 203–06, 210–20). The resemblance between Barbee's tribute to the Founder and grand eulogies of Lincoln (for example,
the poetic tribute by Walt Whitman, "When Lilacs Last in the Dooryard
Bloom'd") has reminded various critics that Ellison may have intended
here to invoke not just early black founders such as Frederick Douglass
and Washington, but also the white founders of America, such as George
Washington, Thomas Jefferson, and Abraham Lincoln (Callahan 135).

FURTHER READING: Booker T. Washington, *Tuskegee and Its People:
Their Ideals and Achievements* (New York: Appleton, 1906); William
Hardin Hughes, ed., *Robert Russa Moton of Hampton and Tuskegee*
(Chapel Hill: U of North Carolina P, 1956); Addie Louise Joyner Butler,
The Distinctive Black College: Talladega, Tuskegee, and Morehouse
(Metuchen, NJ: Scarecrow, 1977).

The stage was now set for the first attempt on the part of the
state government in Alabama, or in any one of the Gulf states, to
tackle seriously the problem of Negro education through the training
of teachers. A cooperative spirit on the part of the four groups named
was assured, but nothing could be done without a leader. In the providence of God the leader appeared in the person of Booker Washington. The life of this truly great man is told with extraordinary mod-
esty, humor, and vividness in *Up from Slavery* — one of America's
classics.

Born as we now know from the records in the family Bible of
James Burroughs, his owner in slavery, on a large plantation near
Hale's Ford Post Office, Franklin County, Virginia, 45 miles from
Lynchburg, on April 5, 1856; ignorant of his father's name; valued in
his owner's inventory when five years old at $400; living for about
the first seven years of his life with his brother, sister and honored
mother, who was cook for the plantation owner, in a one-room log
cabin about 14 by 16 feet, without wooden floor or glass windows;
sleeping "on a bundle of filthy rags laid upon the dirt floor"; living
almost entirely on corn bread and pork with now and then a glass of
milk or a potato, and two large spoonfuls of molasses from "the big
house" on Sunday; wearing only a flax shirt, whose roughness was a
living torture; removing after emancipation to Malden in the
Kanawha Valley in West Virginia, the family belongings being all carried in a cart; working in the salt furnace and the coal mine; begin-

ning to teach himself how to read from a "Blue-back" Webster's
Spelling book; studying under Mr. William Davis, a colored man and
a former Union soldier (by whose presence at the ripe age of 83 we
are honored today) at the first night school to be opened for colored
people in the region, at a time when not a single one of them in his
neighborhood could read a book, working faithfully for the good,
but strict Mrs. Viola Ruffner, of Charleston, West Virginia, at $5 a
month, while snatching every minute he could for study; starting off
at the age of 16 to drive and walk the 500 miles to Hampton to sat-
isfy his thirst for an education; spending several nights under the side-
walk in Richmond, while unloading pig iron in the day-time to get
money for his meals; passing the famous test of recitation-room-
cleaning to enter Hampton — four times with a broom, three times
with a dust cloth; not knowing whether to sleep over, beneath, or between the sheets that were provided him; gaining there through character and industry the position of janitor; paying off his debts by
summer work in a restaurant; graduating with the respect of all in
1875; teaching the school in his home-village of Malden, where he
also taught Sunday school, and started a night school, a debating society, and a reading room; spending a winter studying at Wayland
Seminary in Washington; returning to Hampton to deliver the "post-
graduate address" on "The Force that Wins"; becoming a member of
the Institute staff as a sort of "house-father" to the Indian young
men; and taking charge of the newly established "night school" there.

Such in brief was the career of our hero up to May, 1881, when at
the age of 25, on the suggestion of General Armstrong and, apparently, with the complete concurrence of the whole Hampton family,
young Washington was chosen to lead the new Normal School in Alabama. Unfortunately the original correspondence between Mr. Mur-
fee, Mr. Campbell and General Armstrong has been lost, but the letter of the last named made such an impression that the memory of its
wording has been handed down almost verbatim in Mr. Campbell's
family. It was: "I know of no one better qualified to take charge of
that school than one of our graduates, a bright mulatto, who had two
years' experience in charge of our Indian boys and training at Wayland Seminary. His name is Booker T. Washington." . . .

> "The old order changeth, yielding place to new,
> And God fulfills Himself in many ways,
> Least one good custom should corrupt the world."

So wrote Tennyson in his *Morte d'Arthur* and so we may say today as we think of the great events here in the late autumn of 1915. Booker Washington died, November 14, 1915. The whole nation mourned his loss. No fairer or finer tribute may be found among the hundreds in the Institute's files than that of the late Governor O'Neal of this state, and of the late Mr. Charles W. Hare, then editor of the "Tuskegee News." In a message from Washington, D. C. to his widow, a woman of real intellectual and moral force and a noble helpmate in all his labors, the former said: "The South as well as the nation mourns the loss of a great man. He had won the confidence of our people, and no man since the Civil War did more to create harmonious relations between the races." Mr. Hare's tribute in the local paper was equally impressive: "Locally almost to a man our own Tuskegee and Macon County citizens are realizing as never before how wonderfully the man had wrought for himself a place in the confidence and esteem of this community and country. In a thousand ways his influence for helpfulness has been felt and everybody mourns his going away." By request of the Mayor of Tuskegee, all stores were closed at the time of his funeral, and by order of the Mayor of Boston, all flags on municipal buildings were placed at half-mast.

It is not too much to say that as impartial critics, North and South, tried to estimate the significance of his achievement its significance began to dawn upon them. Colonel Henry Watterson, the leading southern journalist, and by many considered the most representative American journalist of his day, in a letter to the chairman of the Board of Trustees, wrote: "No man, since the War of Sections, has exercised such benevolent influence and done such real good to the country, especially to the South." Thoughtful men even went so far as to place him among that small group of American models which includes George Washington, Thomas Jefferson, Robert E. Lee, Abraham Lincoln, and perhaps a dozen others, and with the lapse of the years, this estimate does not seem exaggerated.

Men called to mind his greatness as an orator shown at the Atlanta Exposition in Georgia, at the dedication of the Shaw Monument in Boston, at the National Educational Association meeting at Madison, Wisconsin, and elsewhere. They praised his writings. But it was Booker Washington, the modest, courageous, clear-thinking, forceful Negro who had founded and developed one of the great educational institutions of America, and made it a power for intelligent and righteous living and for a sympathetic approach to the problems of race adjustment, to whom the nation paid its deepest homage. And it was, of course, appropriate that here at Tuskegee the beautiful national memorial was erected through the contributions of nearly 100,000 Negroes. It shows America's second Washington lifting the veil from the face of ignorance, and turning the crouching slave into a freeman capable of effective independent labor and thought.

On all sides the questions being asked after his death were: "Will the work of Tuskegee go on?" "Who will take up the mantle of Elijah?" The Trustees, through a committee of which ex-President Low of Columbia University was chairman, acted promptly and, in the Providence of God, wisely. I have no hesitation in saying that time has completely justified their choice.

Major Moton's experience at Hampton, his sterling character, his clear-thinking mind, his lovable personality, his large administrative ability, and the known confidence of Dr. Washington in him made him foreordained to fill the great gap. And just as everyone today when speaking of Hampton refers to both General Armstrong and Dr. Frissell, although General Armstrong has the eternal honor of founding Hampton, and so Washington must ever have the supreme honor of founding Tuskegee, yet increasingly with the years will Tuskegee suggest both Washington and Moton.

In selecting Major Moton, the Trustees took a step in advance in the field of Negro leadership. Booker Washington was a mulatto. As he stated in *Up from Slavery* it was rumored on the plantation that his father was a white man, and the rumor was probably correct.

Some people who did not understand the potentiality of the Negro, as such, believed that Booker Washington's powers were mainly due to some good white blood in his ancestry. But now a man was chosen of pure Negro stock, with an ancestry, by the way, which is known to go back to a Mandingo chief of the eighteenth century: Tuskegee was going to put to the test the power of pure Negro leadership. Dr. Washington had shown that some Negro blood did not prevent the highest character, the broadest vision, and the most remarkable ability. Now it was to be shown that a man with only Negro blood could effectively fill an office with a great tradition and most exacting duties. Fortunately, he was as proud of his Negro blood as was Booker Washington, and with his dark countenance he could not have disguised it even had he wanted to!

The new Principal's inaugural address was reassuring to all concerned, in that it showed conclusively that the principles for which Booker Washington stood were to be adhered to, the methods being merely adjusted to meet the changed conditions of Negro life. The following extract from Major Moton's inaugural is worth quoting at this time:

"In order that this institution shall continue to carry forward the ideas and ideals of its great Founder; in order that it shall not cease to render large service to humankind; in order that we shall keep the respect and confidence of the people of this land, we must, first, every one of us, principal, officers, teachers, graduates, and students, use every opportunity and strive in every reasonable way, to develop and strengthen between white and black people, North and South, that unselfish cooperation which has characterized the Tuskegee Institute from its very beginning. Second, we must patiently and persistently and in the spirit of unselfish devotion, follow the methods of education, which, in this school, have been so distinctive, so unique, and so helpful. Third, we must consecrate and reconsecrate our lives to this work as instruments in God's hands for the training of black men and women for service, in whatever capacity, or in whatever locality they may find a human need. Fourth, there must be no cantankerousness here — we must all work absolutely together."

. . . Tuskegee stands for showing the white man all that is best in the Negro, and for showing the Negro all that is best in the white man, and for helping both to work together to advance their common interests.

Here are some of the main features of Tuskegee's educational creed as illustrated by the Founder's sayings:

We believe in the dignity of labor. "We shall prosper in proportions as we learn to dignify labor and put brains and skill into the common occupations of life."

We believe in doing what we do well. "The man who has learned to do something better than anyone else, has learned to do a common thing in an uncommon manner, is the man who has a power and influence that no adverse circumstances can take from him."

We believe in the power of education. "Ignorance is not a cure for anything." "There is no defense or security for any of us except in the highest intelligence and development of all."

We believe in the life of service. "The only thing worth living for is the lifting up of our fellowmen" . . . "The greatest thing you can learn is the lesson of brotherly love, of usefulness, and of charity."

We believe in the spirit of cooperation between all individuals and groups. "Cast down your bucket where you are. Cast it down in making friends, in every honorable way, of the people of all races by whom you are surrounded."

We believe in fitting all men to exercise the responsibilities of American citizenship. "It is important and right that all privileges of the law be ours, but it is vastly more important that we be prepared for the exercise of these privileges" . . . "Let the very best educational opportunities be provided for both races, and add to this the enactment of an election law that shall be incapable of unjust discrimination, at the same time providing that in proportion as the ignorant secure education, property, and character, they will be given the rights of citizenship."

Such are some of the fundamental convictions on which Tuskegee's work has been built up. They have helped to give the South confidence in the movement to educate the Negro, and have helped to give the Negro confidence in himself as a Negro and as an American, to develop and to play a useful part in our American life. The emphasis on Negro self-consciousness was necessary in the decades following the Civil War to give the Negro a feeling of racial solidarity and confidence, but now that this has been attained there is some danger of its over-emphasis. It is undoubtedly important when certain matters are under scientific investigation or consideration to remember that an Anglo-Saxon is an Anglo-Saxon, an Oriental an Oriental, and a Negro a Negro, but it is even more important, under these and all other circumstances, to remember that men of the white, black, and yellow races are first of all human beings. Probably, therefore, more can now be accomplished in matters involving Negro rights and Negro progress by emphasis on the constitutional rights of all our citizens and on human justice, rather than by stressing too much the rights of any one group, although there are times when the latter is still a necessity. Furthermore when we wish to consider racial differences, let it be done objectively and fairly without any smug pre-suppositions as to the essential and permanent superiority of any one group, or of the essential and permanent inferiority of any other. Brothers may differ in many ways, but they are still brothers!

Tuskegee is a radiating center for these ideals which have the same universal applicability as the ideals of the Sermon on the Mount — on which they are so largely based. They *were* the foundations on which a simple industrial school was founded here. They were equally vital when it became a great Normal and Industrial Institute. They *are* equally vital now that the Institute is developing increasingly on the college grade. They *will be* equally vital if Tuskegee ever develops into a vocational university of a new type. Let us learn all we can from modern pedagogy, and modern science, and modern psychology, and modern sociology, and develop this institution fearlessly with their aid, but let us in the process never cast loose from these original moorings.

Langston Hughes

Cowards from the Colleges

James Langston Hughes (1902–67), one of the leading African American writers of the early twentieth century and a key figure in the Harlem Renaissance, is best known for his poetry in volumes such as *Weary Blues* (1926), *Fine Clothes to the Jew* (1927), and *Montage of A Dream Deferred* (1951), fiction such as *Not Without Laughter* (1930) and *The Ways of White Folks* (1934), and two autobiographies, *The Big Sea* (1940) and *I Wonder as I Wander* (1956). Hughes's jazz and blues–inflected verse and his landmark essay "The Negro Artist and the Racial Mountain" (1926) broke with conservative artistic traditions of the past and argued for a new, highly vernacular black cultural voice of the kind so often featured in *Invisible Man*. Born in Joplin, Missouri, Hughes developed an artistic voice that combined the languages of the South and the Midwest with the urban East. He was accomplished as a musical lyricist and wrote a number of plays, including *Mulatto* (1935) and *The Sun Do Move* (1942), while in his later career he edited several anthologies, wrote books for children and pictorial accounts of African American culture, and produced *A History of the NAACP* (1962).

Especially in the 1930s and 1940s, however, Hughes's work was also driven by protest against racial intolerance. His short stories built around the character Jesse B. Semple (or "Simple"), first published beginning in 1942 in the prominent black newspaper the *Chicago Defender*, contain acerbic commentary on race relations. In several noteworthy poems and plays he denounced the injustice of the famous Scottsboro case in Alabama, where several young black men were wrongly charged with the rape of white women. "Cowards from the Colleges," which first appeared in 1934 in the NAACP magazine *Crisis*, edited by W. E. B. Du Bois, is in this same spirit, and it belongs as well to a genre of essays by African American intellectuals in which the accommodation practiced by some black colleges and members of the black middle class is held up to judgment.

Hughes's sharp-edged essay embraces general policies as well as specific incidents that would have been well known to Ellison and that bear on his protagonist's experience at college. Although African American

students of the 1920s and 1930s did often protest both local and national racism, Hughes focused on the institutional pressures that could
easily suppress student activism. His argument, in brief, is that black colleges often conformed to rigid and politically safe policies in order to
court white sponsorship and, as Ellison's protagonist discovers, repri-
manded or punished those whose actions might put the school at risk.
One might also compare the harsh critique of some black southern colleges for their reactionary social codes and tyrannical administrations
published by J. Saunders Redding in *No Day of Triumph* in 1942. Redding's catalog includes an account of one college president who runs his
school — as illustrated in an evening chapel address — through a combination of intimidation and humiliation but whose favorite hymn is "Live
Humble." Dr. Bledsoe's favorite hymn (*Invisible Man* 106), "Live-a-
Humble," as it is usually called, is itself a paean to Christian subservience: "A-live a-humble, humble / Humble yourself, the bell's-a
done-a rung," runs the chorus of a version issued by the great singer
Roland Hayes in 1948 (Hayes 106). But it is also an apt characterization
not only of the posture of passivity that whites expected of blacks in the
era of segregation but also of the masquerade performed by leaders like
Bledsoe in preserving their own fragile power. Like Bledsoe, moreover,
the president in Redding's narrative keeps various relics of the college
site's plantation history in his office because of their "symbolical significance," and when Redding visits him the following morning, the president is having a student shine his shoes, his foot resting on the young
man's knee (Redding 121–32).

FURTHER READING: E. Franklin Frazier, *Black Bourgeoisie* (Glencoe,
IL: Free P, 1957); Raymond Wolters, *The New Negro on Campus: Black
College Rebellions of the 1920s* (Princeton: Princeton UP, 1975); Arnold
Rampersad, *The Life of Langston Hughes*, 2 vols. (New York: Oxford
UP, 1986–88); Edward J. Mullen, ed., *Critical Essays on Langston
Hughes* (Boston: Hall, 1986).

Two years ago, on a lecture tour, I visited more than fifty colored
schools and colleges from Morgan College in Baltimore to Prairie
View in Texas. Everywhere I was received with the greatest kindness
and hospitality by both students and faculties. In many ways, my
nine months on tour were among the pleasantest travel months I have
ever known. I made many friends, and this article is in no way meant

as a disparagement of the courtesies and hospitality of these genial people — who, nevertheless, uphold many of the existing evils which I am about to mention, and whose very geniality is often a disarming cloak for some of the most amazingly old-fashioned moral and pedagogical concepts surviving on this continent.

At every school I visited I would be shown about the grounds, and taken to view the new auditorium or the modern domestic science hall or the latest litter of pigs born. If I took this tour with the principal or some of the older teachers, I would often learn how well the school was getting on in spite of the depression, and how pleasant relationships were with the white Southerners in the community. But if I went walking with a younger teacher or with students, I would usually hear reports of the institution's life and ways that were far from happy.

For years those of us who have read the Negro papers or who have had friends teaching in our schools and colleges, have been pretty well aware of the lack of personal freedom that exists on most Negro campuses. But the extent to which this lack of freedom can go never really came home to me until I saw and experienced myself some of the astounding restrictions existing at many colored educational institutions.

To set foot on dozens of Negro campuses is like going back to mid-Victorian England, or Massachusetts in the days of the witch-burning Puritans. To give examples, let us take the little things first. On some campuses grown-up college men and women are not allowed to smoke, thus you have the amusing spectacle of twenty-four-year-old men sneaking around to the back doors of dormitories like little boys to take a drag on a forbidden cigarette. At some schools, simple card playing is a wicked abomination leading to dismissal for a student — even though many students come from homes where whist and bridge are common amusements. At a number of schools, dancing on the campus for either faculty or students is absolutely forbidden. And going to dancing parties off campus is frequently frowned upon. At one school for young ladies in North Carolina, I came across an amusing rule which allowed the girls to dance with each other once or twice a week, but permitted no young men at their frolics. At some schools marching in couples is allowed instead of dancing. Why this absurd ban on ballroom dancing exists at colored schools, I could never find out — doubly absurd in this day and age when every public high school has its dances and "proms," and the very air is full of jazz, North and South, in inescapable radio waves.

One of the objects in not permitting dancing, I divined, seems to be to keep the sexes separated. And in our Negro schools the technique for achieving this — boys not walking with girls, young men not calling on young ladies, the two sexes sitting aisles apart in chapel if the institution is co-education — in this technique Negro schools rival monasteries and nunneries in their strictness. They act as though it were unnatural for a boy and girl to ever want to walk or talk together. The high points of absurdity during my tour were campuses where young men and women meeting in broad daylight in the middle of the grounds might only speak to one another, not stand still to converse lest they break a rule; and a college in Mississippi, Alcorn, — where to evening lectures grown-up students march like school kids in and out of the hall. When I had finished my lecture at Alcorn, the chairman tapped a bell and commanded, "Young ladies with escorts now pass." And those few girls fortunate enough to receive permission to come with a boy rose and made their exit. Again the bell tapped and the chairman said, "Unescorted young ladies now pass." And in their turn the female section rose and passed. Again the bell tapped. "Young men now pass." I waited to hear the bell again and the chairman saying, "Teachers may leave." But apparently most of the teachers had already left, chaperoning their grown-up charges back to the dormitories. Such regimentation as practiced in this college was long ago done away with, even in many grammar schools of the North.

Apparently the official taboo on male and female companionship extends even to married women teachers who attend summer seminars in the South, and over whom the faculty extends a prying but protective arm. The wife of a prominent educator in the South told me of being at Hampton for one of their summer sessions a few years ago. One night her husband called up long distance just to hear his wife's voice over the phone. Before she was permitted to go to the phone and talk to a MAN at night, however, she had to receive a special permit from, I believe, the dean of women, who had to be absolutely assured that it really was her husband calling. The long distance phone costs mounted steadily while the husband waited but Hampton did its part in keeping the sexes from communicating. Such interference with nature is a major aim of many of our campuses.

Accompanying this mid-Victorian attitude in manners and morals, at many Southern schools there is a great deal of official emphasis placed on heavy religious exercises, usually compulsory, with required daily chapels, weekly prayer meetings, and Sunday services. Such a stream of dull and stupid sermons, uninspired prayers, and monotonous hymns — neither intellectually worthy of adult minds nor emotionally exciting in the manner of the old time shouts — pour into students' ears that it is a wonder any young people ever go to church again once they leave college. The placid cant and outworn phrases of many of the churchmen daring to address student groups today makes me wonder why their audiences are not bored to death. I did observe many young people going to sleep.

But there are charges of a far more serious nature to bring against Negro schools than merely that of frowning on jazz in favor of hymns, or their horror of friendly communication between boys and girls on the campuses. To combine these charges very simply: Many of our institutions apparently are not trying to make men and women of their students at all — they are doing their best to produce spineless Uncle Toms, uninformed, and full of mental and moral evasions.

I was amazed to find at many Negro schools and colleges a year after the arrest and conviction of the Scottsboro boys, that a great many teachers and students knew nothing of it, or if they did the official attitude would be, "Why bring that up?" I asked at Tuskegee, only a few hours from Scottsboro, who from there had been to the trial. Not a soul had been so far as I could discover. And with demonstrations in every capital in the civilized world for the freedom of the Scottsboro boys, so far as I know not one Alabama Negro school until now has held even a protest meeting. (And in Alabama, we have the largest colored school in the world, Tuskegee, and one of our best colleges, Talladega.)

But speaking of protest meetings — this was my experience at Hampton. I lectured there the week-end that Juliette Derricotte was killed. She had been injured in an automobile wreck on her way home from Fisk University where she was dean of women, and the white Georgia hospitals would not take her in for treatment, so she died. That same week-end, a young Hampton graduate, the coach of Alabama's A.&M. Institute at Normal was beaten to death by a mob in Birmingham on his way to see his own team play. Many of the Hampton students and teachers knew Juliette Derricotte, and almost all of them knew the young coach, their recent graduate. The two happenings sent a wave of sorrow and of anger over the campus where I was a visitor. Two double tragedies of color on one day — and most affecting to students and teachers because the victims were "of their own class," one a distinguished and widely travelled young woman, the other a popular college graduate and athlete.

A note came to me from a group of Senior students asking would I meet with a student committee. When a young man came to take me to the meeting, he told me that it would concern Juliette Derricotte and their own dead alumnus. He said that the students wanted to plan a protest on the campus against the white brutality that had brought about their death.

I was deeply touched that they had called me in to help them, and we began to lay plans for the organization of a Sunday evening protest meeting, from which we would send wires to the press and formulate a memorial to these most recent victims of race hate. They asked me would I speak at this meeting and I agreed. Students were chosen to approach the faculty for permission to use the chapel. We were to consult again for final plans in the evening.

At the evening committee meeting the faculty had sent their representative, Major Brown, a Negro (who is, I believe, the dean of men), to confer with the students. Major Brown began by saying that perhaps the reports we had received of the manner of these two deaths had not been true. Had we verified those reports?

I suggested wiring or telephoning immediately to Fisk and to Birmingham for verification. The Major did not think that wise. He felt it was better to write. Furthermore, he went on, Hampton did not like the word "protest." That was not Hampton's way. He, and Hampton, believed in moving slowly and quietly, and with dignity.

On and on he talked. When he had finished, the students knew quite clearly that they could not go ahead with their protest meeting. (The faculty had put up its wall.) They knew they would face expulsion and loss of credits if they did so. The result was that the Hampton students held no meeting of protest over the mob-death of their own alumnus, nor the death on the road (in a Negro ambulance vainly trying to reach a black hospital) of one of the race's finest young women. The brave and manly spirit of that little group of Hampton students who wanted to organize the protest was crushed by the official voice of Hampton speaking through its Negro Major Brown.

More recently, I see in our papers where Fisk University, that

great (?) center of Negro education and of Jubilee fame has expelled
Ishmael Flory, a graduate student from California on a special honor
scholarship, because he dared organize a protest against the Univer-
sity singers appearing in a Nashville Jim-crow theatre where colored
people must go up a back alley to sit in the gallery. Probably also the
University resented his organizing, through the Denmark Vesey
Forum, a silent protest parade denouncing the lynching of Cordie
Cheek who was abducted almost at the very gates of the University.

Another recent news item tells how President Gandy of Virginia
State College for Negroes called out the cracker police of the town to
keep his own students from voicing their protest as to campus conditions. Rather than listen to just grievances, a Negro president of a
large college sends for prejudiced white policemen to break his students' heads, if necessary.

And last year, we had the amazing report from Tuskegee of the
school hospital turning over to the police one of the wounded Negroes shot at Camp Hill by white lynchers because the sharecroppers
have the temerity to wish to form a union — and the whites wish no
Negro unions in Alabama. Without protest, the greatest Negro
school in the world gives up a poor black, bullet-riddled sharecropper
to white officers. And awhile later Tuskegee's president, Dr. Moton,
announces himself in favor of lower wages for Negroes under the
N.R.A., and Claude Barnett, one of his trustees, voices his approval
of the proposed code differentials on the basis of color.

But then, I remember that it is Tuskegee that maintains a guest
house on its campus for *whites only!* It also maintains a library that
censors all books on race problems and economics to see that no volumes "too radical" get to the students. And during my stay there several young teachers whispered to me that a local white trustee of the
school receives his Negro visitors only on the porch, not in his home.
It is thus that our wealthiest Negro school with its two thousand six
hundred students expects to turn out men and women!

Where then would one educate "Uncle Toms?"

Freedom of expression for teachers in most Negro schools, even
on such unimportant matters as to rouge or not to rouge, smoke or
not smoke, is more or less unknown. Old and mossbacked presidents,
orthodox ministers or missionary principals, control all too often
what may or may not be taught in the classrooms or said in campus
conversation. Varied examples of suppression at the campuses I visited are too numerous to mention in full in a short article, but they

range all the way from an Alabama secondary school that permitted no Negro weeklies like the *Chicago Defender* or the *Pittsburgh Courier* in its library because they were "radical," to the great university of Fisk at Nashville where I asked a nationally known Negro professor and author of several books in his field what his attitude toward communism was, and received as an answer, "When I discuss communism on this campus, I will have a letter first from the president and the board of trustees."

There is at the Negro schools in the South, even the very well-endowed and famous ones that I have mentioned, an amazing acquiescence to the wishes of the local whites and to the traditions of the Southern color-line. When programs are given, many schools set aside whole sections in their own auditoriums for the exclusive use of whites. Often the best seats are given them, to the exclusion of Negro visitors. (But to insert into this article a good note, Mary McLeod Bethune, however, permits no such goings-on at Bethune-Cookman Institute in Daytona, one of the few campuses where I lectured that had not made "special provisions" for local white folks. A great many whites were in the audience but they sat among the Negroes.)

Even where there is no official campus segregation (such as Tuskegee's white guest house, or Hampton's hospital where local whites are given separate service), both teachers and students of Negro colleges accept so sweetly the customary Jim Crowing of the South that one feels sure the race's emancipation will never come through its intellectuals. In North Carolina, I was given a letter to the state superintendent of the Negro schools, a white man, Mr. N. C. Newbold. When I went to his office in Raleigh to present my letter, I encountered in his outer office a white woman secretary busy near the window quite a distance from the door. She gave me a casual glance and went on with what she was doing. Then some white people came into the office. Immediately she dropped her work near the window and came over to them, spoke to them most pleasantly, and ignored me entirely. The white people, after several minutes of how-are-you's and did-you-enjoy-yo'self-at-the-outing-last-week, said that they wished to see Mr. Newbold. Whereupon, having arrived first and having not yet been noticed by the secretary, I turned and walked out.

When I told some Negro teachers of the incident, they said, "But Mr. Newbold's not like that."

"Why, then," I asked, "does he have that kind of secretary?"

Nobody seemed to know. And why had none of the Negro teachers who call at his office ever done anything about such discourteous secretaries? No one knew that either.

But why (to come nearer home) did a large number of the students at my own Lincoln University, when I made a campus survey there in 1929, declare that they were opposed to having teachers of their own race on the faculty? And why did they then (and probably still do) allow themselves to be segregated in the little moving picture theatre in the nearby village of Oxford, when there is no Jim-Crow law in Pennsylvania — and they are some four hundred strong? And why did a whole Lincoln University basketball team and their coach walk docilely out of a cafe in Philadelphia that refused to serve them because of color? One of the players explained later, "The coach didn't want to make a fuss."

Yet Lincoln's motto is to turn out leaders! But can there be leaders who don't want to make a fuss?

And can it be that our Negro educational institutions are not really interested in turning out leaders at all? Can it be that they are far more interested in their endowments and their income and their salaries than in their students?

And can it be that these endowments, incomes, gifts — and therefore salaries — springing from missionary and philanthropic sources and from big Northern boards and foundations — have such strings tied to them that those accepting them can do little else (if they wish to live easy) but bow down to the white powers that control this philanthropy and continue, to the best of their ability, to turn out "Uncle Toms?"

A famous Lincoln alumnus, having read my undergraduate survey of certain deplorable conditions on our campus, said to me when I graduated there, "Your facts are fine! Fine! Fine! But listen, son, you mustn't say everything you think to white folks."

"But this is the truth," I said.

"I know, but suppose," continued the old grad patronizingly, in his best fatherly manner, "suppose I had always told the truth to white folks? Could I have built up that great center for the race that I now head in my city? Where would I have gotten the money for it, son?"

The great center of which he spoke is a Jim Crow center, but he was very proud of having built it.

To me it seems that the day must come when we will not be proud of our Jim Crow centers built on the money docile and lying beggars have kidded white people into contributing. The day must come when we will not say that a college is a great college because it has a few beautiful buildings, and a half dozen Ph.D.'s on a faculty that is afraid to open its mouth though a lynching occurs at the college gates, or the wages of Negro workers in the community go down to zero!

Frankly, I see no hope for a new spirit today in the majority of the Negro schools of the South unless the students themselves put it there. Although there exists on all campuses a distinct cleavage between the younger and older members of the faculties, almost everywhere the younger teachers, knowing well the existing evils, are as yet too afraid of their jobs to speak out, or to dare attempt to reform campus conditions. They content themselves by writing home to mama and by whispering to sympathetic visitors from a distance how they hate teaching under such conditions.

Meanwhile, more power to those brave and progressive students who strike against mid-Victorian morals and the suppression of free thought and action! More power to the Ishmael Florys, and the Denmark Vesey Forum, and the Howard undergraduates who picket the Senate's Jim Crow dining rooms — for unless we develop more and ever more such young men and women on our campuses as an antidote to the docile dignity of the meek professors and well-paid presidents who now run our institutions, American Negroes in the future had best look to the unlettered for their leaders, and expect only cowards from the colleges.

Gunnar Myrdal

Social Equality

The phrase *social equality* played a significant role in American thinking about segregation and race relations throughout the nineteenth and twentieth centuries. Social equality was usually distinguished from political equality (in matters such as legal due process, contract obligations, and voting rights) and referred to equal access to schools, housing, transportation, and other public accommodations — that is, to those arenas of life in which whites and blacks might most likely come into closer physical contact. Famous legal decisions in support of segregation, such as *Plessy* v. *Ferguson* (1896), and much sociological writing about race and racism proved, however, that distinctions between social and political equality were often blurred, for few whites were willing to grant political or legal equality, out of fear that it might lead to other forms of equality. In a great many instances, "social equality" was in essence a coded phrase that meant racial mixing — the right of blacks and whites to date, intermarry, and have children. The prohibition against miscegenation, as it was usually called during the era of segregation, was so great as to guarantee a hysterical reaction among those whites opposed to integration when the taboo of social equality seemed threatened. As the black writer and activist Kelly Miller wrote in 1908, for example, the phrase "social equality" is "like a savage warwhoop [that] arouses the deepest venom of race, which slumbers only skin deep beneath a thin veneer of civilization" (Miller 123).

When Ellison's protagonist mistakenly says "social equality" rather than "social responsibility" during his graduation speech at the men's smoker (*Invisible Man* 31), he touches a sore spot in the white southern psyche. The selection "Social Equality," from Gunnar Myrdal's classic study of American racism, *An American Dilemma*, offers a clear evocation of the climate of opinion about social equality at the time Ellison was writing. Commissioned by the Carnegie Corporation in 1938 to study the problem of American racism, the Swedish social economist Myrdal (1898–1987) led a group of researchers in writing a massive volume that stood for more than a generation as the authoritative study of America's abiding dilemma — that racial prejudice directly contradicts

66

America's proclaimed commitment to equality. Not all readers were equally impressed. Among the challenging reviews of *An American Dilemma* was one by Ellison himself, who criticized Myrdal for portraying African American life, whether pathologically or not, as principally a *reaction* against white racism and white institutions. As Ellison pointed out, blacks are not "simply the creation of white men" but have themselves engaged in a complex, dualistic, if sometimes hidden, creation of their own culture and of American culture itself. Ellison's review, written in 1944 but unpublished at that time, is revealing both for its general critique of sociological studies of race relations and for its several clear premonitions of *Invisible Man*, including a remark that points to the very first pages of the novel: "In our society it is not at all unusual for a Negro to experience a sensation that he does not exist in the real world at all. He seems rather to exist in the nightmarish fantasy of the white American mind as a phantom that the white mind seeks unceasingly, by means both crude and subtle, to lay" (*"An American Dilemma:* A Review" 315, 304).

FURTHER READING: Oliver Cromwell Cox, *Caste, Class, and Race: A Study in Social Dynamics* (New York: Doubleday, 1948); David W. Southern, *Gunnar Myrdal and Black-White Relations: The Use and Abuse of* An American Dilemma, *1944–1969* (Baton Rouge: Louisiana State UP, 1987); Walter A. Jackson, *Gunnar Myrdal and America's Conscience: Social Engineering and Racial Liberalism, 1938–1987* (Chapel Hill: U of North Carolina P, 1990).

In his first encounter with the American Negro problem, perhaps nothing perplexes the outside observer more than the popular term and the popular theory of "no social equality." He will be made to feel from the start that it has concrete implications and a central importance for the Negro problem in America. But, nevertheless, the term is kept vague and elusive, and the theory loose and ambiguous. One moment it will be stretched to cover and justify every form of social segregation and discrimination, and, in addition, all the inequalities in justice, politics, and breadwinning. The next moment it will be narrowed to express only the denial of close personal intimacies and intermarriage. The very lack of precision allows the notion of "no social equality" to rationalize the rather illogical and wavering system of color caste in America.

The kernel of the popular theory of "no social equality" will, when pursued, be presented as a firm determination on the part of the whites to block amalgamation and preserve "the purity of the white race." The white man identifies himself with "the white race" and feels that he has a stake in resisting the dissipation of its racial identity. Important in this identification is the notion of "the absolute and unchangeable superiority of the white race." From this racial dogma will often be drawn the *direct* inference that the white man shall dominate in all spheres. But when the logic of this inference is inquired about, the inference will be made *indirect* and will be made to lead over to the danger of amalgamation, or, as it is popularly expressed, "intermarriage."

It is further found that the ban on intermarriage is focused on white women. For them it covers both formal marriage and illicit intercourse. In regard to white men it is taken more or less for granted that they would not stoop to marry Negro women, and that illicit intercourse does not fall under the same intense taboo. Their offspring, under the popular doctrine that maternity is more certain than paternity, become Negroes anyway, and the white race easily avoids pollution with Negro blood. To prevent "intermarriage" in this specific sense of sex relations between white women and Negro men, it is not enough to apply legal and social sanctions against it — so the popular theory runs. In using the danger of intermarriage as a defense for the whole caste system, it is assumed both that Negro men have a strong desire for "intermarriage," and that white women would be open to proposals from Negro men, *if* they are not guarded from even meeting them on an equal plane. The latter assumption, of course, is never openly expressed, but is logically implicit in the popular theory. The conclusion follows that the whole system of segregation and discrimination is justified. Every single measure is defended as necessary to block "social equality" which in its turn is held necessary to prevent "intermarriage."

The basic role of the fear of amalgamation in white attitudes to the race problem is indicated by the popular magical concept of "blood." Educated white Southerners, who know everything about modern genetic and biological research, confess readily that they actually feel an irrational or "instinctive" repugnance in thinking of "intermarriage." These measures of segregation and discrimination are often of the type found in the true taboos and in the notion "not to be touched" of primitive religion. The specific taboos are characterized, further, by a different degree of excitement which attends their violation and a different degree of punishment to the violator: the closer the act to sexual association, the more furious is the public reaction. Sexual association itself is punished by death and is accompanied by tremendous public excitement; the other social relations meet decreasing degrees of public fury. Sex becomes in this popular theory the principle around which the whole structure of segregation of the Negroes — down to disfranchisement and denial of equal opportunities on the labor market — is organized. The reasoning is this: "For, say what we will, may not all the equalities be ultimately based on potential social equality, and that in turn on intermarriage? Here we reach the real *crux* of the question." In cruder language, but with the same logic, the Southern man on the street responds to any plea for social equality: "Would you like to have your daughter marry a Negro?"

This theory of color caste centering around the aversion to amalgamation determines, as we have just observed, the white man's rather definite rank order of the various measures of segregation and discrimination against Negroes. The relative significance attached to each of those measures is dependent upon their degree of expediency or necessity — in the view of white people — as means of upholding the ban on "intermarriage." In this rank order, (1) the ban on intermarriage and other sex relations involving white women and colored men takes precedence before everything else. It is the end for which the other restrictions are arranged as means. Thereafter follow: (2) all sorts of taboos and etiquettes in personal contacts; (3) segregation in schools and churches; (4) segregation in hotels, restaurants, and theaters, and other public places where people meet socially; (5) segregation in public conveyances; (6) discrimination in public services; and, finally, inequality in (7) politics, (8) justice and (9) breadwinning and relief.

The degree of liberalism on racial matters in the white South can be designated mainly by the point on this rank order where a man stops because he believes further segregation and discrimination are not necessary to prevent "intermarriage." We have seen that white liberals in the South of the present day, as a matter of principle, rather unanimously stand up against inequality in breadwinning, relief, justice, and politics. These fields of discrimination form the chief battleground and considerable changes in them are, as we have seen, on the way. When we ascend to the higher ranks which concern social relations in the narrow sense, we find the Southern liberals less prepared to split off from the majority opinion of the region. Hardly anybody in the South is prepared to go the whole way and argue that even the ban on intermarriage should be lifted. Practically all agree, not only upon the high desirability of preventing "intermarriage," but also that a certain amount of separation between the two groups is expedient and necessary to prevent it. Even the one who has his philosophical doubts on the point must, if he is reasonable, abstain from ever voicing them. The social pressure is so strong that it would be foolish not to conform. Conformity is a political necessity for having any hope of influence; it is, in addition, a personal necessity for not meeting social ostracism. . . .

The fixation on the purity of white womanhood, and also part of the intensity of emotion surrounding the whole sphere of segregation and discrimination, are to be understood as the backwashes of the sore conscience on the part of white men for their own or their compeers' relations with, or desires for, Negro women. These psychological effects are greatly magnified because of the puritan *milieu* of America and especially of the South. The upper class men in a less puritanical people could probably have indulged in sex relations with, and sexual day-dreams of, lower caste women in a more matter-of-course way and without generating so much pathos about white womanhood. The Negro people have to carry the burden not only of the white men's sins but also of their virtues. The virtues of the honest, democratic, puritan white Americans in the South are great, and the burden upon the Negroes becomes ponderous.

Our practical conclusion is that it would have cleansing effects on race relations in America, and particularly in the South, to have an open and sober discussion in rational terms of this ever present popular theory of "intermarriage" and "social equality," giving matters their factual ground, true proportions and logical relations. Because it is, to a great extent, an opportunistic rationalization, and because it refers directly and indirectly to the most touchy spots in American life and American morals, tremendous inhibitions have been built up against a detached and critical discussion of this theory. But such inhibitions are gradually overcome when, in the course of secularized education, people become rational about their life problems. It must never be forgotten that in our increasingly intellectualized civilization even the plain citizen feels an urge for truth and objectivity, and that this rationalistic urge is increasingly competing with the opportunistic demands for rationalization and escape.

There are reasons to believe that a slow but steady cleansing of the American mind is proceeding as the cultural level is raised. The basic racial inferiority doctrine is being undermined by research and education. For a white man to have illicit relations with Negro women is increasingly meeting disapproval. Negroes themselves are more and more frowning upon such relations. This all must tend to dampen the emotional fires around "social equality." Sex and race fears are, however, even today the main defense for segregation and, in fact, for the whole caste order. The question shot at the interviewer touching any point of this order is still: "Would you like to have your daughter (sister) marry a Negro?"

Supreme Court Brief

Brown v. Board of Education: The Effects of Segregation

The 1954 Supreme Court decision in *Brown* v. *Board of Education* declared that segregation by race, even if so-called "separate but equal" facilities were provided (which was almost never the case), was unconstitutional. Coming close to one century after the end of the Civil War, the decision capped a long struggle by the NAACP and others, centering on public schools, to break down the barriers of segregation. Even though by 1960 only 6 percent of public schools in the South had complied with the orders issued by the Court in its decree of implementation in 1955, the landmark ruling had nonetheless provided the legal underpinnings necessary to the civil rights movement of the 1950s and 1960s. Because segregation was an issue not just in schools but in all walks of American life, legal historian Richard Kluger chose an apt inversion of Ellison's epithet for a chapter in which he described the new world of the African American in the wake of *Brown* as that of "visible man" (Kluger 748–78). Black men and women would remain subject to prejudice and racial hatred for years to come, but their legal, civic, and social rights henceforth had to become visible to white America.

Invisible Man appeared two years before the ruling in *Brown* v. *Board of Education,* but because the collective cases that went under that title had been in the process of litigation and appeal for several years, it may be more than a coincidence that the protagonist receives his scholarship and brief case from his local Board of Education (*Invisible Man* 32). Still, the novel is infused with the ethos of segregation captured at the limits of absurdity (see pp. 1–6 of this book), and its concluding episodes, depending on how one reads the historical scheme, strand the protagonist somewhere in the years leading directly to the Court's decision. Beyond its great ramifications for American public life, the *Brown* decision was notable to jurists and legal scholars because it evaded precedent and relied heavily on moral argument and sociological investigations of the detrimental effects of segregation. Among the works cited in an unusual array of footnotes in the decision, for instance, were Myrdal's *An Ameri-*

can Dilemma and a famous study conducted by Kenneth Clark, in which he used black and white dolls to demonstrate that young black children were accustomed by prevailing racial attitudes, at a very early age, to think of whiteness as preferable and more pretty or nice. In place of the Court's ruling itself (347 U.S. 483 [1954]), which is of constitutional rather than literary interest, the selection here is from the brief filed by the appellants in *Brown*, a team led by the future Supreme Court justice, and then legal counsel for the NAACP, Thurgood Marshall.

FURTHER READING: Richard Kluger, *Simple Justice: The History of Brown v. Board of Education and Black America's Struggle for Equality* (New York: Random, 1975); Doug McAdam, *Political Process and the Development of Black Insurgency, 1930–1970* (Chicago: U of Chicago P, 1982); Andrew Kull, *The Color-Blind Constitution* (Cambridge, MA: Harvard UP, 1992); Mark V. Tushnet, *Making Civil Rights Law: Thurgood Marshall and the Supreme Court, 1936–1961* (New York: Oxford UP, 1994).

The problem of the segregation of racial and ethnic groups constitutes one of the major problems facing the American people today. It seems desirable, therefore, to summarize the contributions which contemporary social science can make toward its resolution. There are, of course, moral and legal issues involved with respect to which the signers of the present statement cannot speak with any special authority and which must be taken into account in the solution of the problem. There are, however, also factual issues involved with respect to which certain conclusions seem to be justified on the basis of the available scientific evidence. . . .

In dealing with the question of the effects of segregation, it must be recognized that these effects do not take place in a vacuum, but in a social context. The segregation of Negroes and of other groups in the United States takes place in a social milieu in which "race" prejudice and discrimination exist. It is questionable in the view of some students of the problem whether it is possible to have segregation without substantial discrimination. Myrdal states: "Segregation . . . is financially possible and, indeed, a device of economy only as it is combined with substantial discrimination." The imbeddedness of segregation in such a context makes it difficult to disentangle the effects of segregation *per se* from the effects of the context. Similarly, it is

difficult to disentangle the effects of segregation from the effects of a
pattern of social disorganization commonly associated with it and reflected in high disease and mortality rates, crime and delinquency,
poor housing, disrupted family life, and general substandard living
conditions. . . .

At the recent Mid-century White House Conference on Children
and Youth, a fact-finding report on the effects of prejudice, discrimination, and segregation on the personality development of children
was prepared as a basis for some of the deliberations. This report
brought together the available social science and psychological studies which were related to the problem of how racial and religious
prejudices influenced the development of a healthy personality. It
highlighted the fact that segregation, prejudices, and discriminations,
and their social concomitants potentially damage the personality of
all children — the children of the majority group in a somewhat different way than the more obviously damaged children of the minority
group.

The report indicates that as minority group children learn the inferior status to which they are assigned — as they observe the fact that
they are almost always segregated and kept apart from others who
are treated with more respect by the society as a whole — they often
react with feelings of inferiority and a sense of personal humiliation.
Many of them become confused about their own personal worth. On
the one hand, like all other human beings they require a sense of personal dignity; on the other hand, almost nowhere in the larger society
do they find their own dignity as human beings respected by others.
Under these conditions, the minority group child is thrown into a
conflict with regard to his feelings about himself and his group. He
wonders whether his group and he himself are worthy of no more respect than they receive. This conflict and confusion leads to self-
hatred and rejection of his own group.

The report goes on to point out that these children must find ways
with which to cope with this conflict. Not every child, of course, re-
acts with the same patterns of behavior. The particular pattern depends upon many interrelated factors, among which are: the stability
and quality of his family relations; the social and economic class to
which he belongs; the cultural and educational background of his
parents; the particular minority group to which he belongs; his personal characteristics, intelligence, special talents, and personality pattern.

Some children, usually of the lower socio-economic classes, may react by overt aggressions and hostility directed toward their own group or members of the dominant group. Anti-social and delinquent behavior may often be interpreted as reactions to these racial frustrations. These reactions are self-destructive in that the larger society not only punishes those who commit them, but often interprets such aggressive and anti-social behavior as justification for continuing prejudice and segregation.

Middle class and upper class minority group children are likely to react to their racial frustrations and conflicts by withdrawal and submissive behavior. Or, they may react with compensatory and rigid conformity to the prevailing middle class values and standards and an aggressive determination to succeed in these terms in spite of the handicap of their minority status.

The report indicates that minority group children of all social and economic classes often react with a generally defeatist attitude and a lowering of personal ambitions. This, for example, is reflected in a lowering of pupil morale and a depression of the educational aspiration level among minority group children in segregated schools. In producing such effects, segregated schools impair the ability of the child to profit from the educational opportunities provided him.

Many minority group children of all classes also tend to be hypersensitive and anxious about their relations with the larger society. They tend to see hostility and rejection even in those areas where these might not actually exist.

The report concludes that while the range of individual differences among members of a rejected minority group is as wide as among other peoples, the evidence suggests that all of these children are unnecessarily encumbered in some ways by segregation and its concomitants.

With reference to the impact of segregation and its concomitants on children of the majority group, the report indicates that the effects are somewhat more obscure. Those children who learn the prejudices of our society are also being taught to gain personal status in an unrealistic and non-adaptive way. When comparing themselves to members of the minority group, they are not required to evaluate themselves in terms of the more basic standards of actual personal ability and achievement. The culture permits and, at times, encourages them to direct their feelings of hostility and aggression against whole groups of people the members of which are perceived as weaker than themselves. They often develop patterns of guilt feelings, rationalizations, and other mechanisms which they must use in an attempt to protect themselves from recognizing the essential injustice of their unrealistic fears and hatreds of minority groups.

The report indicates further that confusion, conflict, moral cynicism, and disrespect for authority may arise in majority group children as a consequence of being taught the moral, religious, and democratic principles of the brotherhood of man and the importance of justice and fair play by the same persons and institutions who, in their support of racial segregation and related practices, seem to be acting in a prejudiced and discriminatory manner. Some individuals may attempt to resolve this conflict by intensifying their hostility toward the minority group. Others may react by guilt feelings which are not necessarily reflected in more humane attitudes toward the minority group. Still others react by developing an unwholesome, rigid, and uncritical idealization of all authority figures — their parents, strong political and economic leaders. As described in *The Authoritarian Personality,* they despise the weak, while they obsequiously and unquestioningly conform to the demands of the strong whom they also, paradoxically, subconsciously hate.

With respect to the setting in which these difficulties develop, the report emphasized the role of the home, the school, and other social institutions. Studies have shown that from the earliest school years children are not only aware of the status differences among different groups in the society but begin to react with the patterns described above.

Conclusions similar to those reached by the Mid-century White House Conference Report have been stated by other social scientists who have concerned themselves with this problem. The following are some examples of these conclusions:

Segregation imposes upon individuals a distorted sense of social reality.

Segregation leads to a blockage in the communications and interaction between the two groups. Such blockages tend to increase mutual suspicion, distrust, and hostility.

Segregation not only perpetuates rigid stereotypes and reinforces negative attitudes toward members of the other group, but also leads to the development of a social climate within which violent outbreaks of racial tensions are likely to occur.

We return now to the question, deferred earlier, of what it is about the total society complex of which segregation is one feature that produces the effects described above — or, more precisely, to the question of whether we can justifiably conclude that, as only one feature of a complex social setting, segregation is in fact a significantly contributing factor to these effects.

To answer this question, it is necessary to bring to bear the general fund of psychological and sociological knowledge concerning the role of various environmental influences in producing feelings of inferiority, confusions in personal roles, various types of basic personality structures, and the various forms of personal and social disorganization.

On the basis of this general fund of knowledge, it seems likely that feelings of inferiority and doubts about personal worth are attributable to living in an underprivileged environment only insofar as the latter is itself perceived as an indicator of low social status and as a symbol of inferiority. In other words, one of the important determinants in producing such feelings is the awareness of social status difference. While there are many other factors that serve as reminders of the differences in social status, there can be little doubt that the fact of enforced segregation is a major factor.

Charles S. Johnson
The Shadow of the Plantation

In *Shadow of the Plantation* (1934) and *Growing Up in the Black Belt* (1941), Charles S. Johnson (1893–1956) produced two of the most important and lasting African American interpretations of black life in the early twentieth-century South. Trained as a sociologist at the University of Chicago, Johnson in 1921 became director of research for the National Urban League and founding editor of its journal *Opportunity*. In a long and varied career, Johnson went on to publish a number of landmark works on black social and educational issues, and to hold a variety of important governmental and educational positions, including the presidency of Fisk University from 1946 until his death. His volume *Patterns of Negro Segregation* (1943) was part of the far-reaching study directed by Gunnar Myrdal for the Carnegie Corporation that included *An American Dilemma* (see p. 66 of this book).

The following selection from Johnson's most influential study bears the burden of some irony. On the one hand, it is a trenchant portrait of the rural black underclass of Macon County, Alabama, in the area surrounding Tuskegee Institute where the novel's protagonist takes Mr. Norton, the white college trustee, on his ill-fated encounter with the sharecropper Jim Trueblood. On the other hand, Johnson's study may represent just the sort of sociological investigation that is being lampooned in Trueblood's account of having become famous, even comparatively well off, because of the intellectuals who want to study his act of incest as an instance of black pathology. If the "biggity school folks" from the college want to get rid of Trueblood, the response of white social scientists appears to be just the reverse: "I done the worse thing a man could ever do in his family and instead of chasin' me out of the country, they gimme more help than they ever give any other colored man" (*Invisible Man* 52, 67). Johnson's work, of course, takes no such perspective on rural black family life; but its detailed account of the wrenching poverty of the area around Tuskegee in the 1930s, and of the sometimes tense relations between the rural folk and those privileged to attend the college, must be answered by Ellison's elaborate invention in

Trueblood's tale of a blues story in which pain, racism, sexism, and stunning lyricism are combined.

In a 1961 interview (see p. 17 of this book), Ellison provided another vantage point on Johnson's study (and his own novel) when he recalled that during graduation ceremonies at Tuskegee, "high-powered word artists," both black and white, would descend on the school to tell us "what our lives were and what our goals should be," while black people from the surrounding farm community, some of whose children were participating in the ceremonies, would remain outside dancing, picnicking, and visiting "as though the ceremonies across the wide lawns did not exist; or at best had no connection with the lives they led" ("That Same Pain, That Same Pleasure" 20–21).

FURTHER READING: Horace Mann Bond, *Negro Education in Alabama: A Study in Cotton and Steel* (Washington, DC: Associated Publishers, 1939); John Dollard, *Caste and Class in a Southern Town* (New Haven: Yale UP, 1937); S. P. Fullinwider, *The Mind and Mood of Black America: Twentieth-Century Thought* (Homewood, IL: Dorsey, 1969); James E. Blackwell and Morris Janowitz, eds., *Black Sociologists: Historical and Contemporary Perspectives* (Chicago: U of Chicago P, 1974).

The area of Macon County covered by this study extends over 200 square miles and is virtually the total lower third of the county. There are the small village concentrations, but over four-fifths of the population live out in the open country on and around the farms which they own or rent, or the plantations on which they are employed. The village communities are, as a rule, so loosely identified by the names that confusion exists even among the residents as to where one begins and the other ends. Since the towns are so largely built for the convenience of the white folks and there is so little advantage to the Negro farming population in living in the towns, these locations are scarcely more than post-office addresses and occasional market places for Negroes.

The center of this population is about ten miles down the highway from Tuskegee and from four to ten miles in the country back of the highway. Tuskegee, if reached by horse and wagon, which is a popular method of travel, despite the vogue of the automobile, is a full day's journey away. The school is known, but visits there are rare.

Occasionally produce or chickens are carried to the village to be marketed. Jerry Wilson, living in Shorter, admitted a certain interest in the place. He said: "If I had some money I'd hire somebody to take me to Tuskegee. I went up dere once to commencement." In Sambo a group of cabins had been whitewashed eighteen years before in anticipation of a visit from Booker T. Washington. That was the last coating they had had, and to all appearances the last effective contact with the institution. The nearest large city of the state is Montgomery; there has been some migration back and forth from this city and across the Georgia line.

The distribution of these families conforms to the physical arrangement of the plantations. The most frequent layout is the cabin, or small cluster of cabins, for each convenient agricultural unit suitable for renting or tenant-farmer use. The very large plantations have close-set rows of cabins on the edge of vast stretches of cotton land. Occasionally some fortuitous division of land throws a group of cabins or frame dwellings together. Traveling through the country, one may observe, standing stark and alone at the crossroads, a church or a store, with no dwelling in sight. It is a part of the character of this community, it would seem, to be bound together over a wide area by crooked little footpaths which serve as the threads of neighborliness. Such loose physical association must, of necessity, foreclose certain advantages of cooperation for social improvement and protection; and make difficult, if not impossible, the development of a sense of community such as might be found in more closely knit villages or in town life.

Here live almost hidden in the fields, or at wide intervals along the country road, over 11,000 Negroes. There is, however, scarcely a stretch of this territory which does not give some sign of life. Along the dusty roads men in the universal garb of blue-denim overalls are forever trudging, casually going somewhere. They are interested in every happening that crosses their vision. Around the cabins or small frame dwellings, visible from the roadway, children are at play, old folks are puttering about or chatting idly in the cooling shade of the dog-run. Pots of soiled clothing are boiling in the yard, attended with a stick by women too old for the fields. Old men tinker with rickety plows or the intricate disrepair of a mule's harness. A loud laugh from out the cluttered spaces calls attention to another cabin set far back from the road. Slinking, hungry dogs infest the region of the houses. Adolescent girls, their hair twisted and held in thin stiff braids by tough threads, sit idly, dangling bare legs, scaly with pellagra. A wagon in which chairs have been placed, and occasionally an excessively noisy and antiquated Ford, carry teeming families to town. . . .

The irony of the situation seems to be in the fact that the life of a tenant in the economic system under which they live is not always congenial when he begins to broaden his horizon. The more alert and ambitious of the men seem to drift away to southern or northern cities. A few of the women also leave. This may explain why the women still living in the county represent a level of education slightly above the men. Curiously, when income of families is divided according to the grades — illiterate, little education, education above the fifth grade — the illiterates were at the bottom of the scale, those with more than fifth-grade education ranked next, and those with little education ranked highest. For example, in the four highest-income brackets — $200–$299, $300–$399, $400–$499, $500 and over — there were 19 illiterates, 26 with five years or less of schooling, and 24 with more than five years of schooling. In the highest of these, $500 and over, there was a practical advantage for those with five and six years of schooling but a pronounced falling-off of those with eight years and more. If the logic of these figures is to be followed, it appears that the environment is less hostile to men with little education than to men with enough to read and write easily. Practically considered, the most successful families financially are those who are neither too illiterate to take advantage of their surroundings nor have more schooling than is demanded by their dependent economic situation. They would be expected to thrive best in an environment that bred few landowners, tolerated few innovations, and placed a penalty upon too much book-learning.

Occasionally a tragedy gives dramatic vividness to the conflict arising under the system. Henry Harding had tried for eighteen years to get somewhere. He studied and read and tried to apply his knowledge, but without effect. Every time he tried to help himself his situation tightened. But a tenant trying to support a family on fifteen acres and send some of his children to school has a small chance. He began to brood. His wife, Mary Harding, told briefly his story:

> My husband was an intelligent man. He nearly finished Tuskegee. He had worked hard but we had lost all we had. On his fiftieth birthday, the twenty-fourth of November, we worked in the field all day and he

kept saying he wouldn't be here long, and he wanted us to hurry up and get the cotton picked. It made me nervous. Every time he'd come home I'd send the boy behind him 'cause I didn't know what he might do. We took some potash from him one night. He wouldn't eat no supper. When I got through supper I was reading a "true story." I likes to read *True Stories* and he knowed so much he took it from me and told me ter stop reading that junk. Hit was on Thanksgiving Day and they was bringing my girl home from Tuskegee School to visit. I always will believe that he lost his mind, for he got outta bed and wandered out dere in the field. Then he got holt of some more potash and et it, and died and never said what he lost hisself fer. He just suicided and killed hisself.

The influence of Tuskegee extended into the community and in an interesting manner. In point of distance this institution was from ten to twenty miles removed from the families of this study. There was also a cultural and social distance. There were members of the community who had attended school, learned trades, and returned. Booker T. Washington was remembered and liked by some of the older individuals. He was twice referred to in course of comment upon themselves and their interests. In Sambo the cabins had been whitewashed in preparation for a visit from him about twenty years ago. He came — a great man with a personality which took them in, which understood them, and which they could understand. On another occasion an old woman had remembered an antipathy which he expressed toward fishing as a recreation. He had said that it was a lazy man's sport, and she confessed to having adopted his prejudice. . . .

Moses Green learned the trade of carpentry and bricklaying at Tuskegee, over twenty years ago. This is what he said about himself:

> I got seven children and they're all mine and my wife's.
>
> Pretty big family now since times are so hard, but I manage to get along. I do little carpenter work for the white and colored folks out here whenever there is any to be done. Didn't get much work last year 'cause people ain't building no houses. I guess I did 'bout $100 worth of carpenter work last year. I learned my trade at Tuskegee, carpentry and bricklaying. Don't get much bricklaying to do.
>
> It's hard to say just how much money I spend for clothes. Got such a big family. Last year I bought a suit for $50, so I won't have to buy none this year. My wife bought a suit last year for $15, and my daughter bought one for $40. That's the one I told you goes to school in Montgomery. Come here, Marguerite, and tell about your school.

MARGUERITE: I've been going to school in Montgomery for three years, taking nurse training. Ain't had but six months' training. The first year I was sick and had to come home; the second year I was sick and stayed there in the hospital; and this year I didn't get but six months' training. I stay sick all the time, but I'm determined to be a nurse. I don't know just what my trouble is; the doctor calls it some kind of funny name. [Girl tried to think for fully ten minutes but could not give the name. She didn't mention how the illness affected her.]

MOTHER: I think they done worked her too hard.

FATHER: I didn't make much of a crop last year. I made a bale of cotton and got enough to pay back the $40 on the government loan. The government loan works this way: The government man comes out to see you and he takes a synopsis of what you have. The owner then waives the rent until the government is paid, then he has to put in for his part afterwards. If you don't make anything the government carries it over. They [the government] deal with the man straight, not the landlord. They leave a government man who comes around and notifies each man when the money is due.

I worked with the Bradley Lumber Company from November to June of this year. Got $60 every two weeks. Worked till the company went busted, but I've got to do a cash business this year 'cause I made enough money when I was working.

Beyond the sense of sharing the new values of the Institute, there is indication of further social distance. The spirit of race consciousness has entered and identifies itself with color consciousness in a manner that places the Tuskegee school in a different world of relations. A man who hopes to send his son to school expressed some apprehensions about his ability to fit into the color scheme.

I wants to send my son to school as far as he can go, but somebody's got to speak a word for him up there at Tuskegee. That school ain't got no race pride. They ain't so much on the black ones. All them black men up to Tuskegee marries yellow women, if they're able to keep 'em. You know yellow women want more than black ones. That's the reason me and my wife ain't never separated — she's good and black. . . . I suppose if I'd a gone to Tuskegee and had schooling I'd a married a yellow woman too. . . . So many colored folks only want to be with white folks. All of them Tuskegee people is like that.

It was evident in this case that there was some confusion between color and culture, and a conviction that to get along one must "either look like white or act like white." The same man, when talking to a Negro visitor of his own complexion but of considerably different education and cultural background, asked, "What nationality is you? You looks colored, but you don't talk like it, so I ain't sure. Do you love colored folks?" Then ruminating further on the question of color he confided: "I got a cousin. Her pappy is white. Old Dr. ———. Everybody knows that. Well, he sent her off to school. Now she's married some white-looking nigger and teaches school. She warn't no better'n me but just 'cause she's white-skinned she got ahead. I ain't never done nothing in my life but I've tried to live right and do good."

During much of the early twentieth century, sharecropping was a common way of life for many black southerners, including the novel's Jim Trueblood and his family (*Invisible Man* 46–70) and the families described in the selections in this volume by Charles S. Johnson (p. 78) and Bernice Kelly Harris (p. 86).

Bernice Kelly Harris

Tore Up and a-Movin'

During the depression of the 1930s, President Franklin Roosevelt's administration established the Works Progress Administration to provide federally funded employment in public works to those who had lost their jobs. Among the organizations that made up the WPA was the Federal Writers' Project, which published a number of volumes based on recorded oral narratives of the people of the United States. Ralph Ellison's participation in the interviews and transcriptions of such narratives after he arrived in New York was crucial to his development as a writer (see pp. 21–22 and pp. 132–33 of this book). In many cases, the narratives gave a public and artistic voice to impoverished and marginalized people whose stories would otherwise have disappeared from view. Some were anecdotal, some heartrending, and some humorously creative; many, like this one by Bernice Kelly Harris (a pseudonym) taken from a 1939 volume that recorded stories by both black and white rural southerners, amounted to life histories of a family and a region in miniature. In the words of the collection's editor, W. T. Couch, *These Are Our Lives*, like other Federal Writers' Project collections, was based on the belief that the people "must be given representation, somehow they must be given voice and allowed to speak, in their essential character" (Couch xiii–xiv).

Harris's oral narrative provides a context in which to think about the partial origins of Ellison's own style in the southern vernacular of black sharecroppers and in a mode of oral narrative that corresponds in some signal ways to Jim Trueblood's tale. No less a blues story in its own right, Harris's "Tore Up and a-Movin'" carries the anguish of poverty alongside an unmistakable tone of resilience. In this regard, one might also compare to Trueblood's story the long life history published in Theodore Rosengarten's *All God's Dangers: The Life of Nate Shaw* (1974). The volume records the first-person vernacular narrative of an Alabama black sharecropper (Nate Shaw was a pseudonym for Ned Cobb) and his family over much of the early half of the twentieth century; but the anonymous woman captured in the shorter story of Bernice Kelly Harris no less gives the lie to any pretense that the shadow of slavery did not still fall especially hard on blacks in the Depression South.

FURTHER READING: Arthur F. Raper and Ira D. Reid, *Sharecroppers All* (Chapel Hill: U of North Carolina P, 1941); David Eugene Conrad, *The Forgotten Farmers: The Story of Sharecroppers in the New Deal* (Urbana: U of Illinois P, 1969); Jerre G. Mangione, *The Dream and the Deal: The Federal Writers' Project, 1935–1943* (Boston: Little, Brown, 1972); Monty N. Penkower, *The Federal Writers' Project: A Study in Government Patronage of the Arts* (Urbana: U of Illinois P, 1977).

We hain't had no Christmas here, not a apple or a nut or nothin': I told the chil'en not to look for no Santa Claus this year, but to thank their God if they had meat and bread." Gracie Turner folds her arms across her husband's brown shirt which she wears over her worn red dress for a sweater and leaves her wash tub in the back yard to show the way to the cheerless fire-place where green wood smolders.

"Dis here is my father, Sam Horton. He has seen some years. He's ninety-one and in tole'ble good health, except his 'memb'ance ain't strong and he can't eat much grease. I've been takin' care o' him now for seven years, best I could. For the past three months he's been gettin' seven dollars and a half for de old age pension, and dat's been a help here.

"Dat's Ola in de corner." Gracie indicates an attractive mulatto girl who looks almost dainty in spite of her ragged clothes. Her feet are bare. "Ola is twenty-four. Awhile back she married a drinkin' man, but he scrapped so bad she couldn't stay wid him; so she come back home to live. Dis girl is Amy, fourteen years old. She's got bad kidney trouble; her leg swells up big as two sometimes. Dr. Simpson started givin' her treatments in de clinic, but she ain't had none in some weeks now." Amy is also barefooted.

"De littlest boy is Raymond Farmer. Dr. Farmer 'fore he died named him for his brother, Judge Raymond Farmer. Stephen is de oldest boy at home. Sam and Will belongs to my daughters, but I raised 'em. Will, go tote in some wood and stir up dis here fire! Will's mama married de second time, and I didn't know how dat new man would treat de child. Wid my husband, James Turner, and Papa and me, dat makes nine of us to stay in dese two rooms. Come on; I'll show you over de house.

"Most of us sleeps on dese three beds in here where we keeps de fire. In here is de kitchen. Mr. Jake Anderson give me dat range; it's de one Miss Bettie fust cooked on when she was married." The old stove is coated with grease, but the kitchen is orderly and fairly clean. At the table, covered with colorful oilcloth, are two long benches where the Turners sit to dine. The bowl of cold collards gives off a penetrating odor even to the front door.

"Right across de hall is de other bedroom. Come on see dat too. De girls covered dese chairs and dis settee wid de flowered cloth dey-selves. Dat victrola ain't no good now. We tries to keep dis room sort o' dressed up for comp'ny, but dey ain't no fire in de heater; so we better set in de fireplace room. Today's a cold day if you ain't about stirrin'.

"Now, 'bout de other chil'en: Hattie May lives on some island down here 'bout Portsmith — Hattie May Williams she is now. Her husband does public work and seems to be a right good man, but I didn't know where he'd be good to Hattie May's Will or not. May married Montgomery, and dey sharecraps for Miss Sallie Simpson over toward Benton. Edward's married and farms for Mr. Peter Ellis at Martinsburg. Lillian Turner — now I can't tell you 'bout her, 'cause I hain't heard from her in three years. Marcy works for rich folks in Philadelphia. She sent us a box o' old clothes 'fore Christmas, and dat's de onliest string we've had this fall. De rich folks is always givin' Marcy wrist watches and necklaces and things for presents. Dey sends her down town any time wid a hund'ed dollars to buy things for 'em, and she takes every cent back to 'em it don't cost. Dey has learnt to trust Marcy. I's tried to raise my chil'en to be trusty and mannerable, to mind dey mama and papa, to be honest. 'Show favor to your mother and father,' I tells 'em, 'dat your days may be length-ened on God's earth.' If dey does wrong it shore ain't 'cause I hain't tried to learn 'em right.

"Dey ain't been much schoolin' for none of 'em. Will's in de fif', and Lillian got to de ninth. None de rest got past de fou'th grade. Turner went to school enough to write his name, but he can't do no figgerin' to 'mount to nothin'. I never went a day in my life, can't write my name or add or keep track of our account on de farm. I want dese youngest chil'en to go long enough to do dat much.

"'Tain't no while to say dis is de hardest year we's ever had. Every year's been hard, de forty-nine years I been here. Dat's all dey is to expect — work hard and go hongry part time — long as we lives on de other man's land. Dey ain't nothin' in sharecrappin', not de way

it's run. My folks has always sharecrapped. Papa farmed round Gum
Springs when I was a girl, and all I learnt was to work in de field.
When I married Turner, we lived in Hawley, Virginia, 'bout six
months. He done public work, railroadin' and sech dere. From Hawley we moved to a farm near Gum Springs, where we worked by de
day for a year. From dere we moved to my brother's and sharecrapped for him five years. Den we moved to Mr. Calep Jones',
where we stayed three years. Next we moved to Mr. Hughes White-
head's and farmed wid him two years. Our next move was to No'th
Ca'lina on Mr. Jake Anderson's farm at de Woollen place. We stayed
wid him thirteen years. Den last year we moved here to de Willis
place, dat Mr. Dick Henry rents from Mr. Bob Willis in Gum
Springs, and here we is now. But we got to move somewhere dis next
year. Another man's a-comin' here. I don't know where we'll go;
houses is sca'ce and hard to find. Mr. Makepeace told Turner he'd
help him all he could, but he ain't got no house we can live in. Plenty
o' land everywhere, but no house! Turner has been huntin' a place for
weeks, and every night when he comes home I runs to de door to
hear de news. Every day it's de same tale: 'I hain't found no place
yet.' I hates to move; nobody knows how I hates to move!"

"Yonder's somebody movin' now," Ola exclaims, looking out the
window. All eyes turn toward the road. Over the deep ruts in the
sand, wagon wheels grind slowly eastward; two wagons loaded with
shabby furnishings wind around the curve out of sight.

"Dat's de way we'll be soon — tore up and a-movin'. I wish I
could have me one acre o' land dat I could call mine. I'd be willin' to
eat dry bread de rest o' my life if I had a place I could settle down on
and nobody could tell me I had to move no more. I hates movin'.

"We left Mr. Jake Anderson 'cause he didn't treat us right. Me and
him fussed de whole thirteen years we stayed dere, and I said if I kept
livin' wid Mr. Anderson I'd go to de devil shore. When Mr. Anderson
use to give de money to Turner, he'd tell him: 'Don't you give none of
it to dat fussy woman.' I quarreled all de time 'bout him givin' money
to de boys and chargin' it 'gainst our account. We always had trouble
settlin' wid Mr. Anderson. One year I got me a book and ask him to
set down everything he charged us wid in my book, so I'd have it in
his own figgers when de year ended. But he said he wouldn't have it
dat way; one set o' books was all he aimed to keep. So den I got to
askin' him every week what he was chargin' us wid, and my daughter
set it down. At de end o' de year we got Mr. James to add it up on

de addin' machine. We handed it to Mr. Anderson when we went to settle, and it made him mad. He said we'd settle by his figgers or get off'n de place, dat nobody should keep books but him on his farm.

"Another time when we wanted a car, he bought us one over in Weldon, but made us put up the two mules we owned den against de car. De boys was in a wreck and damaged de car right smart. Mr. Anderson come and took in de mules and de car too. After he had it fixed up, we tried to get him to sell it back to us. He wouldn't but went and sold it to another man. So we was lackin' a car and mules too.

"Mr. Anderson was all time orderin' us to get off'n his place. He's mighty fitified anyhow, and when somethin' didn't suit him he'd order us to move. One Christmas we ask him for fifty dollars for some clothes and a little Santy Claus for the chil'en. Dey was 'bout twelve of us den to take care of. Mr. Anderson said we shouldn't have de money and for us to move. We done it. Dey was a little house close to Maryton where we moved into, but 'twa'n't long 'fore here come Mr. Anderson orderin' us to move back. He finally offered us de fifty dollars, 'cause he knowed we was good hands. We was mighty slow dat time 'bout movin' back to his farm; he got uneasy 'fore we did go back.

"We never made nothin' much wid Mr. Anderson. De most we cleared was $179, after we'd paid out, two years. Most years it was fifty and sixty dollars after de account was paid. Every settlement day me and him had a round. I'd tell him he had too much charged against us, and he'd say I was de fussin'est woman he ever saw, and to go to de devil! De last year we was wid him we made 'leben bales o' cotton and three hund'ed bags o' peas. When we settled, we didn't have accordin' to his figgers but five dollars for our part o' de crap, nothin' to buy a string o' clothes wid, nothin' to eat but meat and bread. We left him. We had to sell de hogs we raised to eat to buy us some clothes. We hain't never got no rent money. I said somethin' to Mr. Anderson last time I saw him 'bout de rent. We needs it for clothes and shoes; the chil'en's feet is on de ground. It made him mad; he said he hadn't got no rent. Turner went over to Benton and ask about it. Dey said it wa'n't right, but Mr. Anderson was holdin' de cotton and peas for higher prices dey reckoned; de rent would come by 'n' by dey reckoned.

"When we started farmin' in March for Mr. Dick Henry, he 'lowed us five dollars a week. On de tenth o' June dey took him to de

State Horspital, and Miss Annie got her brother, Mr. Bates, to tend to de farm for her. He owned up he didn't know nothin' 'bout farmin'. Fust, dey started out lettin' us have $3.50 a week; den it dwindled down to two, den to nothin'. Miss Annie said she dreaded for Sad'dys to come 'cause we was lookin' to her for money for rations, and she didn't have it. I couldn't fuss wid her, 'cause I knowed she was tellin' de truth. Mr. Bates brought some hogs here and told us to raise 'em on halves. I toted 'em slops all th'ugh de summer and fed 'em co'n; here dis fall he took 'em away from us, on our debt he claimed. Turner traded his gun for a mother hog and three little pigs, all we got now. De same way wid de co'n. Mr. Bates commenced haulin' it away. I told him le's wait and see what de cotton and peanuts 'mounted to and den divide de co'n equal 'tween us. He said naw, he wa'n't goin' to dat way. Cou'se I knowed we couldn't make much, but looked like we was bound to have some co'n for our bread. I went in de field and begun loadin' me a one-ho'se wagon o' co'n, but he objected. So all I got out'n de crap was a barrel o' nubbins dat I took anyhow.

"Mr. Henry come home 'fore Christmas and 'pears to be all right now. We hain't had no settlement wid him yet, but he told us dey wouldn't be nothin' for us this year, not to look for it. De account on de book 'gainst us is $300. How it got dat much I can't tell you. We raised 224 bags o' peas and 1800 pounds o' seed cotton on twenty acres. I knowed we couldn't make no crap, wid just twenty-four bags o' plaster 'lowed us to fertilize twenty acres. We was just about to get hongry here, with all de money cut off and no crap comin' in. Long as dey was cotton to pick or peas to shake some of us could get a day o' work now and then, enough to buy a sack o' flour and a little strip o' meat. Work has been sca'ce dis fall though. So Turner got him a WP and A job a-diggin' stumps. He's done had three pay days, $12.80 at de time, though he don't get but $12 'cause eighty cents has to go to Mr. Sickle for haulin' him to work. I makes dat twelve dollars do all it will, but dey's eight of us to live out'n it four weeks to de month.

"Turner ought not to be a-workin' wid de WP and A. De gover'-ment's got no business a-payin' out relief money and a-givin' WP and A jobs to farmers. De old age pensions is all right for old folks dat's 'flicted and can't do. Take Papa dere; he can't work in de field now. He knocks up our wood to burn in de fire-place, but he's seen too many years to get out and work by de day. But able-bodied landers

has got no business a-havin' to look to de gover'ment for a livin'. Dey
ought to live of'n de land. If 'twas fixed right dey'd make all de livin'
dey need from de ground. Dey ain't no sense in diggin' stumps for
dollars to buy co'n and flour-bread and meat, when here's plenty o'
land to raise 'em on. Every lander ought to raise his somethin' t' eat
de whole year round and some to sell. Everybody's got to eat; dat's
'bout all wages comes to anyhow, somethin' t' eat. If I had de say half
de land would be planted in stuff to eat; nobody would have to fur-
nish me and overcharge me when settlement time come.

"I always tries to raise my meat and bread and lard, collards and
sweet 'taters for de winter, and a gyarden for de summer. I keeps a
cow. Milk and butter and biscuit is de biggest we live on now. I has
to use butter in my biscuits for lard part de time. My collards hain't
flourished dis year like usual. You see 'em dere at de front. Looks like
hot water has been poured over 'em. De soil here don't suit collards;
it's too pore to raise anything without plenty fertilize. Mr. Henry fur-
nished de mule dis year and we de fertilize, but dey wouldn't stand
for much; cou'se dey wouldn't sell it to us on our say. I believes de
bugs dats eatin' up stuff now is sent 'cause folks is so mean. If dey
don't do better, plagues is goin' to take de land. I tries to live a Christian, tell de truth, and be honest, but de world is full of dem dat
don't. It ain't often I gets to church. I hain't been in over twelve
months. Roanoke-Salem is where we 'tends, but I'm tellin' you de
God's truth: I hain't had nothin' fittin' to wear to church lately; de
chil'en neither. Amy had a print dress she could wear dis summer, but
soon as cold weather come, she had to quit church and school both
'cause she didn't have no jacket to wear. I don't go nowheres, never
been nowheres, but to work. Picture show? I never saw one in my
life. De onliest far ways I ever been was on a excursion one time to
Portsmith.

"No, it's been nothin' but hard work for Gracie, and de boss man
gettin' it all. I's known some good uns. Mr. Calep Jones was a pore
man, but he was straight and fair in his dealin's. We got every cent
we was due when we lived wid him. De years we was wid him we
cleared $200, de most we ever made. Mr. Jones's dead, but if he ain't
in heb'n ain't nobody dere. Once Papa farmed for a rich man, and he
was good too. Every Christmas dat come he give all de tenants on his
place a sack o' apples and nuts and candy."

Amy rises from her corner to warm her bare feet at the dying fire.
Gracie looks from the window and sees the mother hog rooting in the

front yard. "Sam, go run de hog out'n de yard." She pushes her tin snuff box more securely in the shirt pocket and leans her head an instant on the foot of the bed. "My head's been afflicted a long time; somethin' pops and rings in it right constant. It ain't bad as it was once though; it use to run corruption th'ugh my years, and I had to keep 'em washed out wid salt water. Dey don't ooze corruption now. Turner's health is pretty good; he's 'flicted with rheumatism, but he works as hard at sixty-five as he ever done. I don't have de doctor much; dey's old home remedies I tries fust, and if dey fails den de doctor has to try his hand. Dat bottle o' castor oil up dere on de mantel is de old stand-by here. When de flu was goin' round so bad I mixed castor oil and turpentine and sprinkled a few drops on de chil'en's hair, and not a one o' dem had de flu. Fluck is good too; it's a weed I use for a purkitive. When de chil'en was teethin' I use to tie fluck round dey necks. It costs too much to send for de doctor. Right now we owes de Roanoke Rapids Horspital $1.50 for Amy. She was in a wreck up here 'bout Camp's store and got five teeth knocked out and her legs bruised up right bad. Dey took her to de horspital where she ought to stayed two or three days, but we wa'n't able to pay, so we had to bring her home. She gets in a quare fix some nights, just lies dere and can't speak or move." . . .

Gracie droops dejectedly in her chair and covers her face momentarily with her hands. "Farmin's all I ever done, all I can do, all I want to do. And I can't make a livin' at it."

"I reckon I soon farm as anything else," Amy observes.

"I rather go in service. I want to be a cook or a maid for white folks," Ola adds. "I can cook some already and I could learn more."

Gracie raises her head, but she remains downcast in spirit. "Dis year has been so hard we've had to drop our burial insurance. We enrolled wid de burial association in Ga'ysburg some years back. All it costs is twenty-five cents when a member dies. But dey don't come many twenty-five centses in dis house.

"Every night I prays to de Lord: 'Please keep death off till I get out'n dis shape.' Dey ain't a decent rag to bury me if I was to die right now, and I hates for de county to have to put me away."

William N. Colson

An Analysis of Negro Patriotism

Every war fought by the United States in the century after emancipation presented African Americans an opportunity, as many saw it, to prove their willingness to fight for the democratic ideals of the nation. Until the late twentieth century, however, each war had also been an occasion for black soldiers to endure discrimination and abuse in the service while achieving few gains that had any value once they returned to civilian life. During World War I some 370,000 black Americans served in the armed forces, but more than half served with segregated, all-black divisions, and the majority were assigned to service duties; very few were allowed to be officers. Several race riots, as well as lesser incidents of violence, occurred at domestic military bases and abroad. Nonetheless, black combat forces fought with great distinction in France and Germany, especially the 369th Infantry Regiment of the 93rd Division, the first Allied troops to reach the Rhine River in the offensive against Germany. When black soldiers returned home only to face renewed hatred and labor discrimination during the race-baiting post-war era, many recalled the equal treatment they had received in Europe. Like the mad vet encountered by Ellison's protagonist at the bar and brothel called the Golden Day, a man who claims to have been a successful surgeon prevented from practicing by "ten men in masks [who] drove me out from the city at midnight and beat me with whips for saving a human life" (*Invisible Man* 93), many African American veterans found democracy realized abroad but, once they returned to the United States, quickly came to feel their service had been in vain.

Ellison's re-creation of the predicament of black veterans grew in part from the history of Tuskegee Veterans Hospital, which in the 1920s had been the site of a significant struggle for the right to staff a black veterans facility with black doctors and nurses (Daniel 368–88); but the "insanity" of the novel's vets is a suitable analogy for the shattered expectations of those who served in the war. The following essay by William N. Colson, a former infantry officer in the United States Army, is drawn from the black labor periodical the *Messenger* and is representative of the many responses by veterans and other blacks to the war. Important book-length studies of the day included Kelly Miller's *World War for Human Rights* (1919), Emmett J. Scott's *American Negro in the World War* (1919), and Arthur W. Little's *From Harlem to the Rhine* (1936). W. E. B. Du Bois, who had faced considerable criticism for initially espousing a policy of "closing ranks" — that is, of accepting segregation during the war in the hopes of greater gains afterward — grew embittered with the treatment of black troops and wrote a famous editorial in the May 1919 issue of *Crisis* entitled "Returning Soldiers," which called on black veterans to "marshal every ounce of our brain and brawn to fight a sterner, longer, more unbending battle against the forces of hell in our own land" (Du Bois, "Returning Soldiers" 14).

FURTHER READING: Arthur E. Barbeau and Florette Henri, *Unknown Soldiers: Black American Troops in World War I* (Philadelphia: Temple UP, 1974); Marvin Fletcher, *The Negro Soldier and the United States Army, 1891–1917* (Madison, WI: n.p., 1968); Gerald W. Patton, *War and Race: The Black Officer in the American Military, 1915–1941* (Westport, CT: Greenwood P, 1981).

An outstanding feature of the late war was the manifest patriotism of the American Negro. Whether willingly or unwillingly, as volunteer or draftee, in France or America as fighting man or stevedore, as shipbuilder, miner or farm hand, he far surpassed every other racial group in America in his relative proportion of effectual loyalty to the United States. He likewise exceeded in patriotic expression every other oppressed group living under the same general circumstances whether in India, Ireland, or Africa. And Negro women and children did their bit no whit less than the men. In household economics, in churches, and in schools they went over the top just as the men did, whether in the Bois de Frehaut or in breaking labor records at Brest, at Hog Island, at Newport News, or at Baltimore. They vied with each other in the purchase of Liberty Bonds. In North Carolina, as a fair example, Negroes pledged and bought War Saving Stamps more extensively in comparison with their ability than white people. Contrary to the general infamous practice in this country, it was not necessary to coerce them into buying bonds and stamps. They thought that some great good would come out of the war for them. The country promised it and their Old Crowd leaders reiterated it. Befuddled by the hysteria of the times, overwhelmed by the crush of

mass opinion, and sharing in the exaggerated but superficial appro-
bation of the public, the Negro race turned itself into a vast singing
army, singing at work, singing at the cantonments, singing on the
march and even under the blasphemy of the guns. . . .

Except as to color, the Negro takes on the externals of civilization
as readily as any minority class in America. When the international
bankers led this country into war, the Negro exhibited the most striking reactions of his teachings and traditions. The teaching of patriotism the world over has usually been a mass of silly and mendacious
fact. The average Negro is taught in the South and from a southern
point of view. Jefferson Davis, Stonewall Jackson, and Robt. E. Lee
are still the great historical figures South of the Mason and Dixon
line. All American schools naturally teach that the United States is the
freest and most democratic country, the world over. The entire world
has been deluded into this belief since 1917. Especially are the American Negroes taught that not only the United States but the South is
the best place on earth for them to live forever. There are three patri-
otisms abroad in the United States: a state, a sectional, and a national. All southern states project organized propaganda in behalf of
state's rights and their respective educationalists have taught the Negroes that their own particular State is the best place under the sun
for the Negroes of that state. At a recent anti-lynching conference
held in New York City, a white Southerner solemnly declared that he
believed Mississippi to be the best state in the Union for Negroes. The
Hampton-Tuskegee group are paid by Northern capitalists to advise
and keep Negroes contentedly in the South. All of this teaching is
done under the guise that the Negro is a common inheritor of rights
and duties and that it is his common responsibility to join unquali-
fiedly in every burst of patriotism.

All patriotism is spontaneous in proportion to the thoughtlessness
of the people. In 1917, white and colored leaders harangued the colored population, while they in their reaction and spontaneity made
quick response to aid in the perpetuation of their own undoing. Con-
scription drove the situation home. Once in the army and navy, once
in the government employ, it was like an incident that took place in
Richmond, Virginia, several years ago. It was the annual football
game between the Universities of Virginia and North Carolina. Negroes are prohibited by law from attending either these state schools.
Special excursion trains were run to the scene of the conflict from all
over the two states where those institutions were situated. Many ig-

norant and gullible Negroes took advantage of the popular enthusiasm to travel to the game on the trains. They bought huge pennants and streamers but when they presented themselves for admission at the ball park they were refused entrance on account of their color. Some remained, however, to view the spectacle through the holes in the fence, others still merrily flaunted in the public streets their pennants marked with the names of the two schools, but a few, the disillusioned, had the good sense to burn their banners up. Negro patriotism is much like that of those silly and unsuspecting folk who came to see the football game.

Here we are principally concerned with the disillusioned, the new Negro and his new patriotism. The Negro soon found that the treachery of the white American was infinitely more damaging to him than that of the Hun. He was refused a square deal in the army and navy, and discriminations became more gruelling in the South. There was more exploitation of labor, more personal insult, more segregation, more degradation of women, more racial limitation and restriction than ever before. Now this state of affairs multiplies race antagonism. Class antagonism is destructive of national unity, which is one of the necessary elements of the new patriotism. Therefore, any lack of patriotism on the part of the Negro was and is the natural and logical consequence of unjust practices perpetrated against him.

It is noteworthy that this new patriotism was born during the time of the Negroes' active participation in all forms of war work, military and otherwise. Nor does it exist solely in the hearts of officers and true leaders for it is a sentiment which has gained its widest currency among the rank and file of the black soldiery and working class. Before the embarkation overseas of the 92d Division, it was frequently a matter of difficulty to instill the qualities of dash and vim into the enlisted personnel. The men asked without hesitation the reason for their fighting in the war. "Safe for democracy" became to them a mere mockery. They had no faith in their white officers and not much in the colored in that emergency. When discriminations were practiced at the cantonments like the customary equipping of white organizations before colored units and the assignments of the whites to the best camp locations, the most unlettered and provincial Negro soldiers often spent hours in discussing the justice of American military authority. In the 92d Division, the enlisted men as a whole were more outspoken and overt in their resentments than their colored officers. A few of them manifested their qualified loyalty by expressing

sentiments of conscientious objection, nor was their conscientious objection always based on religious scruples. It was often a challenge to
a mischievous patriotism. When black officers taught black men bay-
onet practice they usually substituted the picture of the rabid white
Southerner for that of the Hun. This method often times inspirited
the soldier with the necessary dash and form.

What was the soul of the Negro in war-time? In the mood of seri-
ousness it was the most usual thing for the Negroes to turn in their
discussions to the fitness of their participation in the business of war.
And in trench or camp, factory or school, the undeniable fact is that
Negroes felt that they were fighting for false ideals.

While in France, the Negro soldiers got their bearings. They discovered that the only white men that treated them as men, were native Europeans, and especially the French with their wider social experience and finer social sense. The Frenchman was unable to
comprehend American color prejudice. The Englishman was much
more democratic than the American. Then the soldiers began to get
letters from home. They brought the news that conditions in the
States were no better than before; they were worse! For instance, a
successful business man from the South wrote that he felt relieved
that his son was fighting on French soil for France, because France
was at least democratic. A Negro clergyman whose church members
subscribed $10,000 worth of Liberty Bonds wrote that he had no pa-
triotism whatever. He had promoted the subscription in a spirit of
hypocritical public service. A leading Negro banker, who had bought
many thousands of dollars worth of bonds stated in confidence that
he joined in the public movement merely for the sake of retaining the
good-will of his white business friends. But there was not one of these
persons who would not have been glad to have given his all if he had
felt that the war was fought for freedom and opportunity at home.
Some Negro officers, just as many white officers did, largely volun-
teered and trained for commissions, not because of any real patriotism but because they wished to escape the draft and because they
sought the distinction and remuneration which went with the officer-
ship. In all fairness, however, it may be said that many of the colored
men trained for commissions out of a sense of race pride and
prospect. Many of the black soldiers were divested of the little patriotism they possessed on their return from France. Their hearts sank as
they hove in sight of these shores. The only reason for their joy in seeing America, was the fact that it meant speedy discharge from a bru-

tal military system and a meeting with home folks and friends. The way soldiers were discharged from the army and navy without prospective employment, is one of the national disgraces. The colored officer, maltreated and thrust aside, has cursed the flag and the country for which it stands a thousand times. Thousands of these soldiers now possess weapons to demonstrate if need be their legal right to self-defense against Southern encroachments and lynch-law.

Intelligent Negroes have all reached the point where their loyalty to the country is conditional. The patriotism of the mass of Negroes may now be called doubtful. The new Negro has put the question: "What will the shot of my bolt mean?"

It was on last November tenth that a black platoon lay near the crest of a hill overlooking the placid Moselle. With their faces towards the battlements of mighty Metz, the soldiers awaited the order to attack. There was less singing and more thought. In one tense and bloody moment the voice of a real doughboy, a new patriot, was heard amid the uncanny hiss of hot steel. It was the fervent wish that across the lines were the Huns of America, the convict leasers, the slave drivers, their domineering white American officers, the lynchers, their oppressors, instead of the Boches. The sentiment was that with the Huns of America over there the incitement necessary to the proper dash and courage would be forthcoming. They would then be fighting to make America safe for all classes. Shortly after the armistice members of this same platoon were anticipating the return home. Most of them were from the South. An ingenious fellow caused an endless round of merriment when he cleverly placed each Southern state on an imaginary map of military operations. Georgia, Mississippi, Texas and Alabama were put in No Man's Land. The border states like Virginia and Kentucky were the third line trenches, etc. The soldiers, all seated beneath an old apple tree, scarred by four years of German shrapnel, finally concluded that their next war for "democracy" would be in the land of "THE STAR SPANGLED BANNER."

War has never given a race its rights. Rights must be worked out along social and economic lines. But before the participation in a war of an oppressed group, a part of a nationality, that group can bargain collectively like the Irish are doing or like the Soviets. The Negro race in America is now beginning to learn that its loyalty has been of little avail. True loyalty permits of no mental reservation. The Negro does possess and will possess a mental reservation until this country is made safe for him and for every other class. Patriotism needs moralization. "Intelligent self-interest is the basis of all morality." For the Negro to be patriotic under the present circumstances would be unmoral. To be nationalistically patriotic the group must will national social enlargement. Many Negroes wished to see America humbled in the war, because America needs to learn the lesson of justice within its own borders before it can vaunt itself as the proponent of world ideals of democracy. A patriotism is moral when the country to which it is subject recognizes and provides for the interests of all classes within its national scope. Nationalistic patriotism is based upon common interests set in motion through common methods to meet the common need. The new Negro is beginning to realize that he is not identified with the common ends, except as to his exclusion from economic, social and political benefits. He is not a party to the conclusion. In short, patriotism should be the expression of free peoples who are ready and willing to lay down their lives in the defense of those things which they enjoy to the whole end of human betterment.

The most enlightened view is that the American Negro can best attack his problem from without. The Irish are using this method with success. White America fears any criticism by foreigners of its policy toward classes within its bounds. This country is committed to a policy of race repression. Evolution is too slow a process to secure the Negro his rights from within the United States. This must be secured by the force of international judgment and injunction as a substitute for physical force. The Negro must appeal to the outside world for justice and opportunity at home. William Monroe Trotter has hit the nail on the head. He is appealing the Negro problem from the lower court of barbaric America to the supreme court of the civilized world.

While black leaders continue to make compromises, the Negro embodying the new patriotism becomes an appreciator of social values. A few months ago a giant Cunarder swung up New York Harbor jammed to the rails with black soldiers returning from la belle France. As the ship hove past that unproved symbol, the Statue of Liberty, one of the soldiers reverentially snapped a salute to Bartholdi's emblematic creation. An officer standing near, curious to know the reason for such an action, made the query why. "Because France gave it" came back the firm reply. The new patriotism will see the Statue of Liberty a proved symbol — and proved even in America.

W. T. Andrews

The Black Migration

The migration of African Americans out of the agricultural South to the urban areas of the industrial North is among the most significant events of black American history. At times the term "Great Migration" is used to describe a period from World War I through 1960, when an estimated five million African Americans moved from the South to the North; but the term often refers more particularly to the migration during and after World War I, which had perhaps the greatest impact on the evolution of American social and cultural life, as cities such as Chicago, Detroit, and New York became centers for African American labor and artistic creation. The combination of a depression in the South, a labor shortage in the urban North caused by a decline in immigration from Europe, and continued racial injustice caused an unprecedented acceleration in migration — several hundred thousand blacks left the South in these years for better opportunities and the promise of equality in the North. A key role in stirring the dreams of countless southern blacks was played by northern black newspapers, none more so than the *Chicago Defender*, which increased its circulation tenfold between 1916 and 1918 by vigorously promoting the migration in editorials and advertisements that proclaimed a new Black Diaspora, a new Exodus to the Promised Land. Some white southerners welcomed such an exodus, but others fought desperately — sometimes through economic intimidation and violence — to keep their cheap pool of labor from dwindling.

The migration quickly became the subject of social and economic study in articles such as "Negroes Move North" (1918), by George Edmund Haynes, director of the Division of Negro Economics in the Department of Labor, and in books such as Louise Venable Kennedy's *The Negro Peasant Turns Cityward* (1930). Letters from prospective migrants were collected in a special issue of the *Journal of Negro History* (July 1919). The following selection, originally presented as a speech at a 1917 race conference in Columbia, South Carolina, by W. T. Andrews, a writer and Methodist minister from Alabama, is drawn from the editorial opinions and public addresses reproduced in Emmett Scott's *Negro*

Migration During the War (1920), a study funded by the Carnegie Corporation. It is representative of the view that the migration was a response to the combination of economic deprivation and racial injustice faced daily by most southern African Americans. Although *Invisible Man* contains no specific dramatization of the mass migration, the novel's protagonist, like Ellison himself and other southern blacks, especially in this previous generation, travels to the urban North, where he expects to find employment and a greater degree of freedom.

FURTHER READING: George W. Groh, *The Black Migration: The Journey to Urban America* (New York: Weybright and Talley, 1972); Carole Marks, *Farewell — We're Good and Gone: The Great Black Migration* (Bloomington: Indiana UP, 1989); Joe William Trotter, ed., *The Great Migration in Historical Perspective: New Dimensions of Race, Class, and Gender* (Bloomington: Indiana UP, 1991); Alferdteen Harrison, *Black Exodus: The Great Migration from the American South* (Jackson: U of Mississippi P, 1991).

In my view the chief causes of negro unrest and disturbance are as follows: the destruction of his political privileges and curtailment of his civil rights; no protection of life, liberty, and property under the law; Jim Crow car; residential and labor segregation laws; no educational facilities worthy of the name in most of the southern States. These, I believe, are the most potent causes which are now impelling the southern negro to seek employment and find homes in northern and western sections of the country.

In South Carolina, and I believe it is equally true of every southern State, except those classed as "border States," statute after statute has been passed to curtail the rights of the negro, but in not a single instance can a law be pointed to which was enacted for the purpose of enlarging his opportunity, surrounding himself and his family with the protection of the law, or for the betterment of his condition. On the contrary every law passed relating to the negro has been passed with the intent of controlling his labor and drawing his circle of freedom into smaller and smaller compass.

In the rural districts the negro is not only at the mercy of the lawless white individual citizen, but equally at the mercy of the rural police, the constables, and magistrates. There is hardly a record in modern history of greater oppression by judicial officers than that dealt to the negroes by a large majority of the magistrates and other officials who preside over the inferior courts of South Carolina.

In towns and cities, as a rule, mayors' and recorders' courts are mills for grinding out negro convicts; negroes charged with petty offenses are brought into these courts, convicted, and sentenced with lightning speed, before they even realize that they are on trial unless they are able to hire attorneys, whose fees often equal the fine that would be imposed. They are beaten at will by arresting officers, frequently shot, and many killed if attempt is made to escape by running away from the officer, and for any such shooting, officers are seldom put to the inconvenience of trial, even if the victim die.

In tragic truth it must be confessed that there is in the South — South Carolina, more certainly — no protection for the life or person of any negro of whatever standing, sex, age, against the intent of the bloody-minded white man.

The negro does not ask for special privileges or social legislation in his behalf. He does not ask to be measured by any standard less than the white man's standard, but he insists that the same test shall apply to all men of all races. He refuses to accept the declaration of men who claim to be earthly agents and representatives of the Almighty, the interpreters of His will and laws, and who solemnly assert that the God of the Christian ordained and decreed the negro race to be in slavery or semislavery to the white race.

The negro believes that the world is built on a moral foundation with justice as its basic rock. He believes that the Almighty is just, merciful and benevolent, and that He included all men in His plan of human development and reaching out for protection.

He asks only for justice. Nothing less than justice will stay the movement of negroes from the South. Its continued refusal will drive in the next two years a third or more of its negro population to other portions of the country.

Richard Wright
12 Million Black Voices

Richard Wright's influence on Ralph Ellison was as profound as Ellison's subsequent renunciation of that influence (see p. 8 and pp. 16–21 of this book). Wright (1908–1960) was the foremost literary chronicler of the black migration to Chicago, as Ellison became the foremost literary chronicler of the cultural transformation of black New York in the first half of the twentieth century. Born into a poor Mississippi sharecropping family, Wright in 1927 went to Chicago, where he joined the Federal Writers' Project in 1935 and became active in Communist Party circles. His short stories, collected in *Uncle Tom's Children* (1938), his first published novel, *Native Son* (1940), and the first volume of a longer autobiography, *Black Boy* (1945), exemplify the naturalist tradition of race writing, in which economic injustice and racial violence are shown to constitute the strongest shaping forces in African American life. After moving to New York in 1937, Wright was the Harlem editor of the communist newspaper the *Daily Worker* and of the magazine *New Challenge*. In addition, he was a mentor to the young Ralph Ellison, who had just arrived from the South in search of work and artistic training. Although each writer grew disaffected with communism, the two writers grew apart within a few years, with Wright taking a greater interest in world politic movements and the struggle for African independence and Ellison remaining devoted to working for black equality in America through the channels of democracy. In the late 1940s Wright moved to France, where he became an ardent spokesman for Third World liberation in such volumes as *Black Power* (1954) and *White Man, Listen!* (1957) but also returned to fiction in an existentialist novel entitled *The Outsider* (1953) and in a further story of Mississippi racism titled *The Long Dream* (1958).

Despite the greatness of Wright's fiction and autobiography, it was in a work of nonfiction, *12 Million Black Voices* (1941), that he most fully expressed the combined anguish, fear, and passionate hope instilled in black migrants by their collective journey to the North. Subtitled *A Folk History of the Negro in the United States* on its first publication, *12 Mil-*

lion Black Voices grew out of Wright's own migration but was immediately occasioned by his employment in the Federal Writers' Project. His text was written to accompany over one hundred photographs selected from the files of the Farm Security Administration, which were themselves a vivid, often searing account of the transformation of black families moved from southern sharecropping to northern urban life. Although Wright's volume was focused on Chicago, it also effectively conveyed, as in the following selection, the sweep and magnitude of black migration to a number of destinations from the Midwest to New York and thus helps to set the context for the new urban environment discovered by the protagonist of *Invisible Man* when he arrives in Harlem.

There is no question about the influence on Ellison of *12 Million Black Voices*. In a personal letter to Wright, Ellison said that the book stirred his "deepest memories and thoughts; those which are sacred and those which bring the bitterest agonies and the most poignant remembrances and regrets." Identifying with Wright as one "for whom the trauma of passing from the country to the city of destruction brought no anesthesia of consciousness, but left our nerves peeled and quivering," Ellison elevated *12 Million Black Voices* above *Native Son*, adding that Wright's history of the migration "seizes hold to [sic] epochs and a continent . . . squeezes out of us what we leave unspoken" (letter of November 3, 1941, quoted in Fabre 210–12).

In addition to Wright's work, in fiction and nonfiction alike, other novels of the migration such as Waters Turpin's *O Canaan!* (1939), William Attaway's *Blood on the Forge* (1941), and Dorothy West's *The Living Is Easy* (1948) are an important prelude to *Invisible Man* not least because Ellison reviewed several of them. In his review of Attaway's powerful labor novel, cited in the Introduction of this book (p. 22), Ellison looked forward to his own protagonist's experience in the industrial world represented by the Liberty Paints factory, noting that Attaway "grasped the destruction of the folk, but missed its rebirth on a higher level. The writer did not see that while the folk individual was being liquidated in the crucible of steel, he was also undergoing fusion with new elements" (Ellison, "Transition" 90).

FURTHER READING: Allan H. Spear, *Black Chicago: The Making of a Negro Ghetto, 1890–1920* (Chicago: U of Chicago P, 1967); David Gordon Nielson, *Black Ethos: Northern Urban Negro Life and Thought, 1890–1930* (Westport, CT: Greenwood, 1977); James R. Grossman, *Land of Hope: Chicago, Black Southerners, and the Great Migration*

(Chicago: U of Chicago P, 1989); Michel Fabre, *The Unfinished Quest of Richard Wright,* 2nd ed., trans. Isabel Barzun (Urbana: U of Illinois P, 1993).

Lord in heaven! Good God Almighty! Great Day in the Morning! It's here! Our time has come! We are leaving! We are angry no more; we are leaving! We are bitter no more; we are leaving! We are leaving our homes, pulling up stakes to move on. We look up at the high southern sky and remember all the sunshine and the rain and we feel a sense of loss, but we are leaving. We look out at the wide green fields which our eyes saw when we first came into the world and we feel full of regret, but we are leaving. We scan the kind black faces we have looked upon since we first saw the light of day, and, though pain is in our hearts, we are leaving. We take one last furtive look over our shoulders to the Big House — high upon a hill beyond the railroad tracks — where the Lord of the Land lives, and we feel glad, for we are leaving. . . .

For a long time now we have heard tell that all over the world men are leaving the land for the streets of the city, so we are leaving too. As we leave we see thousands of the poor whites also packing up to move to the city, leaving the land that will not give life to her sons and daughters, black or white. When a man lives upon the land and is cold and hungry and hears word of the great factories going up in the cities, he begins to hope and dream of a new life, and he leaves.

In 1890 there were 1,500,000 of us black men and women in the cities of the nation, both north and south. In 1900 there were 2,000,000 of us. In 1920 there were 3,500,000 of us in the cities of the nation and we were still going, still leaving the land. So many of us crowded into New York City that Harlem's black population doubled between 1900 and 1920. In Philadelphia our influx increased the number of black people by one-third in a few years. In Chicago our endless trek inflated the Black Belt population by more than 125,000 from 1920 to 1930. And our tide continued to roll from the farm to the factory, from the country to the city.

Perhaps never in history has a more utterly unprepared folk wanted to go to the city; we were barely born as a folk when we headed for the tall and sprawling centers of steel and stone. We, who were landless upon the land; we, who had barely managed to live in family groups; we, who needed the ritual and guidance of institutions to hold our atomized lives together in lines of purpose; we, who had known only relationships to people and not relationships to things; we who had never belonged to any organizations except the church and burial societies; we, who had had our personalities blasted with two hundred years of slavery and had been turned loose to shift for ourselves — we were such a folk as this when we moved into a world that was destined to test all we were, that threw us into the scales of competition to weigh our mettle. And how were we to know that, the moment we landless millions of the land — we men who were struggling to be born — set our awkward feet upon the pavements of the city, life would begin to exact of us a heavy toll in death?

We did not know what would happen, what was in store for us. We went innocently, longing and hoping for a life that the Lords of the Land would not let us live. Our hearts were high as we moved northward to the cities. What emotions, fears, what a complex of sensations we felt when, looking out of a train window at the revolving fields, we first glimpsed the sliding waters of the gleaming Ohio! What memories that river evoked in us, memories black and gloomy, yet tinged with the bright border of a wild and desperate hope! The Ohio is more than a river. It is a symbol, a line that runs through our hearts, dividing hope from despair, just as once it bisected the nation, dividing freedom from slavery. How many desperate scenes have been enacted upon its banks! How many grim dramas have been played out upon its bosom! How many slave hunters and Abolitionists have clashed here with fire in their eyes and deep convictions in their hearts! This river has seen men whose beliefs were so strong that the rights of property meant nothing, men whose feelings were so mighty that the laws of the land meant nothing, men whose passions were so fiery that only human life and human dignity mattered.

The train and the auto move north, ever north, and from 1916 to 1928, 1,200,000 of us were moving from the South to the North and we kept leaving. Night and day, in rain and in sun, in winter and in summer, we leave the land. Already, as we sit and look broodingly out over the turning fields, we notice with attention and hope that the dense southern swamps give way to broad, cultivated wheat farms. The spick-and-span farmhouses done in red and green and white crowd out the casual, unpainted gingerbread shacks. Silos take the place of straggling piles of hay. Macadam highways now wind over the horizon instead of dirt roads. The cheeks of the farm people are

full and ruddy, not sunken and withered like soda crackers. The slow
southern drawl, which in legend is so sweet and hospitable but which
in fact has brought down on our black bodies suffering untold, is su-
perseded by clipped Yankee phrases, phrases spoken with such rapid-
ity and neutrality that we, with our slow ears, have difficulty in understanding. And the foreigners — Poles, Germans, Swedes, and
Italians — we never dreamed that there were so many in the world!
Yes, coming north for a Negro sharecropper involves more strange-
ness than going to another country. It is the beginning of living on a
new and terrifying plane of consciousness.

We see white men and women get on the train, dressed in expen-
sive new clothes. We look at them guardedly and wonder will they
bother us. Will they ask us to stand up while they sit down? Will they
tell us to go to the back of the coach? Even though we have been told
that we need not be afraid, we have lived so long in fear of all white
faces that we cannot help but sit and wait. We look around the train
and we do not see the old familiar signs: FOR COLORED and FOR
WHITE. The train speeds north and we cannot sleep. Our heads sink
in a doze, and then we sit bolt-upright, prodded by the thought that
we must watch these strange surroundings. But nothing happens;
these white men seem impersonal and their very neutrality reassures
us — for a while. Almost against our deeper judgment, we try to
force ourselves to relax, for these brisk men give no sign of what they
feel. They are indifferent. O sweet and welcome *indifference*!

The miles click behind us. Into Chicago, Indianapolis, New York,
Cleveland, Buffalo, Detroit, Toledo, Philadelphia, Pittsburgh, and
Milwaukee we go, looking for work. We feel freer than we have ever
felt before, but we are still a little scared. It is like a dream. Will we
wake up suddenly and find that none of this is really true, that we are
merely daydreaming behind the barn, snoozing in the sun, waiting to
hear the hoarse voice of the riding boss saying: "Nigger, where do
you think you are? Get the hell up from there and move on!"

Timidly, we get off the train. We hug our suitcases, fearful of pick-
pockets, looking with unrestrained curiosity at the great big brick
buildings. We are very reserved, for we have been warned not to act
"green," that the city people can spot a "sucker" a mile away. Then
we board our first Yankee street car to go to a cousin's home, a
brother's home, a sister's home, a friend's home, an uncle's home, or
an aunt's home. We pay the conductor our fare and look about ap-
prehensively for a seat. We have been told that we can sit where we

please, but we are still scared. We cannot shake off three hundred years of fear in three hours. We ease into a seat and look out of the window at the crowded streets. A white man or a white woman comes and sits beside us, not even looking at us, as though this were a normal thing to do. The muscles of our bodies tighten. Indefinable sensations crawl over our skins and our blood tingles. Out of the corners of our eyes we try to get a glimpse of the strange white face that floats but a few inches from ours. The impulses to laugh and to cry clash in us; we bite out lips and stare out of the window.

There are so many people. For the first time in our lives we feel human bodies, strangers whose lives and thoughts are unknown to us, pressing always close about us. We cannot see or know a *man* because of the thousands upon thousands of *men*. The apartments in which we sleep are crowded and noisy, and soon enough we learn that the brisk, clipped men of the North, the Bosses of the Buildings, are not at all *indifferent*. They are deeply concerned about us, but in a new way. It seems as though we are now living inside of a machine; days and events move with a hard reasoning of their own. We live amid swarms of people, yet there is a vast distance between people, a distance that words cannot bridge. No longer do our lives depend upon the soil, the sun, the rain, or the wind; we live by the grace of jobs and the brutal logic of jobs. We do not know this world, or what makes it move. In the South life was different; men spoke to you, cursed you, yelled at you, or killed you. The world moved by signs we knew. But here in the North cold forces hit you and push you. It is a world of *things*. . . .

It is when we seek to express ourselves that the paradoxical cleavage in our lives shows most. Day after day we labor in the gigantic factories and mills of Western civilization, but we have never been allowed to become an organic part of this civilization; we have yet to share its ultimate hopes and expectations. Its incentives and perspectives, which form the core of meaning for so many millions, have yet to lift our personalities to levels of purpose. Instead, after working all day in one civilization, we go home to our Black Belts and live, within the orbit of the surviving remnants of the culture of the South, our naïve, casual, verbal, fluid folk life.

Alone together with our black folk in the towering tenements, we play our guitars, trumpets, and pianos, beating out rough and infectious rhythms that create an instant appeal among all classes of people. Why is our music so contagious? Why is it that those who deny us are willing to sing our songs? Perhaps it is because so many of those who live in cities feel deep down just as we feel. Our big brass horns, our huge noisy drums and whirring violins make a flood of melodies whose poignancy is heightened by our latent fear and uneasiness, by our love of the sensual, and by our feverish hunger for life. On the plantations our songs carried a strain of other-worldly yearning which people called "spiritual"; but now our blues, jazz, swing, and boogie-woogie are our "spirituals" of the city pavements, our longing for freedom and opportunity, an expression of our bewilderment and despair in a world whose meaning eludes us. The ridiculousness and sublimity of love are captured in our blues, those sad-happy songs that laugh and weep all in one breath, those mockingly tender utterances of a folk imprisoned in steel and stone. Our thirst for the sensual is poured out in jazz; the tension of our brittle lives is given forth in swing; and our nervousness and exhaustion are pounded out in the swift tempo of boogie-woogie.

We lose ourselves in violent forms of dances in our ballrooms. The faces of the white world, looking on in wonder and curiosity, declare: "*Only* the Negro can play!" But they are wrong. They misread us. We are able to play in this fashion because we have been excluded, left behind; we play in this manner because all excluded folk play. The English say of the Irish, just as America says to us, that only the Irish can play, that they laugh through their tears. But every powerful nation says this of the folk whom it oppresses in justification of that oppression. And, ironically, they are angered by the exhibition of any evidence to the contrary, for it disturbs their conscience with vague and guilty doubts. They smile with cold disdain when we black folk say that our thirst can be slaked in art, that our tensions can be translated into industry, that our energies can be applied to finance, that our delight in the world can be converted into education, that our love of adventure can find fulfillment in aviation. But in one way or another, the white folk deny us these pursuits, and our hunger for expression finds its form in our wild, raw music, in our invention of slang that winds its way all over America. Our adoration of color goes not in murals, but into dress, into green, red, yellow, and blue clothes. When we have some money in our pockets on payday, our laughter and songs make the principal streets of our Black Belts — Lenox Avenue, Beale Street, State Street, South Street, Second Street, Auburn Avenue — famous the earth over.

The Bosses of the Buildings would have the world believe that we black folk, after these three hundred years, have locked in our veins blood of a queer kind that makes us act in this "special pattern." In their classrooms and laboratories they attempt to harness science in defense of their attitudes and practices, and never do they so vigorously assail us as "trouble-makers" as when we say that we are "this way" because we are made to live "this way." They say we speak treasonably when we declare that human life is plastic, that human nature is malleable, that men possess the dignity and meaning of the environmental and institutional forms through which they are lucky or unlucky enough to express themselves. They solemnly assert that we seek to overthrow the government by violence when we say that we live in this manner because the Black Belt which cradles our lives is created by the hands and brains of men who have decreed that we must live differently. They brand us as revolutionists when we say that we are not allowed to react to life with an honest and frontal vision.

We live on, and our music makes the feet of the whole world dance, even the feet of the children of the poor white workers who live beyond the line that marks the boundary of our lives. Where we cannot go, our tunes, songs, slang, and jokes go. Some of the white boys and girls, starved prisoners of urban homes, even forget the hatred of their parents when they hear our sensual, wailing blue melodies. The common people of the nation grow to love our songs so much that a few of us make our living by creating a haven of song for those who are weary of the barren world of steel and stone reared by the Bosses of the buildings. But only a few of those who dance and sing with us suspect the rawness of life out of which our laughing-crying tunes and quick dance-steps come; they do not know that our songs and dances are our banner of hope flung desperately up in the face of a world that has pushed us to the wall.

Louis Armstrong, both as a trumpeter and as a vocalist, exercised a profound influence on the development of jazz from the 1920s through the 1960s. At both the beginning and the end of the novel, Ellison's protagonist meditates on the way in which Armstrong's music represents the deep social message of the blues as well as the centrality of improvisation in African American art and life (*Invisible Man* 12, 581).

Part Two

"A HEAP OF SIGNIFYING"

Vernacular Culture

Andy Razaf
(What Did I Do to Be So) Black and Blue

The song from which Ellison's protagonist derives his most searching quotation from a piece of music — "what did I do to be so black and blue?" (*Invisible Man* 12) — was recorded in several versions by Louis Armstrong, the era's most famous jazz musician. Armstrong has a multidimensional role in *Invisible Man* (see pp. 11 and 14–15 of this book), but "(What Did I Do to Be So) Black and Blue" is of special significance in its own right. Armstrong first encountered the song in 1929 on the black musical stage of New York, where it had been belatedly inserted into a show running as *Hot Chocolates,* with music principally by Fats Waller and lyrics by Andy Razaf (1895–1973). Apparently written to order at the command of the mobster Dutch Schultz (the show's financial backer), who wanted a "funny song" about the tragedy of being black, "Black and Blue" in fact explored very serious ground about prejudice and evoked a mixture of laughter and stunned discomfort in the first audience who heard it sung on stage by Edith Wilson (Singer 12–20). Armstrong recorded it the same year, and the song came to be regarded as one of the first overt instances of racial protest in American popular music. *Hot Chocolates* also featured another famous Waller-Razaf collaboration, "Ain't Misbehavin'," and the work of composer and lyricist gained a new life with the Broadway production in 1978 of *Ain't Misbehavin',* which closes with a poignant rendition of "Black and Blue."

The lyricist of "Black and Blue" shortened his real name of Andrea Razafkeriefo (his father was from Madagascar) to Andy Razaf when he embarked on a writing career that was equally successful up in Harlem and downtown in Tin Pan Alley. He composed the lyrics for more than eight hundred songs, among them many recorded by Armstrong, Billie Holiday, Duke Ellington, Ethel Waters, and others. Also a recorded vocalist and a writer of poems published in *Negro World* in the early 1920s, some attacking Anglo-Saxon racism and lynching (Martin 173, 244), Razaf was best known for the shows *Keep Shufflin* (1928) and *Blackbirds* (1930), in addition to *Hot Chocolates.* Other Razaf songs that may have a bearing on scenes and motifs in *Invisible Man* include "What Harlem Is to Me" and "Sambo's Syncopated Russian Dance," which mocked African American

infatuation with communism and thus might have inspired Tod Clifton's
street-corner marketing of the grotesque Sambo dolls in the novel.
   FURTHER READING: Allen L. Woll, *Black Musical Theatre: From
Coontown to Dreamgirls* (Baton Rouge: Louisiana State UP, 1989);
Barry Singer, *Black and Blue: The Life and Lyrics of Andy Razaf* (New
York: Schirmer, 1992).

> Out in the street, shufflin' feet,
> Couples passing two by two,
> While here am I, left high and dry,
> Black, and 'cause I'm black I'm blue.
>
> Browns and yellers all have fellers,
> Gentlemen prefer them light,
> Wish I could fade, can't make the grade,
> Nothin' but dark days in sight.
>
> Cold empty bed, springs hard as lead,
> Pains in my head, feel like old Ned,
> What did I do to be so black and blue?
>
> No joys for me, no company,
> Even the mouse ran from my house,
> All my life through, I've been so black and blue.
>
> I'm white inside, it don't help my case,
> 'Cause I can't hide what is on my face.
>
> I'm so forlorn, life's just a thorn,
> My heart is torn, why was I born?
> What did I do to be so black and blue?
>
> Just 'cause you're black, folks think you lack,
> They laugh at you and scorn you too,
> What did I do to be so black and blue?
>
> When you are near, they laugh and sneer,
> Set you aside and you're denied,
> What did I do to be so black and blue?
>
> How sad I am, each day I feel worse,
> My mark of Ham seems to be a curse.
>
> How will it end? Ain't got a friend,
> My only sin is in my skin,
> What did I do to be so black and blue?

African American Folk Song
Run, Nigger, Run

One central motif of *Invisible Man* is set in motion at the end of the first chapter by the protagonist's dream about the engraved document in his briefcase, which reads: "To Whom It May Concern: Keep This Nigger-Boy Running." The line recurs to Ellison's narrator when he discovers the message of Bledsoe's letter to his prospective northern employers, and the idea dominates the remainder of the novel, from his migration north to the moment he drops into a coal cellar while running down the street during the riot. In building into his plot the protagonist's continual movement, at once forced and futile, Ellison recapitulates a common theme in black folklore and literature. He later connected it to "double-dealing" sociological theories such as "benign neglect" and "reverse discrimination," which, he remarked, translate: "Keep those Negroes running — but in their same old place" (*Invisible Man* 33, 191, xv).

The theme of running can be traced in early African American culture to the theme of escape from slavery memorialized in poetry, folktales, and songs. The selection "Run, Nigger, Run" is a version of one of the earliest transcribed African American songs, first appearing in William Allen's 1867 collection of black spirituals, work songs, and ballads, *Slave Songs in the United States* (Allen 89). Numerous variants appear in later collections, most of them, like this example, narrating a slave's escape or offering advice about avoiding capture by slave patrols ("patter-rollers") or dogs. As in many black folk songs, nonsense rhymes can sometimes disguise or encode a serious message of resistance, as in this variation:

> Dis nigger run, he run his best,
> Stuck his head in a hornet's nest,
> Jumped de fence and run fru de paster;
> white man run, but nigger run faster.
> (Scarborough 24)

FURTHER READING: Henry E. Krehbiel, *Afro-American Folksongs: A Study in Racial and National Music* (1914; rpt. New York: Frederick

Ungar, 1962); Miles Mark Fisher, *Negro Slave Songs in the United States* (New York: Russell and Russell, 1953); Paul Oliver, *Savannah Syncopators: African Retentions in the Blues* (New York: Stein and Day, 1970).

Do, please, marster, don't ketch me,
Ketch dat nigger behin' dat tree;
He stole money en I stole none,
Put him in the calaboose des for fun!

Chorus:
　　Oh, run, nigger, run! de patter-roller ketch you.
　　Run, nigger, run! hit's almos' day!
　　Oh, run, nigger, run! de patter-roller ketch you.
　　Run, nigger, run! hit's almos' day!

Some folks say dat a nigger won't steal,
But I kotch one in my corn-fiel';
He run ter de eas', he run ter de wes',
He run he head in a hornet nes'!

De sun am set, dis nigger am free;
De yaller gals he goes to see;
I heard a man cry, "Run, doggone you,"
Run, nigger, run, patter-roller ketch you.

Wid eyes wide open and head hangin' down,
Like de rabbit before de houn',
Dis nigger streak it for de pasture;
Nigger run fast, white man run faster.

And ober de fence as slick as a eel
Dis nigger jumped all but his heel;
De white man ketch dat fast, you see,
And tied it tight aroun' de tree.

Dis nigger heard dat old whip crack,
But nebber stopped fur to look back;
I started home as straight as a bee
And left my heel tied aroun' de tree.

My ol' Miss, she prommus me
Dat when she die, she set me free;
But she done dead dis many year ago,
En yer I'm hoein' de same ol' row!

I'm a-hoein' across, I'm a-hoein' aroun',
I'm a-cleanin' up some mo' new groun'.
Whar I lif' so hard, I lif' so free,
Dat my sins rise up in front er me!

But some er dese days my time will come,
I'll year dat bugle, I'll year dat drum,
I'll see dem armies a-marchin' along,
I'll lif' my head en jine der song —
I'll dine no mo' behin' dat tree,
W'en de angels flock fer to wait on me!

African American Folk Song

Jack the Rabbit! Jack the Bear!

Jack the Rabbit and Jack the Bear are common figures of African American folklore. As in the folktales reprinted below (pp. 127–30), they frequently represent characters who survive by wit and trickery; and throughout the black narrative tradition descended from slavery, animals often enact an allegory of the relationship between master and slave. A traditional black folk song uses the rabbit figure to point to the anonymity of storytellers and singers alike in the history of slave culture: "Anybody should ask you who made up this song, / Tell 'em Jack the Rabbit, he's been here and gone." As the following selection from a railroad work song suggests, however, Jack the Rabbit and Jack the Bear could be cited as comparatively wide-ranging metaphors of African American experience in the world of bondage, labor, and racism whose effects and meaning remained especially sharp in the era of segregation.

In this song the act of lining the track refers to the backbreaking labor, with sledge hammers and pry-bars, of putting railroad track in proper alignment. In African American folklore, a "jack" sometimes refers to a charm or conjure (Puckett 168, 206ff.); in many tales Jack (or John) appears simply as a cunning black man; and as a grizzly bear Jack figures in convict work songs (Courlander 106). A variant of the railroad work song published in 1925 offers less of a narrative line than the selection below but includes a transcription of the grunting and breathing ("um-uh") that melds with the song:

> Brother Rabbit, Brother Bear,
> Can't you line them just a hair?
> Shake the iron, um-uh!
>
> Down the railroad, um-uh!
> Well, raise the iron, um-uh!
> Raise the iron, um-uh!
> (Odum and Johnson, *The Negro and His Songs* 262)

In "Out of the Hospital," a section of *Invisible Man* attached to the Liberty Paints episode that Ellison excised during revision, the protagonist thus recalls a version of the railroad song as he strains to lift an iron lid after fleeing from the hospital:

Jack the Rabbit
Jack the Bear
Lift it, lift it,
Just a hair ...

This leads the protagonist to reflect in his own improvisatory way on the need to *"sing a song in silence in a strange land, Jack it up, bear it in the dark, it's heavy as the world"* (Ellison, "Out of the Hospital" 263). Likewise, when Ellison's narrator speaks from his state of hibernation, having escaped what Peter Wheatstraw calls the bear's den of Harlem, he recalls his earlier identity as Jack the Bear (*Invisible Man* 6, 168, 174). As the title of a Duke Ellington composition and the stage name of a 1920s Harlem pianist, however, Jack the Bear is also a folk epithet evoking survival and wisdom in the modern world of urban black performance (Savery 67). As in the following example, work songs frequently included limitless improvised stories alternating with a rhythmic chorus such as "Jack the Rabbit! Jack the Bear!"

FURTHER READING: Alan Dundes, ed., *Mother Wit from the Laughing Barrel: Readings in the Interpretation of Afro-American Folklore* (1973; rpt. New York: Garland, 1981); Roger D. Abrahams, *Afro-American Folktales: Stories from Black Traditions in the New World* (New York: Pantheon, 1985).

Jack the rabbit! Jack the bear!
Can't you line him just a hair,
Just a hair, just a hair?
Annie Weaver and her daughter
Ran a boarding house on the water.
She's got chicken, she's got ham,
She's got everything I'll be damned.
Old Joe Logan he's gone north
To get the money for to pay us off.

In the early twentieth-century South, prison convicts, especially African Americans such as the novel's Brother Tarp, often performed backbreaking labor while wearing heavy chains and shackles (*Invisible Man* 386–90).

Peetie Wheatstraw
The Devil's Son-in-Law

Soon after he arrives in Harlem, Ellison's protagonist, in one of the most intriguing moments in the novel, encounters a character who identifies himself as Peter Wheatstraw (*Invisible Man* 172–77). Confronted with a flurry of riddles and word games derived from African American folklore and popular songs, the protagonist is recognizably estranged from the provocative blues story half told and half sung by Wheatstraw: "God damn, I thought, they're a hell of a people!" Wheatstraw sings a bawdy chorus from "Boogie Woogie Blues," by Jimmy Rushing and Count Basie, invokes the folk figures of Jack the Rabbit and Jack the Bear (see p. 120 of this book), strings together a thirty-five-syllable word loaded with African American folk beliefs about conjure and prophecy, and identifies himself as the "Devil's only son-in-law." Peetie (or Pete) Wheatstraw was the stage name of William Bunch, an actual blues singer whom Ellison knew from his recordings (more than 160 between 1930 and 1941) and his performances in the Midwest, and with whom Ellison himself played on one occasion in Saint Louis (Oliver, *Blues off the Record* 189–94; Oakley, 186–88). The name was also a pseudonym adopted by other singers. Muriel Longini, the folklorist who reprinted the lyrics below among a broad sampling of black folk songs from Chicago, identified the name of this Peetie Wheatstraw (she wrote "Wheet Straw") as "the pseudonym of a blues singer who makes recordings," although she likely had in mind the real Wheatstraw, whose recordings frequently carried the epithet "high sheriff from hell" or "the devil's son-in-law."

FURTHER READING: Paul Garon, *The Devil's Son-in-Law* (London: Studio Vista, 1971); Giles Oakley, *The Devil's Music: A History of the Blues* (New York: Taplinger, 1977); Robert Palmer, *Deep Blues* (New York: Viking, 1981).

I am Peetie Wheat Straw, the high sheriff of hell,
I am Peetie Wheat Straw, the high sheriff of hell,
And when I lock you up, baby, you're locked in a dungeon cell.

I am Peetie Wheat Straw, the devil's son-in-law,
I am Peetie Wheat Straw, the devil's son-in-law,
The woman I married, old Satan was her paw. . . .

After I married this woman, it was like being tied to a ball and
    chain,
After I married this woman, it was like being tied to a ball and
    chain,
It makes no difference, mama, I'll treat you nice just the same.

African American Spiritual
Many Thousands Gone

"Many Thousands Gone," the spiritual sung spontaneously by the crowd gathered for Tod Clifton's funeral (*Invisible Man* 452), is among the simplest but most profound songs created by African American slaves. First transcribed (as "Many Thousand Go") in William Allen's *Slave Songs in the United States* in 1867 (Allen 48), it has been reproduced in virtually every collection of spirituals since then, including such popular volumes as J. B. T. Marsh's *The Story of the Jubilee Singers* (1872). Frequently performed and recorded by Paul Robeson and others, the song's simple verses are subject to endless elaboration and exist in many variants. Generally dated from the onset of the Civil War (although earlier versions are likely), "Many Thousands Gone" speaks first of all of the time when a slave will be released from bondage — whether through emancipation, escape, or death — but it may also be read as a tribute to the thousands of Africans who have died in the middle passage from Africa to America, under slavery, or through violence and hardship since. Music plays a key role throughout *Invisible Man*, but the arguments over the cultural value and meaning of the spirituals were particularly pointed in the early twentieth century, with the middle class and a number of black schools taking the disdainful view expressed by the protagonist's campus colleagues toward Trueblood and his quartet, whose "earthy harmonies . . . [and] plaintively animal sounds" they find embarrassing (*Invisible Man* 47). In an essay on racial dehumanization whose argument echoes *Invisible Man*, James Baldwin chose the spiritual's title as his own: "The story of the Negro in America is the story of America — or, more precisely, it is the story of Americans. . . . He is a series of shadows, self-created, intertwining, which now we helplessly battle. One may say that the Negro in America does not really exist except in the darkness of our minds" (Baldwin, "Many Thousands Gone" 18).

FURTHER READING: Eileen Southern, *The Music of Black Americans: A History* (New York: Norton, 1971); John Lovell, Jr., *Black Song: The Forge and the Flame* (New York: Macmillan, 1972); Dena J. Epstein, *Sinful Tunes and Spirituals: Black Folk Music to the Civil War* (Urbana: U of Illinois P, 1977).

No more auction block for me,
No more, no more;
No more auction block for me,
Many thousands gone.

No more peck of corn for me,
No more, no more;
No more peck of corn for me,
Many thousands gone.

No more driver's lash for me,
No more, no more;
No more driver's lash for me,
Many thousands gone.

No more pint of salt for me,
No more, no more;
No more pint of salt for me,
Many thousands gone.

No more mistress' call for me,
No more, no more;
No more mistress' call for me,
Many thousands gone.

Emma Backus
Why Mr. Dog Runs Brer Rabbit

Carl Carmer
Brer Rabbit and the Goobers

Although animal folktales are common throughout the world, African American tales have often contained negotiations of authority comparable to that between master and slave and rather explicit dimensions of political resistance. Whether in tales handed down in the African and African American traditions, or in the versions popularized in the nineteenth-century Uncle Remus stories of Joel Chandler Harris, the rabbit in particular has been recognized as a trickster figure who thrives by outwitting his opponent, often a bear, a fox, or a dog. In an urban setting designated characteristics of folk figures might be even more fluid and unpredictable, although in hip slang of the era, the rabbit might be a "cool cat" whereas the bear was a "square" (Fullinwider 220). As Ellison's varied use of Jack the Bear suggests (see p. 120 of this book), any number of animal tales might be relevant to *Invisible Man*, whose protagonist must find his way through a world of tricks, traps, exploitation, illusion, and outright antagonism. His encounter with Peter Wheatstraw — "What I want to know is . . . is you got the *dog?*" — produces the truth about the narrator's current predicament: the dog "got holt to you." That is to say, the narrator is at the mercy of forces he cannot yet control, chased like a running slave or an escaped convict by a vicious dog, which is usually a despised figure in African or African American folktales (*Invisible Man* 174; Puckett 35). Likewise, the remembered childhood figure of Buckeye the Rabbit, who drifts into the narrator's semiconsciousness after his accident at the Liberty Paints factory, derives from a trickster figure with various incarnations, including a rhyme about a rabbit whose short tail is a sign of his close calls and a work song with roots in escape (Talley 175; see p. 25 of this book).

The collection of African American folktales and songs became a major enterprise among ethnographers and editors in the late nineteenth century. The first selection below, "Why Mr. Dog Runs Brer Rabbit," is taken from a set of stories transcribed by Emma Backus for the *Journal of American Folklore* and is characteristic of contemporary material. A central argument among ethnographers and literary scholars alike concerned the degree to which African American culture retained African ideas or narrative styles, a debate dating from the nineteenth century but galvanized by Melville Herskovits's landmark study *The Myth of the Negro Past* (1941) and one that continues to have important implications for present understanding of African American cultural forms. The second selection, "Brer Rabbit and the Goobers," comes from a 1934 collection, *Stars Fell on Alabama*, by Carl Carmer (1893–1976). It was also reprinted in the foremost mid-century collection of black folklore, *Book of Negro Folklore*, edited by Langston Hughes and Arna Bontemps.

Although his novel itself is proof to the contrary, Ellison once lamented that the black achievement in folklore had not often been matched in fiction. In folktales, he argued, we "depict the humor as well as the horror of our living. We project Negro life in a metaphysical perspective and we [see] it with a complexity of vision that seldom gets into our writing" (Ellison, "A Very Stern Discipline" 283).

FURTHER READING: Richard M. Dorson, *American Negro Folktales* (Greenwich, CT: Fawcett, 1967); Lawrence W. Levine, *Black Culture and Black Consciousness: Afro-American Folk Thought from Slavery to Freedom* (New York: Oxford UP, 1978); Joseph E. Holloway, ed., *Africanisms in American Culture* (Bloomington: Indiana UP, 1990); Roger D. Abrahams, *Singer the Master: The Emergence of African American Culture in the Plantation South* (New York: Pantheon, 1992).

Emma Backus

Why Mr. Dog Runs Brer Rabbit

One morning, Mr. Buzzard he say he stomach just hungry for some fish, and he tell Mrs. Buzzard he think he go down to the branch, and catch some for breakfast. So he take he basket, and he sail along till he come to the branch.

He fish right smart, and by sun up he have he basket plum full. But Mr. Buzzard am a powerful greedy man, and he say to hisself, he did, I just catch one more. But while he done gone for this last one, Brer Rabbit he came along, clipity, clipity, and when he see basket plum full of fine whitefish he stop, and he say, "I 'clare to goodness, the old woman just gwine on up to the cabin, 'cause they got nothing for to fry for breakfast. I wonder what she think of this yer fish," and so he put the basket on he head, Brer Rabbit did, and make off to the cabin.

Direc'ly he meet up with Mr. Dog, and he ax him where he been fishing that early in the day, and Brer Rabbit he say how he done sot on the log 'longside of the branch, and let he tail hang in the water and catch all the fish, and he done tell Mr. Dog, the old rascal did, that he tail mighty short for the work, but that Mr. Dog's tail just the right sort for fishing.

So Mr. Dog, he teeth just ache for them whitefish, and he go set on the log and hang he tail in the water, and it mighty cold for he tail, and the fish don't bite, but he mouth just set for them fish, and so he just sot dar, and it turn that cold that when he feel he gin up, sure's you born, Mr. Dog, he tail froze fast in the branch, and he call he chillens, and they come and break the ice.

And then, to be sure, he start off to settle Ole Brer Rabbit, and he get on he track and he run the poor ole man to beat all, and directly he sight him he run him round and round the woods and holler, "Hallelujah! hallelujah!" and the puppies come on behind, and they holler, "Glory! glory!" and they make such a fuss, all the creeters in the woods, they run to see what the matter. Well, sah, from that day, Mr. Dog he run Brer Rabbit, and when they just get gwine on the swing in the big woods, you can hear ole Ben dar just letting hisself out, "Hallelujah! hallelujah!" and them pups just gwine "Glory! glory!" and it surely am the sound what has the music dar, it surely has the music dar.

Carl Carmer

Brer Rabbit and the Goobers

"Brer Rabbit seen Brer B'ar one day a-settin' out to dig goobers wid de donkey draggin' de dump cart. Brer Rabbit say me an' Miss Rabbit an' all them little rabbits sho' is hungry fo goobers. So he go home an' fin' him a red string an' tie it 'roun' his neck an' he run an' lay down in de road where Brer B'ar would be com'n by wid de cart carryin' his sack filled up wid goobers.

By'n by Brer B'ar come along an' de donkey shy so he 'most upset de cart. Brer B'ar git out an' he say: 'If'n it ain't Brer Rabbit as dead as a doornail wid his throat cut. Make good rabbit stew foh me an'

Miss B'ar. So he pick up Brer Rabbit an' fling him in de cart an' go on. Soon's his back is turned Brer Rabbit fling out de bag o' goobers an' jump out heself an' run home. On de way he meet Brer Fox an' Brer Fox say: 'Where you git dat bag o' goobers?' an' Brer Rabbit tell him.

Soon's Brer B'ar come in sight er his house, way behime dem dark pines, he holler to his ole 'oman:

> 'Hello dar. Come heah, Miss B'ar:
> Goobers heah; rabbits dar!'

Miss B'ar she run out de cabin. She run 'roun' de dump cart. She look in. Des a lil' rattlin' load o' goobers in de bottom er de cart.

She say: 'Goobers gone, rabbit gone, bag gone!'

Brer B'ar tu'n 'roun' an' look, he scratch his head, he say: 'Dat 'ar rabbit done left me bar.'

Nex' day he hitch up de donkey to de dump cart an' start to de patch to haul up mo' goobers. His ole 'oman, she tell him: 'Watch out, don' drap noddin' on de big road wid dis nex' load.'

Dis time Brer Fox he 'low he'll git his winter's pervisions by speculatin' wid Brer B'ar's load, labor and land.

Brer Fox git a red string, he do. He tie hit 'roun' his neck.

He go to de big road. Some place what Brer Rabbit done lay down, Brer Fox he done lay down. He keep des' as still. D'reckly heah come Brer B'ar wid 'noder heapin' load o' goobers.

De donkey he shy agin at de same place. Brer B'ar he git off de cart, he look at Brer Fox, he say: 'What dis mean? Un-hum! Maybe perhaps de same thief what stole my goobers yestiddy. You got de same like red 'roun' your th'oat. Maybe perhaps you dead too. He feel Brer Fox, he say: 'You good weight too, I take you to my ole 'oman, maybe you'll make er good stew.'

Wid dat Brer Fox think he sho' goin' git good chance to git his fill er goobers.

Brer B'ar he lif' Brer Fox by de behime legs, he say:

> 'Maybe you be dead, er maybe no,
> But I will make you dead fer sho'!'

and wid dat he swing Brer Fox 'roun' and 'roun' and lam his head 'ginst de wheel er de cart.

Dat lick like to kilt Brer Fox. Hit all he can do to jerk his behime legs loose from Brer B'ar and run home t'rough de dark pines. He had de swole head some seasons frum dat lick. Chillun, de same cunnin' trick ain't apt to work twict."

Racist imagery has been common in the history of American popular culture. This coin bank, similar to the one described in *Invisible Man* (319), depicts a black figure with crudely stereotyped features. When a lever is pressed, the eyes roll back, the lips open wide, and a coin placed in the hand is deposited in the mouth.

Street Market Song

De Sweet Pertater Man

Leo Gurley

Sweet-the-Monkey

The oral narratives collected by the Federal Writers' Project ranged from the story of rural southern poverty (see p. 86 of this book) to simple songs and street hollers such as the marketing call of the "Sweet Pertater Man" in one of the selections that follow. From factory workers to farmers to railroad porters to hustlers to housewives, the oral narrators who allowed the writers to record their life histories and colloquial anecdotes created a richly textured portrait of America. The project was curtailed by the onset of World War II, and only a few volumes of material, notably *These Are Our Lives* (1939) and *Lay Down My Burden: A Folk History of Slavery* (1945), appeared before the postwar period. A 1937 volume entitled *American Stuff*, which included Richard Wright's famous short work "The Ethics of Living Jim Crow," featured six market songs of Harlem. One was "De Sweet Pertater Man," the cry of a sweet potato vendor that may have inspired the vignette of the yam vendor in *Invisible Man*. It also may have fostered the multiple puns on "yam" and "I am," through which Ellison jokingly alludes to the key passage in Exodus wherein Moses begins the story of deliverance from bondage, so important in African American cultural history, and God speaks of his unnameable name: I AM THAT I AM (*Invisible Man* 263–69; Exodus 3:7–15). The street cries were also reproduced in B. A. Botkin's 1956 volume, *New York City Folklore*, and Langston Hughes and Arna Bontemps's 1957 collection, *Book of Negro Folklore*.

Among Ellison's African American colleagues in the Federal Writers' Project were Richard Wright, Margaret Walker, Arna Bontemps, and Zora Neale Hurston, and his own participation in the collecting of oral narratives from 1938 to 1940, as part of the "Living Lore Unit," was instrumental to his discovery of the vernacular voices of Harlem street life that are so important to the dialogue of *Invisible Man* (see pp. 8 and

21–22 of this book). In an interview with Ann Banks, whose *First-Person America* reprints a generous selection of short oral narratives, including several recorded by Ellison, he remarked, "I hung around playgrounds, I hung around the street, the bars. . . . I would tell some stories to get people going and then I'd sit back and try to get it down as accurately as I could" (Banks xvii). As he told another interviewer, however, complete accuracy in such a project was impossible: "I couldn't quite get the tone of the sounds in but I could get some of the patterns and get an idea of what it was like" (McPherson 59). On yet another occasion, it is worth noting, Ellison also recalled that the collecting of street narratives occurred at the same time he was studying essays on the craft of writing by Henry James and Joseph Conrad (Hersey 303). One of the narratives is the source of Mary Rambo's remark to the protagonist "Don't let this Harlem git you. I'm in New York, but New York ain't in me, understand what I mean?" (*Invisible Man* 255; Banks 243). A less extravagant version of the street slang the protagonist finds in Peetie Wheatstraw, the narrative of Sweet-the-Monkey that Ellison recorded in an interview with a Harlemite named Leo Gurley mixes outlaw folklore with a motif of invisibility that Ellison must have found revealing.

FURTHER READING: Jerre G. Mangione, *The Dream and the Deal: The Federal Writers' Project, 1935–1943* (Boston: Little, Brown, 1972); Richard H. Pells, *Radical Visions and American Dreams: Culture and Social Thought in the Depression Years* (New York: Harper, 1973); William Stott, *Documentary Expression and Thirties America* (New York: Oxford UP, 1973); *First Person America,* ed. Ann Banks (New York: Knopf, 1980).

Street Market Song
De Sweet Pertater Man

See des gread big sweet pertaters
Right chere by dis chicken's side,
Ah'm de one what bakes dese taters
Makes dem fit to suit yo' pride

Dere is taters an' mo' taters,
But de ones ah sells is fine

Yo' kin go fum hyeah to yondah
But yo' won't get none lak mine
'Cause Ah'm de tater man!
(Ah mean!)
De sweet pertater man!

Leo Gurley

Sweet-the-Monkey

I hope to God to kill me if this ain't the truth. All you got to do is go down to Florence, South Carolina, and ask most anybody you meet and they'll tell you it's the truth.

Florence is one of those hard towns on colored folks. You have to stay out of the white folks' way. All but Sweet. That the fellow I'm fixing to tell you about. His name was Sweet-the-Monkey. I done forgot his real name, I cain't remember it. But that was what everybody called him. He wasn't no big guy. He was just bad. My mother and grandmother used to say he was wicked. He was bad alright. He was one sucker who didn't give a damn bout the crackers. Fact is, they got so they stayed out of *his* way. I cain't never remember hear tell of any them crackers bothering *that* guy. He used to give em trouble all over the place and all they could do about it was to give the rest of us hell.

It was this way: Sweet could make hisself invisible. You don't believe it? Well here's how he done it. Sweet-the-monkey cut open a black cat and took out its heart. Climbed up a tree backwards and cursed God. After that he could do anything. The white folks would wake up in the morning and find their stuff gone. He cleaned out the stores. He cleaned out the houses. Hell, he even cleaned out the damn bank! He was the boldest black sonofabitch ever been down that way. And couldn't nobody do nothing to him. Because they couldn't never see im when he done it. He didn't need the money. Fact is, most of the time he broke into places he wouldn't take nothing. Lotsa times he just did it to show em he could. Hell, he had everybody in that lil old town scaird as hell, black folks and white folks.

The white folks started trying to catch Sweet. Well, they didn't have no luck. They'd catch im standing in front of the eating joints and put the handcuffs on im and take im down to the jail. You know what that sucker would do? The police would come up and say, "Come on, Sweet," and he'd say, "You all want me?" and they'd put the handcuffs on im and start leading im away. He'd go with em a little piece. Sho, just like he was going. Then all of a sudden he would turn hisself invisible and disappear. The police wouldn't have nothing but the handcuffs. They couldn't do a thing with that Sweet-the-Monkey. Just before I come up this way they was all trying to trap im. They didn't have much luck. Once they found a place he'd looted with footprints leading away from it and they decided to try and trap im. This was bout sunup and they followed his footprints all that day. They followed them till sundown when he came partly visible. It was red and the sun was shining on the trees and they waited till they saw his shadow. That was the last of Sweet-the-Monkey. They never did find his body, and right after that I come up here. That was bout five years ago. My brother was down there last year and they said they think Sweet done come back. But they cain't be sho because he won't let hisself be seen.

Mezz Mezzrow
Hip Language

Although a comparatively small part of *Invisible Man,* the hipster slang of Peetie Wheatstraw or Rineheart and the cool style evinced by the zoot suiters the protagonist meets on the subway platform after Tod Clifton's murder — those who "speak a jived-up transitional language" and who are "outside the groove of history" but certainly in their own groove (*Invisible Man* 441–43) — are manifestations of a street culture centered primarily on black jazz. Ellison's own musical training and his work in recording oral narratives for the Federal Writers' Project make his fascination throughout the novel with contemporary fusions of language and music especially important. Hip language of the era was codified in the jazz musician Cab Calloway's two books, *Cab Calloway's Hepster's Dictionary* (1938) and *Professor Cab Calloway's Swingformation Bureau* (1944), and the proliferation of a black urban vernacular, especially with the advent of bebop, became a subject of interest for the black and white press alike (Anderson 315–16). The 1940s language of hip was part of a much older and continuing evolution of black language interacting with white mainstream culture; but the more particular dress insignia of the war period, the zoot suit — with its thigh-length jacket, wide padded shoulders, and peg pants—belonged to a generation of mostly black youth (but including many Mexican Americans on the West Coast) whose defiance of prejudice coincided with World War II. The zoot suit phenomenon was soon the subject of sociological analyses that focused on racial pathology and urban disorders such as the Harlem riots (Clark, "The Zoot Effect in Personality"), on youth cults and potential gang formation (Redl, "Zoot Suits: An Interpretation"), and, eventually, on the postwar commodification of youth culture (Firestone, "Cats, Kicks, and Color"). Just as bebop became part of the black wartime language of resistance to discrimination (Lott), so the extravagant fashion of the zoot suit, says a recent critic more attuned to the semiotics of material culture, was "a subcultural gesture that refused to concede to the manners of subservience" (Cosgrove 78).

Milton "Mezz" Mezzrow (1899–1972) was a white musician whose book *Really the Blues,* an account of jazz, the blues, and urban street culture principally in Chicago and New York, became an underground classic because his immersion in black culture allowed him to tell its story in an authentic language. Published in 1946, the first-person narrative, composed with the assistance of a folklorist and writer named Bernard Wolfe, contains a number of descriptions and passages that are suggestive for *Invisible Man*. For example, in describing the tendency of unhip listeners to stand in front of the bandstand "snapping their fingers in a childish way, yelling 'Get hot! Yeah man, get hot!'" Mezzrow anticipates the surreal scene in which the protagonist undergoes shock treatment and imagines the doctor to say, "They really do have rhythm, don't they? Get hot, boy! Get hot!" (Mezzrow and Wolfe 142; *Invisible Man* 237)

FURTHER READING: LeRoi Jones (Imamu Amiri Baraka), *Blues People* (New York: Morrow, 1963); Ben Sidran, *Black Talk* (New York: Holt, 1971); Albert Murray, *Stomping the Blues* (New York: McGraw, 1976); Neil Leonard, *Jazz: Myth and Religion* (New York: Oxford UP, 1987); Burton W. Peretti, *The Creation of Jazz: Music, Race, and Culture in Urban America* (Urbana: U of Illinois P, 1992).

What weird kind of polyglot patois was this, that they slung around my head on The Corner? It was nothing but the "new poetry of the proletariat." Dan Burley, famous old Negro newspaperman and editor of Harlem's *Amsterdam News*, describes jive that way, and I got a feeling he's right. It's *the language of action*, says Dan, "which comes from the bars, the dancehalls, the prisons, honkytonks, ginmills, etc., wherever people are busy living, loving, fighting, working, or conniving to get the better of one another." But don't think that it's a kind of petty patter, reserved for small talk. Uh, uh. In it the cats discuss "politics, religion, science, war, dancing, business, love, economics, and the occult." Jive, I found out, is not only a strange linguistic mixture of dream and deed; it's a whole new attitude towards life.

In the snatches of viper conversation up above, and in the bits of jive scattered over some other pages of this story, you don't get the full flavor of this street-corner poetry. This lingo has to be *heard*, not seen, because its free-flowing rhythms and intonations and easy elisions, all following a kind of instinctive musical pattern just like Bessie Smith's mangling of the English language, can only hit the ear,

not the eye. Besides, if I wrote the hip language straight, most everything I said would sound like plain gibberish. (The word *jive* probably comes from the old English word *jibe*, out of which came the
words *jibberish* and *gibberish*, describing sounds without meaning,
speech that isn't intelligible.) This jive is a private affair, a secret
inner-circle code cooked up partly to mystify the outsiders, while it
brings those in the know closer together because they alone have the
key to the puzzle. The hipster's lingo is a private kind of folk-poetry,
meant for the ears of the brethren alone.

   How can any outsider latch on to the real flavor of a secret code in
which *tick twenty* means ten o'clock and *line forty* means the price is
twenty dollars; friends are addressed as *gate* or *slot*, verbal shorthand
for *gatemouth* and *slotmouth*, which are inner-circle racial jokes to
begin with; *they* or *them people* means, not two or more persons, but
a man's wife or mistress; *Tenth Street* isn't a city thoroughfare but a
ten-dollar bill; specific places are known by special nicknames —
New York City as *The Apple*, Seventh Avenue as *The Stroll*, the
Savoy Ballroom as *The Track*; doubletalk nonsense-syllables like
lozeerose, that resemble no regular words in any regular language,
are invented to refer to private matters like marihuana? Guys talk
that way when they don't want to be spied on, resent eavesdroppers;
when they're jealously guarding their private lives, which are lived
under great pressure, and don't want the details known to outsiders
— detectives, square ofay musicians, informers, rivals from white
show business, thrill-hungry tourists who come slumming up to "savage" and "primitive" Harlem to eyeball and gape.

   Another well-known author and journalist, Earl Conrad, talks
about jive as a kind of caricatured twist the Negro gives to the language that was foisted on him. "White America perpetrated a new
and foreign language on the Africans it enslaved. Slowly, over the
generations, Negro America, living by and large in its own segregated
world, with its own thoughts, found its own way of expression,
found its own way of handling English, as it had to find its own way
in handling many other aspects of a white, hostile world. Jive is one
of the end-results. . . . Jive talk may have been originally a kind of
'pig Latin' that the slaves talked with each other, a code — when they
were in the presence of whites. Take the word 'ofay.' Ninety million
white Americans right now probably don't know that that means 'a
white,' but Negroes know it. Negroes needed to have a word like that

in their language, needed to create it in self-defense." *Ofay*, of course, is pig Latin for *foe*.

Conrad's right a hundred times over, but I think you have to make a big distinction between the Southern Negro's strictly cautious and defensive private lingo and the high-spirited, belligerent jive of the younger Northern Negroes. Down South, before the Civil War and for long decades after it, right up to today, the colored folks had to nurse their wounds in private, never show their hurts and resentments, and talk among themselves in conspiratorial whispers. The language was mostly a self-protective code to them, and so it wasn't very elaborate or full of bubbling energy and unshackled invention; it was the tongue of a *beaten* people. But once the big migration got under way and the more adventurous Negroes started trekking northward up the Mississippi, a lot of their pent-up feelings busted out and romped all over the place. They brought their New Orleans music with them, and it exploded over Chicago and the whole North with one hell of a roar. And their talk got more explosive too, more animated, filled with a little hope and spirit. That's when jive as we know it today really got going.

I heard the jive language in its early stages, when I was hanging around the South Side in Chicago. It was the first furious babbling of a people who suddenly woke up to find that their death-sentence had been revoked, or at least postponed, and they were stunned and dazzled at first, hardly able to believe it. Then came the full exuberant waking up, the full realization that the bossman, at least the peckerwood kind with a bullwhip in his hand, was gone. The music got wilder and wilder. The excited rush of talk on street-corners, and in poolrooms and ginmills, swelled up to a torrent. That was the first real jive — the lingo of prisoners with a temporary reprieve. When I got to Harlem I found it had spread to the East, and really come of age. These Harlem kids had decided they wouldn't be led back to jail nohow. They spieled a mile a minute, making that clear.

Jive, Dan Burley says, "is the same means of escape that brought into being the spirituals as sung by American slaves; the blues songs of protest that bubble in the breasts of black men and women believed by their fellow white countrymen to have been born to be menials, to be wards of a nation, even though they are tagged with a whimsical designation as belonging to the body politic. . . . Jive serves a definite need of the people the same as do the Knights of

Pythias, the Elks, or the Sons and Daughters of I Do Arise, with their signs, passwords, handclasps, and so on."

Sure. But I think you've got to keep hammering away at the fact that it *is* a protest, and not so inarticulate at that. That's what makes it entirely unique, a different kind of language from the traditional Southern Negro's, which didn't challenge the white oppressor but only tried to escape from his eagle eye, and those of his watchdogs. Jive does knit together a kind of tight secret society — but it's a society which resents and nourishes its resentment, and is readying to strike back. The hipsters' fraternal order isn't just an escape valve, a defense mechanism; it's a kind of drilling academy too, preparing for future battles.

Jive isn't just a reflection of a primitive state; not by a long shot. The Negro doesn't add action metaphors to abstractions, put movement into static phrases, throw warmth into frozen logical categories, just because he can't understand them any other way. That's open to question. What is sure is that he's got too much poetry and rhythmic feeling in him, still alive and kicking, to be expressed in the bookish accents of educated white speech. He's got to pep up that bedraggled lingo to hold his interest and give vent to his emotions.

It's sure true, as all the writers point out, that the heart of jive is action. That's the most important fact about it. That's why it's peculiarly and uniquely a *Northern* Negro's creation. The ground-down Southern Negroes didn't develop an *action* language anywhere near as rich as this, although they had their own rich folk-poetry, because they couldn't see any possibility of action. But these Northern kids I hung around with were so active they couldn't sit still. Life below the Mason-Dixon line was sluggish, sleepwalking; up above 110th Street it was hyperthyroid. Life meant constant movement to these youngsters. They even called each other *cats* approvingly because they wanted to be as alert and keen-sighted as an alley-cat, that slinks through the dark streets and back lanes all night long, never closing its eyes, gunning everything and ready for all comers. . . . Their language could hardly keep up with their restless, roving activities. It was the poetic expression of an immobilized people who, at last, see the day coming when all the action in the world will be open to them, and all things will become possible.

The young citified Northern Negroes I got to know, unlike a lot of the older colored folks down South, were plenty alert and attentive, keyed-up with the effort to see and hear everything all at once, because that's how bottomdogs got to be unless they want to get lost in the shuffle. And, from where they were standing — blasted at by the radio, drowned in newsprint, suffocated by Hollywood epics — it looked to them like the top-of-the-pile white man is a bulging bundle of words. That T. S. Eliot described us all as hollow men, stuffed with straw. To the colored boys, we were all stuffed with pages from Webster's Dictionary.

Back off a thousand miles and look for yourself — what's the mark of the upper-crust American, the lawyer, the doctor, the financier, the politician? It's his command of the King's English, the way he spouts his high-powered jive so glib and smooth. Colored kids up North, dead-set on bettering themselves, dig the fact that the ofays with the most education have the highest standing, the most money and power — and the first thing that hits you about these high-riding guys is a smooth kind of gab, full of long skullbusting words and cliquish doubletalk.

Well, if talk shows your worth in this world the colored kids never made, then they sure aim to talk some too — not because they believe in it, but just to show they can do it. That's the first step: to prove to others, *and to themselves*, that they're in the running, have got what it takes. You can't get by in the hard American scuffle just by shaking your weary old head and pulling your scraggly whiskers. You got to *talk*, man. If you're Negro, and don't want to stick in a spiritual gallion all your days, you got to talk twice as fast as anybody else. So these high-spirited hip kids I hung out with made up their own private tongue. Most of them didn't even finish grammar school; they were operating just with their own native mother-wit. And in some ways it turned out richer and more human than the ofay's. It was just as complicated and specialized, just as subtle and roundabout, as any lingo the whites ever thought of. And less artificial too, more down-to-earth, alive with a deep-felt poetic sense and a rich imagery born out of Nature, jammed with the profound wisdom of the streets.

And all the while, as I could guess from the oblique kind of humor in the language, from the comic nature of its symbols and images, there was a great bellylaugh hid away in it. The colored boys never stopped to bemoan their fate in this hip language of theirs; there's no time for self-pity in this scuffle. Maybe they *were* schooling themselves in a kind of eloquence they wouldn't aim for on their own; maybe they *were* playing the ofay game of making-with-the-words.

But they were also mocking the game and the rulemakers too, and mocking the whole idea of eloquence, the idea that words are anything but hypes and camouflage. The hip cat plays the game with his tongue almost coming through his cheek.

Once and for all, these smart Northern kids meant to show that they're not the ounce-brained tongue-tied stuttering Sambos of the blackface vaudeville routines, the Lazybones' of the comic strips, the Old Mose's of the Southern plantations. Historically, the hipster's lingo reverses the whole Uncle Tom attitude of the beaten-down Southern Negro. Uncle Tom believes he's good-for-nothing, shiftless, sub-human, just like the white bossman says he is. Uncle Tom scrapes and bows before his ofay "superiors," kills off all his self-respect and manliness, agrees that he's downtrodden because he doesn't deserve any better. Well, the kids who grew up in Northern cities wouldn't have any more of that kneebending and kowtowing. They sure meant to stand up on their hind legs and let the world know they're as good as anybody else and won't take anybody's sass. They were smart, popping with talent, ready for any challenge. Some of them had creative abilities you could hardly match anywhere else. Once they tore off the soul-destroying straitjacket of Uncle Tomism, those talents and creative energies just busted out all over. These kids weren't schooled to use their gifts in any regular way. So their artistry and spirit romped out into their language. They began out-lingoing the ofay linguists, talking up a specialized breeze that would blow right over the white man's head. It gave them more confidence in themselves.

Deny the Negro the culture of the land? O.K. He'll brew his own culture — on the street corner. Lock him out from the seats of higher learning? He pays it no nevermind — he'll dream up his own professional doubletalk, from the professions that *are* open to him, the professions of musician, entertainer, maid, butler, tap-dancer, handyman, reefer-pusher, gambler, counterman, porter, chauffeur, numbers racketeer, day laborer, pimp, stevedore. These boys I ran with at The Corner, breathing half-comic prayers at the Tree of Hope, they were the new sophisticates of the race, the jivers, the sweettalkers, the jawblockers. They spouted at each other like soldiers sharpening their bayonets — what they were sharpening, in all this verbal horseplay, was their wits, the only weapons they had. Their sophistication didn't come out of moldy books and dicty colleges. It came from opening their eyes wide and gunning the world hard. Soon as you stop bow-ing your head low and resting your timid, humble eyes on the ground, soon as you straighten your spine and look the world right in the eye, you dig plenty. . . . Their hipness, I could see, bubbled up out of the brute scramble and sweat of living. If it came out a little too raw and strong for your stomach, that's because you been used to a more refined diet. You didn't come of age on the welfare, snagging butts out of the gutter. You can afford the luxury of being a little delicate, friend.

You know who they were, all these fast-talking kids with their four-dimensional surrealist patter? I found out they were the cream of the race — the professionals of Harlem who never got within reaching distance of a white collar. They were the razor-witted doctors without M.D.'s, lawyers who never had a shingle to hang out, financiers without penny one in their pokes, political leaders without a party, diploma-less professors and scientists minus a laboratory. They held their office-hours and made their speeches on The Corner. There they wrote their prose poems, painted their word pictures. They were the genius of their people, always on their toes, never missing a trick, asking no favors and taking no guff, not looking for trouble but solid ready for it. Spawned in a social vacuum and hung up in mid-air, they were beginning to build their own culture. Their language was a declaration of independence.

I found some signifying clues to the hip lingo in the way it described traits and qualities the young Negro admires. The *cat* he looks up to is *hip*, like a guy who carries a bottle or a bankroll or, more likely, a gun on his hip — in other words, he sure is well-primed and can take care of himself in any situation; he's *solid*, which is short for *solid as the Rock of Gibraltar*, and describes a man who isn't going to be washed away so easy; he's *got his boots on and they're laced up all the way*, meaning that he's torn himself away from the insane-asylum of the South, where the poor beaten Uncle Toms plod around in the gallion barefoot, and only the white boss-man wears boots; he's *righteous*, in the Biblical sense of having justice on your side, and he's *ready*, like a boxer poised to take on all corners, and he's *really in there*, as a prizefighter wades into the thick of it instead of running away from his opponent; he really *comes on*, like a performer making his entrance on the stage, full of self-confidence and self-control, aware of his own talents and the ability to use them; or he really *gets off*, that is, is so capable of expressing himself fully that he gets the load of oppression off, the load that

weighs down poor broken people who are miserable and can't do
anything about it, can't even put it into words; and he's *groovy*, the
way musicians are groovy when they pool their talents instead of
competing with each other, work together and all slip into the same
groove, heading in the same direction, cooperating all the way; and
finally, he's a *solid sender*, he can send your spirit soaring and make
you real happy, because no matter how heavy his burden is he still
isn't brought down, he keeps his sense of humor and his joy in life,
and uses them to make you feel good too.

Those are the qualities the young cats go for, the ones they've invented new phrases to describe. Fitted together, they form a portrait
of Uncle Tom — in *reverse*, a negative print. They add up to something mighty impressive, a real man. As their new American lingo
tells you, that's what these hip kids mean to become. I could see how
hard they worked at it. A heap of them made it.

What struck me as a wonderful thing was that they never lost their
perspective — the language lets you know that too. The hipster stays
conscious of the fraud of language. Where many ofays will hold forth
pompously, like they had The Word, the Negro mimics them sarcasti-
cally. As a final subtle touch, his language is also a parody, a satire
on the conventional ofay's gift of gab and gibberish. A lot of it consists of flowery ofay phrases and puffed-up clichés that are purposely
twisted around to show how corny and funky they are, like a man's
features are twisted in a caricature to show how simply he is inside. I
never once saw those kids get dead serious and all swole up with
pompous airs. It inspired me to realize that these hip cats were half-
conscious comic artists, playing with words. Their lingo was more
than a secret code; it was jammed with a fine sense of the ridiculous
that had behind it some solid social criticism.

Harlem became a mecca for blacks migrating from the South and the center of African American culture early in the twentieth century. Although Harlem was particularly hard hit by the depression of the 1930s, it remained a key arena in the history of black politics and the arts.

Part Three

"THE CITY WITHIN
A CITY"
Harlem, U.S.A.

Federal Writers' Project
Portrait of Harlem

The volume entitled *New York Panorama* (1938), from which the following selection is taken, was published as a companion to the *Guide to New York City*, which itself was part of a series of guides to cities and regions of the United States published through the Federal Writers' Project under the auspices of the WPA (see p. 8 of this book). The product of a collective effort by many writers, *New York Panorama* included chapters on such topics as history, architecture, music, speech, and nationalities. Black New York was portrayed in a chapter devoted to Harlem, reproduced here as a good summary of the historical development of the "city within a city," or "Harlem, U.S.A.," as it has been called, and characteristic of writing about the urban area in which African American arts and social life flourished during the Harlem Renaissance (see p. 159 of this book) and beyond. The Federal Writers' Project also undertook research on the black history of New York that was published many years later as *The Negro in New York: A Social History* (1967). Part of the Federal Writers' Project work of Ellison (see pp. 21–22 of this book), it included research on the early African American writer Jupiter Hammond and the 1863 draft riots in New York for this volume (O'Meally, *Craft of Ralph Ellison* 33).

Contemporaneous books on Harlem that offered panoramas based more on personalities than on cultural institutions include Claude McKay's *Harlem: Negro Metropolis* (1940) and Roi Ottley's *New World A-Coming* (1943). Both books described especially well, if idiosyncratically, the social and business life of Harlem — including the subculture of numbers running — and the impact of leaders such as Marcus Garvey, the popular preacher Father Divine, and labor organizer Sufi Abdul Hamid. Whatever the virtue of Ottley's book, however, one should keep in mind that Ellison himself, in a 1943 review, complained that it made the mistake of thinking Harlem represented black America at large, and he placed it "with those recent movies which, after promising to depict Negroes honestly, slip back into the black-face of traditional burlesque" (Ellison, "New World A-Coming" 67–68). More important, although it comes up only to the end of the 1920s, is James Weldon Johnson's classic

study of the rise of Harlem and modern African American culture, *Black Manhattan* (1930).
FURTHER READING: Allon Schoener, ed., *Harlem on My Mind: Cultural Capital of Black America, 1900–1968* (New York: Random, 1968); Gilbert Osofsky, *Harlem: The Making of a Ghetto, 1890–1930,* 2nd ed. (New York: Harper, 1971); Jervis Anderson, *This Was Harlem: A Cultural Portrait, 1900–1950* (New York: Farrar, 1982).

For several decades after the Civil War, most of New York's well-to-do Negroes enjoyed a fairly stable community life in Brooklyn. But on Manhattan Island, where the poorer class predominated, the Negro population was scattered and shifting, though with its largest numbers in the blighted areas of the lower West Side. Moving slowly northward as the city expanded in that direction, the chief center of Negro population was by 1900 in the region of West Fifty-Third Street and the neighboring San Juan Hill district. But it was not long before the region became so congested that many Negroes were seeking homes still further north.

At this time, scores of modern apartment houses that had been built in Harlem for white tenants were largely empty, owing to a lack of adequate transportation facilities. Philip A. Payton, a shrewd and enterprising Negro realtor, persuaded the owners of one or two buildings on 134th Street to fill them with Negro tenants. Before long, other buildings were taken over and filled. This invasion, as it was termed by white residents of Harlem, evoked an organized social and economic war. As though they were fighting plague carriers, the Hudson Realty Company, acting for white property owners, purchased all West Side property owned or rented by Negroes and evicted the tenants. Payton, with J. B. Nail, Sr., in retaliation organized the Afro-American Realty Company, which purchased buildings occupied by white tenants and in turn evicted them. Also St. Philip's Episcopal Church, one of the oldest and wealthiest Negro churches in New York, purchased 13 apartment houses on West 135th Street, and rented them to Negroes.

The white tenants gave way, and block after block of apartment houses stood deserted. Reluctantly, the landlords leased them to Negroes. As the years passed, the "black blocks" spread and the present "city within a city" took form. The migration to Harlem was immensely augmented by the large-scale influx of southern Negroes who came North during the World War in search of higher wages. At the end of the war, the Negro population of New York was estimated to be four times greater than when the movement to Harlem began.

But after the larger part of New York's Negro population had settled in Harlem, owners of apartments elsewhere refused to rent them to Negroes; consequently, rents in the highly congested Harlem area are often twice as much as in other comparable sections of the city. This district's density of population and the extremely high rentals have created alarming conditions. In 1935 it was found that as many as 3,871 Negroes lived in a single city block, and that many families were paying half or more of their incomes for shelter. Eighty-four percent of the residential buildings are from 20 to 34 years old. These conditions account in some part for a death-rate that has reached 15.5 per thousand. Early in 1934, exasperated tenants organized the Consolidated Tenants' League to combat high rents and improve living conditions. The Federal-built Harlem River Houses, a Public Works Administration project accommodating 527 families, has shown the way to better things although it has accomplished little in relieving the congestion of Harlem's wide-spread slums.

But not all of Harlem is slum area. Scattered throughout the district are many well-built homes. The section on 138th and 139th Streets between Seventh and Eighth Avenues is known locally as "Strivers' Row," because so many middle-class Negroes desire to live there; and "Sugar Hill," on upper Edgecombe and St. Nicholas Avenues, possesses the newest and tallest apartment buildings in Harlem, as well as many fine private homes.

The Negro's restriction to certain trades and professions has made him particularly vulnerable to suffering during times of depression. As early as 1910, when Negroes comprised less than two percent of the city's population, the majority were employed in domestic service. The labor shortage caused by the World War, however, enabled a few to enter the fields of transportation, mechanics, and manufacture. When the depression struck in 1929, many actors, musicians, messengers, porters, and domestic servants were thrown out of work. The extent to which Negro income depends upon domestic employment is evidenced by the fact that more than 85 percent of employed Negro women are in domestic and personal service. Though today

they account for only a little more than five percent of the city's population, Negroes comprise more than 20 percent of the total number
of persons on relief rolls.

Although Harlem is the largest Negro community in the world,
most of its restaurants, hotels, saloons, and retail shops are owned by
Greeks, Germans, Jews, Italians, Irish, and other white groups. In
business, more than in any other field, the Harlem Negro has shown
a lack of initiative that puts Harlem in sharp contrast with many
Negro communities throughout the country. Negro boys and girls are
rarely employed as clerks in Harlem stores, but work downtown as
maids, porters, elevator and errand boys. Most of Harlem's Negro-
owned businesses are in the field of personal service. The community
contains more than 2,000 Negro barber shops and "beauty parlors."
On the other hand, Harlem has proved a haven for the professional
class, which numbers about 5,000. Physicians and dentists are especially numerous.

Catering to the inner man is one of Harlem's chief industries, and
eating-places are to be found everywhere throughout the district.
These range from tiny Negro-owned restaurants in private homes and
basements to large chain-cafeterias controlled by white capital and
the cafes and cabarets that play a prominent part in New York's
night life. Prominent in this field are Father Divine's 15 restaurants,
where a meal featuring chicken or chops is served for 15 cents.

During the Prohibition era, many of the Negro-owned saloons
passed into Italian hands, and remained open in spite of the law.
Most of Harlem's saloons are still Italian-owned; but some of the better known taprooms and cabarets are conducted by Negroes.

Playing the central role in the life of the Harlem Negro is not the
cabaret or cafe, as is commonly supposed, but the church. Thousands
of the early southern migrants met for religious services in apartments and homes. Later they purchased the existing churches of
white Baptists, Methodists, Episcopalians, and Presbyterians in the
Harlem region. The actual surrender of a white church to Negroes
was done with something approaching ritual: a joint service would be
held at which the out-going white congregation would welcome the
in-coming black.

It is difficult to say which is the more numerous of Harlem's two
largest religious sects, the Baptists or the Divinists. The Baptists have
the largest churches, such as the Abyssinia and Mt. Olivet, but it is
possible that Father Divine has more followers in his many "Heav-

ens" throughout the city. There are two general types of churches in Harlem: the conventional, which embraces the long-established orga nizations, including the Methodist, Baptist, Episcopalian, Presbyterian, Congregationalist; and the unconventional, consisting of the tabernacles of "prophets," the "storefront meeting places, the synagogues of Black Jews, and the houses of various sects and cults. The "Church of the Believers of the Commandments" may be across the street from a Daddy Grace "House of Prayer." The "Metaphysical Church of Divine Investigation" may be a few doors from the Black Jews' "Commandment Keepers." Add to these the Moorish Temples, Sister Josephine Becton's churches, the tabernacles of Prophet Costonie, the "Heavens" of Father Divine, and the sanctuaries of Mother Horne, and some conception of Harlem's many diverse religions and cults may be had.

Because of its highly sensitive social and political temper, Harlem has been termed the "focal point in the struggle for the liberation of the Negro people." It was but natural that the long effort to free the Scottsboro boys should begin in Harlem, and the greatest demonstration in connection with the release of four of them occurred when thousands of Negroes jammed the Pennsylvania Station to welcome them to New York. During Italy's invasion of Ethiopia, anything concerning Italy on the movie screen brought forth immediate hisses and catcalls. In the consciousness of this oppressed community, current events are commonly interpreted as gains or set-backs for the Negro people. This social restlessness results in many public demonstrations. Harlemites in increasing numbers attend street meetings protesting evictions; picket stores to compel the hiring of Negroes, or WPA offices to indicate disapproval of cuts in pay or personnel; parade against the subjection of colonial peoples, or to celebrate some new civic improvement; and march many miles in May Day demonstrations.

Harlem's peculiar susceptibility to social and political propaganda is well illustrated in the case of Marcus Garvey, a West Indian, who for a few years in the early 1920's was known as "provisional President of Africa." He advocated the establishment of a Black Republic in Africa, and preached racial chauvinism. As head of the Universal Negro Improvement Association, Garvey was the first Negro leader in America to capture the imagination of the masses, and no one else has so stirred the race consciousness of the Negroes in New York and elsewhere. The *Negro World*, once powerful organ of his Universal

Negro Improvement Association, attracted such contributors as
Edgar Grey, Hubert Harrison, and William Ferris to its pages. Garvey's financial manipulations in connection with his steamship company, the Black Star Line, led to his downfall. He was indicted by the
Federal Government for using the mails to defraud, served a term in
the Atlanta penitentiary, and was later deported.

The most serious rioting that Harlem has known occurred in the
spring of 1935, at a time when many of the white-owned business establishments on West 125th Street were being boycotted for their refusal to employ Negroes. A leading figure in the attendant agitation
was a person calling himself Sufi Abdul Hamid, who in gaudy Egyptian uniform preached anti-Semitism on the street corners and was regarded by Harlem's Jewish merchants as a "Black Hitler." On March
19 a Negro boy was caught stealing in one of the boycotted stores.
Rumors immediately spread throughout Harlem that the boy had
been beaten and killed by the white proprietor; large crowds gathered
in and near West 125th Street, and in spite of police efforts an orgy
of window-smashing and store-looting followed. As emphasized in
the report of an investigating committee appointed by Mayor La
Guardia, the outbreak had its fundamental causes in the terrible economic and social conditions prevailing in Harlem at the time.

When the Federal Emergency Relief Administration began operations, it found a majority of Harlem's population on the verge of starvation, as a result of the depression and of an intensified discrimination that made it all but impossible for Negroes to find employment.
Landlords, knowing that their tenants could not move to other neigh-
borhoods, had raised rents exorbitantly, and wholesale evictions followed. The FERA, with its successors the Civil Works Administration
and the Works Progress Administration, brought a new lease on life
to Harlem's underprivileged. WPA's monthly checks constitute a considerable part of the community life-blood, and white storekeepers
are quick to join with Negro relief workers in protesting against any
threats to their jobs. Today one notes a very decided lessening of the
dangerous tension that pervaded Harlem in the dark winters of 1934
and 1935.

Although New York had had a few scattered Negro writers before
that time, what is sometimes termed the "literary renaissance" of
Harlem dates from about 1925. The movement was in large part initiated by the publication of the *Survey Graphic's* special "Harlem
Number" and of Alain Locke's interpretative anthology entitled *The*

New Negro. A host of young writers made their appearance in the middle and late 1920's, among them Walter White, Eric Walrond, Rudolph Fisher, Jean Toomer, Claude McKay, Countee Cullen, Langston Hughes, Wallace Thurman, Jessie Fauset, Nella Larsen, Zora Neale Hurston, George Schuyler, and Arna Bontemps. Confined almost exclusively to Harlem, this literary movement was notable in that for the first time the American Negro depicted his own life with a wide and varied range of talent and feeling. For a few years Negro writers created more than they ever have before or since that period. Joyce's *Ulysses* influenced some of them; and even the gospel of Gertrude Stein claimed a number of Negro adherents. Some members of the movement were apotheosized in Carl Van Vechten's *Nigger Heaven*, a novel that New York read with avidity. The poetry of McKay, Cullen, and Hughes expressed in new rhythms and beauty and vigor the bitterness and despair of Negro life in America. Toomer, in *Cane*, sounded a new and lyric note in American prose; and Walter White, in *The Fire in the Flint* and *Flight*, dealt with the Negro's struggle in both South and North against the barriers of color. Jessie Fauset, Nella Larsen, and Claude McKay frequently depicted Harlem life in their novels. James Weldon Johnson, long a Harlem resident, and later a professor at Fisk and New York Universities, elaborated in *Black Manhattan* the description of Harlem that was a prominent feature of his earlier *Autobiography of an Ex-Colored Man*. Rudolph Fisher, Wallace Thurman, George Schuyler, and W. E. B. Du Bois wove fantasy and satire into their descriptions of Negro life. With the beginning of the national depression in 1929, the movement largely disintegrated.

Among the Negro artists of Harlem are Augusta Savage, Aaron Douglas, Richmond Barthe, Charles Alston, E. Sims Campbell, Vertis Hayes, Bruce Nugent, Henry W. Barnham, Sara Murrell, Romare Bearden, Robert Savon Pious, and Beauford Delaney. Of these Aaron Douglas, painter and mural artist, Richmond Barthe, sculptor, Augusta Savage, sculptress, and E. Sims Campbell, painter and cartoonist, are the most prominent. Many Negro artists are employed on the Federal Art Project, under whose direction they have executed murals for the new wing of the Harlem Municipal Hospital. Harlem now boasts of 15 art centers, in churches, the Y.M.C.A., the Y.W.C.A., and neighborhood houses, where classes are conducted in painting, ceramics, carving, and sculpture. Best known for its exhibitions is the Uptown Art Laboratory. The Federal Art Project in New York has discovered an immense amount of latent artistic talent among the Negro children of Harlem.

Until very recently the doors of the American theater have not been open to the Negro playwright, who has therefore had no opportunity to master the technique of the stage. Only in rare instances have producers presented plays written by Negroes. Willis Richardson's one-act plays were produced in some of the little and commercial theaters; and in 1925, Garland Anderson's *Appearances* ran in the Frolic Theater. Wallace Thurman collaborated on *Lulu Belle* and *Harlem*, both well known on Broadway. In 1937, Langston Hughes entered the field of the drama with his *Mulatto*. The Krigwa Players were pioneers in the little theater movement. Today Harlem's thespians are for the most part associated with the New Theater League and the Federal Theater Project.

Prominent among those plays written by whites in which Negro actors have had an opportunity to depict the lives of their people are Eugene O'Neill's *The Emperor Jones* and *All God's Chillun Got Wings*, produced in 1920 and 1924; Edward Sheldon and Charles MacArthur's *Lulu Belle*, which opened in New York in 1926; Paul Green's Pulitzer Prize play, *In Abraham's Bosom*, produced in 1926 at the Provincetown Playhouse; Marc Connelly's *The Green Pastures*, which started in 1929 on its long career of sensational success; and Paul Peters' and George Sklar's *Stevedore*, first presented in 1930.

New York, like Boston, Philadelphia, and Chicago, has its celebrated music schools and opportunities for musical expression, which have always attracted Negro artists. The successes of Hall Johnson, Roland Hayes, Paul Robeson, Jules Bledsoe, and Marian Anderson are nationally known. Many of Harlem's Negro musical artists are now associated with the Federal Music Project.

Of all the popular personalities whom Harlem has shared with America, Bill "Bojangles" Robinson has evoked the most lasting and genuine affection. As the world's ace tap dancer, he has appeared on the stage or screen of every city and town in this country, and has earned a reputation as a philanthropist in his private life. In 1934, he was elected "unofficial mayor" of Harlem.

By adoption, Harlem claims the Negro show girl, Josephine Baker, who came out of the slums of St. Louis and earned the title of "Empress Josephine" during her stay in Paris in 1931 with the "Dixie Steppers," a company that had begun by touring the South in a series of one-night stands. She became a European celebrity as star of the Folies Bergère, and married Count Pepito De Albertini.

The late Richard B. Harrison, whose theatrical career knew only one role, made his debut at the age of 66 and achieved the greatest fame of any Negro actor. His life was closely bound up with "De Lawd" of Marc Connelly's play, *The Green Pastures*, and little is recorded of his earlier career. When the play was awarded the Pulitzer Prize in 1930, Lieutenant Governor Herbert Lehman presented "De Lawd" with the Spingarn medal at the Mansfield Theater before an enthusiastic audience. In 1936, the entire nation mourned the death of the man who "brought God to Broadway."

Florence Mills, who ranks as one of America's greatest musical comedy stars, came to New York after a Chicago cabaret career, and was featured by Paul Slavin at the Plantation Cafe. She made her first Broadway appearance in the popular *Shuffle Along*, and achieved her first European triumph in *Dixie to Broadway*. She died in 1927, shortly after a successful European tour in *Blackbirds*.

Paul Robeson, a graduate of Rutgers College who achieved national reputation in his student days as a football star, made his first appearance on the professional stage in Mary Hoyt Wiborg's *Taboo*. Later he replaced Charles Gilpin in *Roseanne*, and in 1924 he became a national figure in the American theater by starring in Eugene O'Neill's *All God's Chillun Got Wings*. After appearing in *Show Boat* in London, he played the title role of O'Neill's *Emperor Jones* in Berlin in 1930. In 1926 he appeared as the star of Jim Tully's *Black Boy*. He has sung and acted throughout Europe, has played prominent roles in many motion pictures, and is the outstanding Negro actor of today.

Though Negroes are considered to be an exceptionally musical people, Harlem's general interest in music is largely limited to those popular jazz orchestras that originated within its boundaries. Some of the greatest of Negro bands — Will Vodery's, Leroy Smith's, Duke Ellington's, and Fletcher Henderson's — acquired their initial fame in downtown New York. It was through their often startling innovations in jazz and swing music that Negro orchestra leaders held sway. Whether it was jazz as it was "jazzed" by Cab Calloway in the 1920's, or swing as it was "swung" by Jimmie Lunceford in the 1930's, the white popular jazz and swing orchestras took most of their cues from Harlem orchestras and their Negro leaders. Most of

the prominent Negro bands have reached a large public through their
phonograph recordings, and Negro band-members are protected by
the powerful Local 802 of the American Federation of Musicians, af-
filiated with the American Federation of Labor — though there are
evidences of discrimination against Negroes in the matter of wages.

Harlem's boast that it is an area where new dance steps are created
is indisputable. Just who initiated the "truck" is not known. Cora La
Redd of the Cotton Club, "Rubber Legs" Williams, Chuck Robinson,
and Bilo and Ashes have all put forward their individual claims. It is
interesting to note that there are many kinds of "trucking," — the
"picket's truck," the "politician's truck," the "Park Avenue truck,"
the "Mae West truck," and the "Hitler truck." Among other contemporary Harlem dances is the "shim-sham," a time-step featuring the
"break" with a momentary pause; and the "razzle-dazzle," which involves a rhythmic clapping of hands and a rolling of hips. The riotous
"Lindy Hop" is a flying dance done by couples in which a girl is
thrown away in the midst of a lightning two-step, then rudely
snatched back to be subjected to a series of twists, jerks, dips, and
scrambles. All of these and many more can be seen in Harlem's dance
halls, at house parties, on beaches, and in the streets in summer to the
tune of WPA Music Project bands.

Alain Locke

The New Negro

Alain Locke's collection of essays and creative writing *The New Negro: Voices of the Harlem Renaissance* (1925) is one of the most famous defining statements of a literary movement. At the same time, the title itself is responsible for some confusion. The term "New Negro" since at least the 1890s had referred to a new generation of post-Reconstruction blacks who, despite the virulent racism of the era, had taken pride in their demand for equal political and economic rights, and had strived to establish an independent voice in African American arts and literature. At whatever point the "New Negro" was said to have arisen, emphasis was placed on difference from the "Old Negro." Whereas one "can hear the clank of the slave's chain in all that [the Old Negro] says and does," wrote J. A. Rogers in a characteristic 1927 essay for the *Messenger,* the New Negro "would rather lose his tongue than betray his people in their struggle for freedom and equality" (Rogers 1).

To the extent that a "renaissance" of black literature began with turn-of-the-century writers such as Charles Chesnutt, Pauline Hopkins, Paul Laurence Dunbar, and W. E. B. Du Bois, the term Harlem Renaissance is perhaps less useful than the once more common term New Negro Renaissance. Nonetheless, given the extraordinary explosion of superior work in poetry, fiction, painting, sculpture, and music, as well as increased activity in historical writing and social science research about black America *by* black Americans, Harlem in the 1920s can appropriately be singled out as a unique moment in cultural history. It saw the intersection of the Jazz age, literary modernism, and the great black migration to the urban North. By the time Ellison arrived in Harlem, the Renaissance had given way to the economic hardships of the depression, and in his apprentice writings Ellison, like other left-wing writers of the day, tended to reject the models of the 1920s as too little concerned with class and political issues. In the more mature writing that led to *Invisible Man,* however, one can find Ellison's discovery of a compromise between the greater aestheticism of the 1920s and the social realism of the 1930s.

Alain Locke's own introductory essay in *The New Negro* is a representative statement of the philosophy animating the activities of the many figures — a number of whom, like Locke himself, did not even live in Harlem — who might be said to compose the movement. The first black Rhodes Scholar and a philosophy professor at Howard University, Locke (1886–1954) helped to edit a special Harlem issue of the magazine *Survey Graphic,* which became the core of *The New Negro.* Except that Marcus Garvey and his circle were not represented, Locke's collection included a virtual catalog of the era's most talented black writers, among them Langston Hughes, Countee Cullen, Jessie Fauset, Zora Neale Hurston, and Jean Toomer. Black music and arts were featured equally, and illustrations by Aaron Douglass and Miguel Covarrubias stressing the African origins of black American art, added to photographs of African sculpture, made the book a landmark in African American culture studies. Robert Moton provided an essay on Tuskegee, E. Franklin Frazier wrote on the black middle class, and Du Bois contributed a far-reaching essay on the political dimensions of the African diaspora. Before it fell victim to the depression, the Harlem Renaissance produced a great range of black art and literature well summed up in Alain Locke's classic volume and in his own introductory essay. Locke himself taught at Howard until his death and wrote or edited several other books, including *The Negro and His Music* (1936) and *The Negro in Art* (1940).

FURTHER READING: Nathan Huggins, *Harlem Renaissance* (New York: Oxford UP, 1971); Arna Bontemps, ed., *The Harlem Renaissance Remembered* (New York: Dodd, 1972); David Levering Lewis, *When Harlem Was in Vogue* (New York: Knopf, 1981); Tony Martin, *Literary Garveyism: Garvey, Black Arts, and the Harlem Renaissance* (Dover, MA: Majority, 1983); Cary D. Wintz, *Black Culture and the Harlem Renaissance* (Houston: Rice UP, 1988); Alain L. Locke, *The Philosophy of Alain Locke: Harlem and Beyond,* ed. Leonard Harris (Philadephia: Temple UP, 1989).

In the last decade something beyond the watch and guard of statistics has happened in the life of the American Negro and the three norns who have traditionally presided over the Negro problem have a changeling in their laps. The Sociologist, the Philanthropist, the Race-leader are not unaware of the New Negro, but they are at a loss to account for him. He simply cannot be swathed in their formulæ. For the younger generation is vibrant with a new psychology; the new spirit is awake in the masses, and under the very eyes of the professional observers is transforming what has been a perennial problem into the progressive phases of contemporary Negro life.

Could such a metamorphosis have taken place as suddenly as it has appeared to? The answer is no; not because the New Negro is not here, but because the Old Negro had long become more of a myth than a man. The Old Negro, we must remember, was a creature of moral debate and historical controversy. His has been a stock figure perpetuated as an historical fiction partly in innocent sentimentalism, partly in deliberate reactionism. The Negro himself has contributed his share to this through a sort of protective social mimicry forced upon him by the adverse circumstances of dependence. So for generations in the mind of America, the Negro has been more of a formula than a human being — a something to be argued about, condemned or defended, to be "kept down," or "in his place," or "helped up," to be worried with or worried over, harassed or patronized, a social bogey or a social burden. The thinking Negro even has been induced to share this same general attitude, to focus his attention on controversial issues, to see himself in the distorted perspective of a social problem. His shadow, so to speak, has been more real to him than his personality. Through having had to appeal from the unjust stereotypes of his oppressors and traducers to those of his liberators, friends, and benefactors he has had to subscribe to the traditional positions from which his case has been viewed. Little true social or self-understanding has or could come from such a situation.

But while the minds of most of us, black and white, have thus burrowed in the trenches of the Civil War and Reconstruction, the actual march of development has simply flanked these positions, necessitating a sudden reorientation of view. We have not been watching in the right direction; set North and South on a sectional axis, we have not noticed the East till the sun has us blinking.

Recall how suddenly the Negro spirituals revealed themselves; suppressed for generations under the stereotypes of Wesleyan hymn harmony, secretive, half-ashamed, until the courage of being natural brought them out — and behold, there was folk-music. Similarly the mind of the Negro seems suddenly to have slipped from under the tyranny of social intimidation and to be shaking off the psychology of imitation and implied inferiority. By shedding the old chrysalis of the Negro problem we are achieving something like a spiritual emancipation. Until recently, lacking self-understanding, we have been almost as much of a problem to ourselves as we still are to others. But the decade that found us with a problem has left us with only a task. The multitude perhaps feels as yet only a strange relief and a new vague urge, but the thinking few know that in the reaction the vital inner grip of prejudice has been broken.

With this renewed self-respect and self-dependence, the life of the Negro community is bound to enter a new dynamic phase, the buoyancy from within compensating for whatever pressure there may be of conditions from without. The migrant masses, shifting from countryside to city, hurdle several generations of experience at a leap, but more important, the same thing happens spiritually in the life-attitudes and self-expression of the Young Negro, in his poetry, his art, his education, and his new outlook, with the additional advantage, of course, of the poise and greater certainty of knowing what it is all about. From this comes the promise and warrant of a new leadership. As one of them has discerningly put it:

> We have tomorrow
> Bright before us
> Like a flame.
>
> Yesterday, a night-gone thing
> A sun-down name.
>
> And dawn today
> Broad arch above the road we came.
> We march!

This is what, even more than any "most creditable record of fifty years of freedom," requires that the Negro of to-day be seen through other than the dusty spectacles of past controversy. The day of "aunties," "uncles," and "mammies" is equally gone. Uncle Tom and Sambo have passed on, and even the "Colonel" and "George" play barnstorm rôles from which they escape with relief when the public spotlight is off. The popular melodrama has about played itself out, and it is time to scrap the fictions, garret the bogeys, and settle down to a realistic facing of facts.

First we must observe some of the changes which since the traditional lines of opinion were drawn have rendered these quite obsolete. A main change has been, of course, that shifting of the Negro population which has made the Negro problem no longer exclusively or even predominantly Southern. Why should our minds remain sectionalized, when the problem itself no longer is? Then the trend of migration has not only been toward the North and the Central Midwest, but city-ward and to the great centers of industry — the problems of adjustment are new, practical, local, and not peculiarly racial. Rather they are an integral part of the large industrial and social problems of our present-day democracy. And finally, with the Negro rapidly in process of class differentiation, if it ever was warrantable to regard and treat the Negro *en masse* it is becoming with every day less possible, more unjust, and more ridiculous.

In the very process of being transplanted, the Negro is becoming transformed.

The tide of Negro migration, northward and city-ward, is not to be fully explained as a blind flood started by the demands of war industry coupled with the shutting off of foreign migration, or by the pressure of poor crops coupled with increased social terrorism in certain sections of the South and Southwest. Neither labor demand, the boll-weevil, nor the Ku Klux Klan is a basic factor, however contributory any or all of them may have been. The wash and rush of this human tide on the beach line of the northern city centers is to be explained primarily in terms of a new vision of opportunity, of social and economic freedom, of a spirit to seize, even in the face of an extortionate and heavy toll, a chance for the improvement of conditions. With each successive wave of it, the movement of the Negro becomes more and more a mass movement toward the larger and the more democratic chance — in the Negro's case a deliberate flight not only from countryside to city, but from medieval America to modern.

Take Harlem as an instance of this. Here in Manhattan is not merely the largest Negro community in the world, but the first concentration in history of so many diverse elements of Negro life. It has attracted the African, the West Indian, the Negro American; has brought together the Negro of the North and the Negro of the South; the man from the city and the man from the town and village; the peasant, the student, the business man, the professional man, artist, poet, musician, adventurer and worker, preacher and criminal, exploiter and social outcast. Each group has come with its own separate motives and for its own special ends, but their greatest experience has been the finding of one another. Proscription and prejudice have thrown these dissimilar elements into a common area of contact and interaction. Within this area, race sympathy and unity have determined a further fusing of sentiment and experience. So what began in terms of segregation becomes more and more, as its elements mix and react, the laboratory of a great race-welding. Hitherto, it must be admitted that American Negroes have been a race more in name than in fact, or to be exact, more in sentiment than in experience. The chief bond between them has been that of a common condition rather than a common consciousness; a problem in common rather than a life in common. In Harlem, Negro life is seizing upon its first chances for group expression and self-determination. It is — or promises at least to be — a race capital. That is why our comparison is taken with those nascent centers of folk-expression and self-determination which are playing a creative part in the world to-day. Without pretense to their political significance, Harlem has the same rôle to play for the New Negro as Dublin has had for the New Ireland or Prague for the New Czechoslovakia.

Harlem, I grant you, isn't typical — but it is significant, it is prophetic. No sane observer, however sympathetic to the new trend, would contend that the great masses are articulate as yet, but they stir, they move, they are more than physically restless. The challenge of the new intellectuals among them is clear enough — the "race radicals" and realists who have broken with the old epoch of philanthropic guidance, sentimental appeal, and protest. But are we after all only reading into the stirrings of a sleeping giant the dreams of an agitator? The answer is in the migrating peasant. It is the "man farthest down" who is most active in getting up. One of the most characteristic symptoms of this is the professional man, himself migrating to recapture his constituency after a vain effort to maintain in some Southern corner what for years back seemed an established living and clientele. The clergyman following his errant flock, the physician or lawyer trailing his clients, supply the true clues. In a real sense it is the rank and file who are leading, and the leaders who are following. A transformed and transforming psychology permeates the masses.

When the racial leaders of twenty years ago spoke of developing race-pride and stimulating race-consciousness, and of the desirability of race solidarity, they could not in any accurate degree have anticipated the abrupt feeling that has surged up and now pervades the awakened centers. Some of the recognized Negro leaders and a powerful section of white opinion identified with "race work" of the older order have indeed attempted to discount this feeling as a "passing phase," an attack of "race nerves" so to speak, an "aftermath of the war," and the like. It has not abated, however, if we are to gauge by the present tone and temper of the Negro press, or by the shift in

popular support from the officially recognized and orthodox spokes-
men to those of the independent, popular, and often radical type who
are unmistakable symptoms of a new order. It is a social disservice to
blunt the fact that the Negro of the Northern centers has reached a
stage where tutelage, even of the most interested and well-intentioned
sort, must give place to new relationships, where positive self-direction
must be reckoned with in ever increasing measure. The American mind
must reckon with a fundamentally changed Negro.

The Negro too, for his part, has idols of the tribe to smash. If on
the one hand the white man has erred in making the Negro appear to
be that which would excuse or extenuate his treatment of him, the
Negro, in turn, has too often unnecessarily excused himself because
of the way he has been treated. The intelligent Negro of to-day is resolved not to make discrimination an extenuation for his shortcomings in performance, individual or collective; he is trying to hold himself at par, neither inflated by sentimental allowances nor depreciated
by current social discounts. For this he must know himself and be
known for precisely what he is, and for that reason he welcomes the
new scientific rather than the old sentimental interest. Sentimental interest in the Negro has ebbed. We used to lament this as the falling
off of our friends; now we rejoice and pray to be delivered both from
self-pity and condescension. The mind of each racial group has had a
bitter weaning, apathy or hatred on one side matching disillusionment or resentment on the other; but they face each other to-day with
the possibility at least of entirely new mutual attitudes.

It does not follow that if the Negro were better known, he would
be better liked or better treated. But mutual understanding is basic
for any subsequent coöperation and adjustment. The effort toward
this will at least have the effect of remedying in large part what has
been the most unsatisfactory feature of our present stage of race relationships in America, namely the fact that the more intelligent and
representative elements of the two race groups have at so many
points got quite out of vital touch with one another.

The fiction is that the life of the races is separate, and increasingly
so. The fact is that they have touched too closely at the unfavorable
and too lightly at the favorable levels.

While inter-racial councils have sprung up in the South, drawing
on forward elements of both races, in the Northern cities manual la-
borers may brush elbows in their everyday work, but the community
and business leaders have experienced no such interplay or far too

little of it. These segments must achieve contact or the race situation in America becomes desperate. Fortunately this is happening. There is a growing realization that in social effort the co-operative basis must supplant long-distance philanthropy, and that the only safeguard for mass relations in the future must be provided in the carefully maintained contacts of the enlightened minorities of both race groups. In the intellectual realm a renewed and keen curiosity is replacing the recent apathy; the Negro is being carefully studied, not just talked about and discussed. In art and letters, instead of being wholly caricatured, he is being seriously portrayed and painted.

To all of this the New Negro is keenly responsive as an augury of a new democracy in American culture. He is contributing his share to the new social understanding. But the desire to be understood would never in itself have been sufficient to have opened so completely the protectively closed portals of the thinking Negro's mind. There is still too much possibility of being snubbed or patronized for that. It was rather the necessity for fuller, truer self-expression, the realization of the unwisdom of allowing social discrimination to segregate him mentally, and a counter-attitude to cramp and fetter his own living — and so the "spite-wall" that the intellectuals built over the "color-line" has happily been taken down. Much of this reopening of intellectual contacts has centered in New York and has been richly fruitful not merely in the enlarging of personal experience, but in the definite enrichment of American art and letters and in the clarifying of our common vision of the social tasks ahead.

The particular significance in the re-establishment of contact between the more advanced and representative classes is that it promises to offset some of the unfavorable reactions of the past, or at least to re-surface race contacts somewhat for the future. Subtly the conditions that are molding a New Negro are molding a new American attitude.

However, this new phase of things is delicate; it will call for less charity but more justice; less help, but infinitely closer understanding. This is indeed a critical stage of race relationships because of the likelihood, if the new temper is not understood, of engendering sharp group antagonism and a second crop of more calculated prejudice. In some quarters, it has already done so. Having weaned the Negro, public opinion cannot continue to paternalize. The Negro to-day is inevitably moving forward under the control largely of his own objectives. What are these objectives? Those of his outer life are happily already well and finally formulated, for they are none other than the ideals of American institutions and democracy. Those of his inner life are yet in process of formation, for the new psychology at present is more of a consensus of feeling than of opinion, of attitude rather than of program. Still some points seem to have crystallized.

Up to the present one may adequately describe the Negro's "inner objectives" as an attempt to repair a damaged group psychology and reshape a warped social perspective. Their realization has required a new mentality for the American Negro. And as it matures we begin to see its effects; at first, negative, iconoclastic, and then positive and constructive. In this new group psychology we note the lapse of senti-mental appeal, then the development of a more positive self-respect and self-reliance; the repudiation of social dependence, and then the gradual recovery from hyper-sensitiveness and "touchy" nerves; the repudiation of the double standard of judgment with its special phil-anthropic allowances and then the sturdier desire for objective and scientific appraisal; and finally the rise from social disillusionment to race pride, from the sense of social debt to the responsibilities of so-cial contribution, and offsetting the necessary working and common-sense acceptance of restricted conditions, the belief in ultimate esteem and recognition. Therefore the Negro to-day wishes to be known for what he is, even in his faults and shortcomings, and scorns a craven and precarious survival at the price of seeming to be what he is not. He resents being spoken of as a social ward or minor, even by his own, and to being regarded a chronic patient for the sociological clinic, the sick man of American Democracy. For the same reasons, he himself is through with those social nostrums and panaceas, the so-called "solutions" of his "problem," with which he and the coun-try have been so liberally dosed in the past. Religion, freedom, educa-tion, money — in turn, he has ardently hoped for and peculiarly trusted these things; he still believes in them, but not in blind trust that they alone will solve his life-problem.

Each generation, however, will have its creed, and that of the pre-sent is the belief in the efficacy of collective effort, in race co-operation. This deep feeling of race is at present the mainspring of Negro life. It seems to be the outcome of the reaction to proscription and preju-dice; an attempt, fairly successful on the whole, to convert a defensive into an offensive position, a handicap into an incentive. It is radical in tone, but not in purpose and only the most stupid forms of opposi-tion, misunderstanding, or persecution could make it otherwise. Of course, the thinking Negro has shifted a little toward the left with the world-trend, and there is an increasing group who affiliate with radical and liberal movements. But fundamentally for the present the Negro is radical on race matters, conservative on others, in other words, a "forced radical," a social protestant rather than a genuine radical. Yet under further pressure and injustice iconoclastic thought and motives will inevitably increase. Harlem's quixotic radicalisms call for their ounce of democracy to-day lest to-morrow they be beyond cure.

The Negro mind reaches out as yet to nothing but American wants, American ideas. But this forced attempt to build his Americanism on race values is a unique social experiment, and its ultimate success is impossible except through the fullest sharing of American culture and institutions. There should be no delusion about this. American nerves in sections unstrung with race hysteria are often fed the opiate that the trend of Negro advance is wholly separatist, and that the effect of its operation will be to encyst the Negro as a benign foreign body in the body politic. This cannot be — even if it were desirable. The racialism of the Negro is no limitation or reservation with respect to American life; it is only a constructive effort to build the obstructions in the stream of his progress into an efficient dam of social energy and power. Democracy itself is obstructed and stagnated to the extent that any of its channels are closed. Indeed they cannot be selectively closed. So the choice is not between one way for the Negro and another way for the rest, but between American institutions frustrated on the one hand and American ideals progressively fulfilled and realized on the other.

There is, of course, a warrantably comfortable feeling in being on the right side of the country's professed ideals. We realize that we cannot be undone without America's undoing. It is within the gamut of this attitude that the thinking Negro faces America, but with variations of mood that are if anything more significant than the attitude itself. Sometimes we have it taken with the defiant ironic challenge of McKay:

> Mine is the future grinding down to-day
> Like a great landslip moving to the sea,
> Bearing its freight of débris far away
> Where the green hungry waters restlessly
> Heave mammoth pyramids, and break and roar
> Their eerie challenge to the crumbling shore.

Sometimes, perhaps more frequently as yet, it is taken in the fervent and almost filial appeal and counsel of Weldon Johnson's:

> O Southland, dear Southland!
> Then why do you still cling
> To an idle age and a musty page,
> To a dead and useless thing?

But between defiance and appeal, midway almost between cynicism and hope, the prevailing mind stands in the mood of the same author's *To America*, an attitude of sober query and stoical challenge:

> How would you have us, as we are?
>   Or sinking 'neath the load we bear,
>   Our eyes fixed forward on a star,
>   Or gazing empty at despair?
>
> Rising or falling? Men or things?
>   With dragging pace or footsteps fleet?
> Strong, willing sinews in your wings,
>   Or tightening chains about your feet?

More and more, however, an intelligent realization of the great discrepancy between the American social creed and the American social practice forces upon the Negro the taking of the moral advantage that is his. Only the steadying and sobering effect of a truly characteristic gentleness of spirit prevents the rapid rise of a definite cynicism and counter-hate and a defiant superiority feeling. Human as this reaction would be, the majority still deprecate its advent, and would gladly see it forestalled by the speedy amelioration of its causes. We wish our race pride to be a healthier, more positive achievement than a feeling based upon a realization of the shortcomings of others. But all paths toward the attainment of a sound social attitude have been difficult; only a relatively few enlightened minds have been able as the phrase puts it "to rise above" prejudice. The ordinary man has had until recently only a hard choice between the alternatives of supine and humiliating submission and stimulating but hurtful counterprejudice. Fortunately from some inner, desperate resourcefulness has recently sprung up the simple expedient of fighting prejudice by mental passive resistance, in other words by trying to ignore it. For the few, this manna may perhaps be effective, but the masses cannot thrive upon it.

Fortunately there are constructive channels opening out into which
the balked social feelings of the American Negro can flow freely.
Without them there would be much more pressure and danger
than there is. These compensating interests are racial but in a new
and enlarged way. One is the consciousness of acting as the advance-
guard of the African peoples in their contact with Twentieth Century
civilization; the other, the sense of a mission of rehabilitating the race
in world esteem from that loss of prestige for which the fate and conditions of slavery have so largely been responsible. Harlem, as we
shall see, is the center of both these movements; she is the home of
the Negro's "Zionism." The pulse of the Negro world has begun to
beat in Harlem. A Negro newspaper carrying news material in English, French, and Spanish, gathered from all quarters of America, the
West Indies, and Africa has maintained itself in Harlem for over five
years. Two important magazines, both edited from New York, maintain their news and circulation consistently on a cosmopolitan scale.
Under American auspices and backing, three pan-African congresses
have been held abroad for the discussion of common interests, colonial questions, and the future co-operative development of Africa. In
terms of the race question as a world problem, the Negro mind has
leapt, so to speak, upon the parapets of prejudice and extended its
cramped horizons. In so doing it has linked up with the growing
group consciousness of the dark-peoples and is gradually learning
their common interests. As one of our writers has recently put it: "It
is imperative that we understand the white world in its relations to
the non-white world." As with the Jew, persecution is making the
Negro international.

As a world phenomenon this wider race consciousness is a different thing from the much asserted rising tide of color. Its inevitable
causes are not of our making. The consequences are not necessarily
damaging to the best interests of civilization. Whether it actually
brings into being new Armadas of conflict or argosies of cultural exchange and enlightenment can only be decided by the attitude of the
dominant races in an era of critical change. With the American
Negro, his new internationalism is primarily an effort to recapture
contact with the scattered peoples of African derivation. Garveyism
may be a transient, if spectacular, phenomenon, but the possible rôle
of the American Negro in the future development of Africa is one of
the most constructive and universally helpful missions that any modern people can lay claim to.

Constructive participation in such causes cannot help giving the Negro valuable group incentives, as well as increased prestigé at home and abroad. Our greatest rehabilitation may possibly come through such channels, but for the present, more immediate hope rests in the revaluation by white and black alike of the Negro in terms of his artistic endowments and cultural contributions, past and prospective. It must be increasingly recognized that the Negro has already made very substantial contributions, not only in his folk-art, music especially, which has always found appreciation, but in larger, though humbler and less acknowledged ways. For generations the Negro has been the peasant matrix of that section of America which has most undervalued him, and here he has contributed not only materially in labor and in social patience, but spiritually as well. The South has unconsciously absorbed the gift of his folk-temperament. In less than half a generation it will be easier to recognize this, but the fact remains that a leaven of humor, sentiment, imagination, and tropic nonchalance has gone into the making of the South from a humble, unacknowledged source. A second crop of the Negro's gifts promises still more largely. He now becomes a conscious contributor and lays aside the status of a beneficiary and ward for that of a collaborator and participant in American civilization. The great social gain in this is the releasing of our talented group from the arid fields of controversy and debate to the productive fields of creative expression. The especially cultural recognition they win should in turn prove the key to that revaluation of the Negro which must precede or accompany any considerable further betterment of race relationships. But whatever the general effect, the present generation will have added the motives of self-expression and spiritual development to the old and still unfinished task of making material headway and progress. No one who understandingly faces the situation with its substantial accomplishment or views the new scene with its still more abundant promise can be entirely without hope. And certainly, if in our lifetime the Negro should not be able to celebrate his full initiation into American democracy, he can at least, on the warrant of these things, celebrate the attainment of a significant and satisfying new phase of group development, and with it a spiritual Coming of Age.

Sterling Spero and
Abram L. Harris

Blacks in the Labor Movement

One consequence of the Great Migration was the significant influx of black workers into northern industry, with the result that labor issues, including unionization and strikes, sometimes acquired a specific racial dimension. The problems were stated succinctly in the opening of a 1935 essay by Lester B. Granger: "Who holds the first claim on the loyalty of the negro worker — his fellow workers who toil side by side with him, or his employer who hires and pays him, sometimes against the wishes of white labor? Is it wisdom for Negro workers to protect the interest of white labor, which has so often kicked them in the face, or should they line up with employers against labor unions, even to the point of scabbing and strike-breaking?" (Granger 234–39).

The Liberty Paints episode of *Invisible Man* (like its longer initial version, published as "Out of the Hospital and Under the Bar") represents the protagonist's extended symbolic encounter with those problems created when the world of northern labor became haltingly more open to African Americans. In the postwar years and during the depression, leading black magazines such as the *Messenger*, the predominantly socialist voice of the most important black union, the Brotherhood of Sleeping Car Porters, and *Opportunity*, the organ of the National Urban League, featured regular articles and editorials devoted to labor issues, which for blacks were inevitably both economic and political in nature. Whether in an industrial or business setting, blacks frequently found themselves confined to particular kinds of work, no matter what their skills or aspirations. Of the "blind alley" service positions that racism forced many African Americans to settle for, Charles S. Johnson remarked: "None of the Horatio Alger ascensions from messenger to manager or from porter to president need to be counted into the labor turnover where Negroes are concerned. Once a porter, barring the phenomenal, always a porter" (C. Johnson 643). *The Black Worker*, a 1931 volume by the scholars and labor activists Sterling Spero and Abram L. Harris from which the following selection is taken, remains even today one of the best comprehensive portraits of black labor in the early twentieth century.

FURTHER READING: George S. Mitchell and Horace R. Cayton, *Black Workers and the New Unions* (Chapel Hill: U of North Carolina P, 1939); Ray Marshall, *The Negro Worker* (New York: Random, 1967); Julius Jacobson, ed., *The Negro and the American Labor Movement* (Garden City, NY: Doubleday, 1968); Philip S. Foner, *Organized Labor and the Black Worker, 1619–1973* (New York: Praeger, 1974); William H. Harris, *The Harder We Run: Black Workers Since the Civil War* (New York: Oxford UP, 1982); Jacqueline Jones, *Labor of Love, Labor of Sorrow: Black Women, Work, and the Family from Slavery to the Present* (New York: Basic, 1985).

The change in the Negro's relation to industry during the last decade and a half has been so sudden that neither the black nor the white working world has been able to grasp its significance and adjust itself to its circumstances. The essence of this change has been the shifting of the Negro's position from that of a labor reserve to a regular element in the labor force of nearly every basic industry. It has brought the Negro face to face with problems of working conditions, which, though they may contain many special elements, are essentially the same as the problems of other workers. They are consequently problems with which the Negro cannot cope successfully without the cooperation of his white fellow workers. Yet ever since the rise to power of the American Federation of Labor both sides have raised obstacles to the consummation of such cooperation. Of all these obstacles none probably has been greater than the narrow and exclusive craft structure and opportunist philosophy of American trade unionism.

The official American labor movement consists of associations of boilermakers and bricklayers, plumbers and carpenters, machinists and railway switchmen, bookbinders and stationary engineers, each interested in its own particular job, jealously guarding its jurisdiction against all encroachments, and highly suspicious of every brother organization whose field approaches its own. The craft is a sort of exclusive club consisting of those who now belong. The smaller it is kept the higher will be the value of the craftsman's service. It is there-

fore made as difficult as possible for new members to join. If whole
classes, such as Negroes, can be automatically excluded, the problem
of keeping the membership down is made that much easier. The organizations may carry the slogan of unity on their banners, but the
ideals of labor solidarity and the brotherhood of all industrial workers have little practical bearing on their conduct. All that they want
are signed agreements with employers. Collective negotiation upon a
business basis is the ideal which really moves their lives. The American Federation of Labor is an agency set up to keep craft separatism
from defeating its own ends. Its purpose is to settle disputes among
the unions, to handle matters of common concern, particularly where
legislation is needed, and to care in some manner for the organization
of those workers who might, if not brought into the system in some
way, ignore its claims and threaten its continuation. The American
Federation of Labor is after all a creature of the trade unions. While
it must have some measure of authority over them in order to fulfill
its purpose, it can hardly, in view of its nature, rise to higher levels
than its dominating elements — the craft internationals.

Although the Negro is but one of the victims of American craft
unionism, he is a victim upon whom the burden falls with special
weight, for his peculiar situation in American society makes it particularly difficult for him to cross craft barriers. To the white trade
unionist the Negro is not merely an outsider trying to get into the
union, but a social and racial inferior trying to force the white man to
associate with him as an equal. And the Negro knows that the white
worker wants to keep him out of the union not merely as a potential
competitor but as a member of a race which must not be permitted to
rise to the white man's level. For three hundred years the Negro has
been kept in a position of social and economic inferiority, and white
organized labor, dominated by the hierarchy of the skilled crafts, has
no desire to see him emerge from that condition.

The educated leaders of the Negro community see only the racial
aspect of this situation. They see that many employers use Negro
labor, thereby giving the black man an opportunity to earn a living
which the policy of most white trade unionists would deny him. They
see white philanthropists and sentimental friends of the black man
trying to help him by giving him schools and social-welfare agencies.
They are impressed with the stories of the poor folks who become
wealthy through thrift and hard work, and with the history of great
institutions which sprang from small beginnings. Here, they say, are

friends of the Negro who have proved their friendship, and here are ways of success which have been tried and found effective. So the race leaders counsel their people to beware of the white working man and to put their trust in the white upper classes. Labor solidarity to which the white unionist appeals when he needs the black man to serve his selfish ends, or which the radical preaches to increase his tiny following from any possible source is, they say, a very dangerous doctrine. It is far safer to give loyal service to the white man who wants it, and by hard work and saving to amass enough wealth to bring comfort and security.

Negro leadership for the past generation has put its stress on the element of race. Their people's plight, they feel, is the plight of a race. They turn a deaf ear to those who say that the Negro's plight is the plight of the working class in general merely aggravated by certain special features. All of the various schools of Negro thought which have had real influence upon Negro life have had one end in view, the elimination of racial discrimination. . . .

The National Association for the Advancement of Colored People has frequently shown its interest in the Negro's relation to labor organizations. It has fought attempts of the plumbers, electricians, railway workers, and others to keep Negroes out of their unions or to force them out of the occupations which those unions attempt to control. But in every case the association has fought for the Negro's admission into the unions on the ground of civil liberty rather than upon the principle of labor solidarity.

Negro administrators of white philanthropy, such as the leaders of the Urban League and the various committees on interracial cooperation scattered throughout the country, have also tried to lift trade-union barriers. They are interested in greater economic opportunity for the colored worker, and they believe that if he can get into the unions he will be able to follow trades which it is almost impossible for him to follow at present. The lifting of trade-union barriers is but one of the methods by which the Urban League and the interracial bodies seek their ends. Their aim is to foster kindly attitudes toward the Negro. Their principal appeal is to employers and the members of the professions. Their efforts to get the Negro into the labor unions have been confined to seeking the cooperation of prominent trade-union officials. Their appeal is an appeal by Negro leaders to the white upper class. It makes no attempt to reach the white or black rank and file.

Historically the most potent influence in the black community has been the evangelical church. It offered the Negro an escape from the economic and social disabilities of this world through salvation in the next. The church won its hold on the race in slave days by giving the slave an emotional outlet for the expression of his earthly misery and heavenly hopes. On the whole the Negro church has either ignored present ills or counselled its communicants to bear with them patiently and to serve their masters, for one should "Render unto Caesar the things that are Caesar's." Such ills as one found in this world were but a preparation for the blessings of the next. The role of the church in Negro life is hard to duplicate in the white world. Religion for the Negro has been a matter of everyday concern. The church has been the very center of the community about which Negro social life revolved.

However, the absorption of the Negro into northern industry is gradually shaking the church's hold and a new philosophy, more in keeping with the dominant thought of the white world, is rising in its place. Like the philosophy of the militant National Association for the Advancement of Colored People and that of the conciliatory interracial movement, this philosophy is decidely individualistic and middle class in outlook. It has its roots in the doctrines of Booker T. Washington and the Hampton and Tuskegee schools, which preach the gospel of salvation through thrift, enterprise, and industrial efficiency. Its flower is the National Negro Business League whose purpose is the encouragement and promotion of business within the race so that eventually an independent petty black capitalism will rise within the limits of white society.

This movement has caught the imagination of the Negro people in a striking manner. The ideal of an independent black economy within the confines of the white is a living force in every black community in the land. Yet how such an independent economy is to rise and function when the white world outside controls credit, basic industry, and the state is something which the sponsors of the movement prefer to ignore. If such an economy is to rise it will have to do so with the aid of white philanthropy and will have to live upon white sufferance. If the great white banks and insurance companies decide that they want Negro business it is hard to see how the little black institutions can compete successfully against them. The same holds for the chain stores and various retail establishments. They will be able to undersell their Negro competitors if they want to, and the Negro world will not continue indefinitely to pay higher prices for its goods merely out of pride of race. Basic industry will continue to remain in the hands of the white world, for even the most ardent supporters of an independent black economy will admit that there is no prospect of the Negro capitalists amassing enough wealth to establish steel mills, build railroads and pipe lines, and gain control of essential raw materials. . . .

The over-sanguine radicals see in the Negro's special racial grievances and his new position in industry the nucleus of a discontented mass movement. But they overlook the fact that the unique social position of the Negro plus the white worker's absence of class consciousness lends force to the separatist preachings of the Negro leaders. It should not be forgotten that the Negro has won his place in industry in the branches in which labor organization has little or no hold and where the white worker's opposition to his employment has consequently carried least weight. Race leaders have not failed to point this out and to drive home the moral that after all the employer is the black man's best friend. And the white trade unionist, using the same facts, points out his moral, that the Negro is an irredeemable scab who breaks the white man's strikes and tears down his hard won standards, and that the unions must exclude him lest he play the traitor in their midst.

A labor movement built upon the principle of working-class unity would of course take the Negro into its ranks and fight to raise the general standard. Self-protection alone should dictate such a course. But the white worker, sharing the prejudices of the rest of the white world, balks at the bugaboo of "social equality" and persists in relegating the black laborer to a place of permanent inferiority.

But side by side with all these forces are tendencies in other directions which in time may destroy their potency. Most important is the machine, which is rapidly changing the meaning of skill and obliterating old craft lines. The machine, rather than any concept of working-class unity or industrial brotherhood, will compel the official labor movement to change its structure and policy if it is not to generate into a mere social relic. Ultimately this will probably redound to the Negro's benefit, but during transitional stages technical changes which reduce the personnel will hurt him along with other workers. And where, as on the railroads, the white men are organized and the Negro is not, the unions will seek to protect their members by compelling the employers to save their jobs at the expense of the Negro's.

The hope of distinctive minorities, like the Negro, which are prone
to become the tools in the industrial struggle first of one side and
then of the other, rests to no small extent upon industrial stabilization. Few Negro railway men would deny that they were better off
under federal control than ever before or since. There is little question that Negroes in government enterprises like the postal service or
in other branches of the public services, despite all sorts of discrimination and inequality in assignments and promotions, are better off
than in competitive industry. Steps towards industrial stabilization,
which would eliminate those competitive elements in industry that redound to the disadvantage of the employees generally and minorities
in particular, require an extension of governmental control. This in
turn can be achieved only through political action of a type in which
the Negro seems especially unlikely to participate. His loyalty to the
Republican party in national politics and his tendency since his recent
settlement in the North to align himself locally with the dominant
machine in the city where he lives make him a bulwark of political
conservatism rather than a promising progressive element.

On the other hand, Negro workers threatened with wholesale
elimination from jobs, or brought face to face with industrial problems which demand united action for solution, have shown a tendency to turn to unions of their own. Frail and ineffective as such organizations have been in the past, they show the beginning of Negro
labor consciousness. They may in time develop a labor leadership
which will help to educate both the Negro workers and the general
labor movement to the realization of the need of black and white
unity. It is here that the rising Negro middle class and the movement
for a self-contained black capitalist economy may strike a snag, for
an organized Negro working class will learn in time that the enrichment of a few Negroes will be of little benefit to the black rank and
file.

But even if the Negro world should change its outlook and ap-
prove of an industrial and political alignment of the working class
cutting across race lines, this change alone would not be sufficient to
affect the situation. No such alignment could be effected by the will
of the outcast minority alone. It must depend upon the will of the
controlling majority, and that majority is white.

Cyril V. Briggs
Race Catechism

Founder of the radical magazine *The Crusader* in 1918, Cyril V. Briggs (1888–1966) was an immigrant West Indian black nationalist who, like W. E. B. Du Bois and others, was spurred by World War I to a militant demand for African American equality. Briggs was an editor of the leading Harlem newspaper, *Amsterdam News*, until 1917, when his antiwar stand led to his dismissal. He then founded *The Crusader*, which became also the official voice of the African Blood Brotherhood, an independent communist organization whose audience for a time significantly overlapped with that of Marcus Garvey, the most famous West Indian black nationalist active in postwar Harlem, because of its appeal to a nationalist philosophy. Within a few years, however, Garvey's Universal Negro Improvement Association (UNIA) embraced capitalism and stood in opposition to communist groups and to the African Blood Brotherhood in particular. By the late 1920s, Briggs and other members found their influence decreasing and abandoned the group in favor of direct action within the Communist Party. Just as Ellison's figure of the Founder in *Invisible Man* is not Booker T. Washington, so his Ras the Exhorter cannot be tied directly to Cyril Briggs, Richard B. Moore (another leader in the African Blood Brotherhood, who was a powerful public orator), or Garvey himself. But Briggs's "Race Catechism" is characteristic of much of the nationalist rhetoric of the day, Garveyite or not, and his racial ideology is one attuned to the views of Ras the Exhorter. At the same time, because the African Blood Brotherhood occupied a middle ground between the UNIA and the Communist Party International, Ellison may have had at least its name in mind as he constructed his own Brotherhood in *Invisible Man* (see p. 19 of this book).

FURTHER READING: E. U. Essien-Udom, *Black Nationalism: A Search for an Identity in America* (Chicago: U of Chicago P, 1963); Harold Cruse, *The Crisis of the Negro Intellectual* (1967; rpt. New York: Quill, 1984); Theodore G. Vincent and Robert Chrisman, eds., *Voices of a Black Nation: Political Journalism in the Harlem Renaissance* (San Francisco: Ramparts, 1973); Alphonso Pinkney, *Red, Black, and Green: Black Nationalism in the United States* (New York: Cambridge UP, 1976).

QUESTION: How do you consider yourself in relation to your Race?

ANSWER: I consider myself bound to it by a sentiment which unites all.

QUESTION: What is it?

ANSWER: The sentiment that the Negro Race is of all races the most favored by the Muses of Music, Poetry, and Art, and is possessed of those qualities of courage, honor, and intelligence necessary to the making of the best manhood and womanhood and the most brilliant development of the human species.

QUESTION: What are one's duties to the Race?

ANSWER: To love one's Race above one's self and to further the common interests of all above the private interests of one. To cheerfully sacrifice wealth, ease, luxuries, necessities and, if need be, life itself to attain for the Race that greatness in arms, in commerce, in art, the three combined without which there is neither respect, honor nor security.

QUESTION: How can you further the interests of the Race?

ANSWER: By spreading Race Patriotism among my fellows; by unfolding the annals of our glorious deeds and the facts of the noble origin, splendid achievements, and ancient cultures of the Negro Race to those whom Alien Education has kept in ignorance of these things; by combatting the insidious, mischievous, and false teachings of school histories that exalt the white man and debase the Negro, that tell of the white man's achievements but not of his ignominy while relating only that part of the Negro's story that pertains to his temporary enslavement and partial decadence; by helping Race industries in preference to all others; by encouraging Race enterprise and business to the ends of an ultimate creation of wealth, employment, and financial strength within the Race; by so carrying myself as to demand honor and respect for my Race.

QUESTION: Why are you proud of your race?

ANSWER: Because in the veins of no human being does there flow more generous blood than in our own; in the annals of the world the history of no race is more resplendent with honest, worthy glory than that of the Negro Race, members of which founded the first beginning of civilization upon the banks of the Nile, developing it and extending it southward to Ethiopia and westward over the smiling Sudan to the distant Atlantic, so that the Greeks who came to learn from our fathers declared that they were "the most just of men, the favorites of the gods."

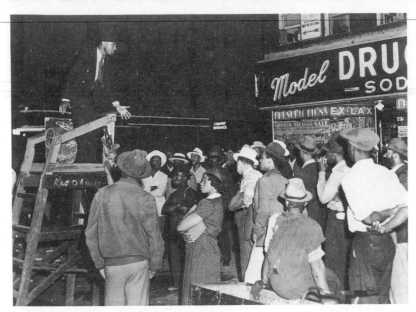

Aspiring political leaders in early twentieth-century Harlem often resorted to speaking from ladders in order to draw a crowd. In Ellison's novel, the narrator hears Ras the Exhorter delivering black nationalist speeches in this manner, and he later speaks from a ladder himself (*Invisible Man* 159, 368).

Marcus Garvey

Africa for the Africans

Speech Delivered at Liberty Hall, August 1921

Marcus Garvey (1887–1940), a Jamaican intellectual and political leader, was one of the most charismatic black figures in Harlem in the post–World War I era. After several years of travel in Europe and Central America, Garvey emigrated to the United States in 1916, where he started a weekly newspaper, *Negro World,* and founded the Universal Negro Improvement Association (UNIA), an organization dedicated to black political self-determination and the affirmation of African cultural history. Although his speeches and writings were strongly influenced by Christian beliefs, Garvey argued that God and Christ were black, and he advocated a form of black separatism and an anticolonialist philosophy of "Africa for the Africans." A "Declaration of Rights of Negro Peoples of the World" issued at a 1920 UNIA convention argued that all black people are "free citizens of Africa, the Motherland of all Negroes," and resolved that "Ethiopia, Thou Land of Our Fathers" should be the "anthem of the Negro race." Garvey's initial popularity derived in part from his skill as a street speaker, where, mounted on a ladder, he competed with other speakers for the attention of Harlem crowds. Garvey's adamant black nationalism especially set him at odds with the Communist Party, which disavowed racial separatism in favor of an integrated class struggle against capitalism. Garvey's promotion of voluntary repatriation to Africa foundered when his steamship company, the Black Star Line, failed and he was convicted of mail fraud. Deported to Jamaica after serving two years in prison, he continued his racial advocacy in a new monthly publication, *Black Man,* and moved to London in 1935.

In Jamaica, Garvey's philosophy of race pride was critical to the founding of Rastafarianism, a religious movement dating from the early 1930s whose members venerate the Ethiopian emperor Haile Selassie (known also as Ras Tafari) and regard Ethiopia as a sacred homeland. The movement, however, has roots in nineteenth-century black nationalism, especially the philosophy of Ethiopianism, which takes its inspiration from a biblical passage — "Princes shall come out of Egypt, and Ethiopia shall soon stretch forth her hands to God" (Psalms 68:31) — to which Ellison alludes on at least two occasions in *Invisible Man* (81, 376). Taking particular inspiration from Ethiopia's resistance to military invasion by Italy in 1936, several proponents of Rastafarian thought — among them Malaku Bayen, author of the pamphlet *The March of Black Men* (1939) — flourished in Harlem alongside other nationalists such as the labor advocate Sufi Abdul Hamid. Ellison's character Ras the Exhorter (also called Ras the Destroyer) is carefully distinguished from Marcus Garvey (*Invisible Man* 367). Nonetheless, his powerful arguments in favor of black nationalism and an Afrocentric philosophy, as well as his street speeches while mounted on a ladder — a common Harlem practice shared by Ellison's narrator (*Invisible Man* 159, 368; see also the illustration on p. 182 of this book) — reflect Garvey's influence and the continuing importance of Ethiopianist thought in the Harlem of the 1930s.

FURTHER READING: Edmund David Cronon, *Black Moses: The Story of Marcus Garvey and the Universal Negro Improvement Association* (Madison: U of Wisconsin P, 1955); John Henrik Clarke, ed., *Marcus Garvey and the Vision of Africa* (New York: Vintage, 1964); Robert Weisbrod, *Ebony Kinship: Africa, Africans, and the Afro-American* (Westport, CT: Greenwood, 1973); Judith Stein, *The World of Marcus Garvey: Race and Class in Modern Society* (Baton Rouge: Louisana State UP, 1986); Wilson J. Moses, *The Golden Age of Black Nationalism, 1850–1925* (1978; rpt. New York: Oxford UP, 1988); Leonard E. Barrett, *The Rastafarians* (Boston: Beacon, 1988).

Africa for the Africans

For five years the Universal Negro Improvement Association has been advocating the cause of Africa for the Africans — that is, that the Negro peoples of the world should concentrate upon the object of building up for themselves a great nation in Africa.

When we started our propaganda toward this end several of the so-called intellectual Negroes who have been bamboozling the race for over half a century said that we were crazy, that the Negro peoples of the western world were not interested in Africa and could not live in Africa. One editor and leader went so far as to say at his so-called Pan-African Congress that American Negroes could not live in Africa, because the climate was too hot. All kinds of arguments have been adduced by these Negro intellectuals against the colonization of Africa by the black race. Some said that the black man would ultimately work out his existence alongside of the white man in countries founded and established by the latter. Therefore, it was not necessary for Negroes to seek an independent nationality of their own. The old time stories of "African fever," "African bad climate," "African mosquitos," "African savages," have been repeated by these "brainless intellectuals" of ours as a scare against our people in America and the West Indies taking a kindly interest in the new program of building a racial empire of our own in our Motherland. Now that years have rolled by and the Universal Negro Improvement Association has made the circuit of the world with its propaganda, we find eminent statesmen and leaders of the white race coming out boldly advocating the cause of colonizing Africa with the Negroes of the western world. A year ago Senator MacCullum of the Mississippi Legislature introduced a resolution in the House for the purpose of petitioning the Congress of the United States of America and the President to use their good influence in securing from the Allies sufficient territory in Africa in liquidation of the war debt, which territory should be used for the establishing of an independent nation for American Negroes. About the same time Senator France of Maryland gave expression to a similar desire in the Senate of the United States during a speech on the "Soldiers' Bonus." He said: "We owe a big debt to Africa and one which we have too long ignored. I need not enlarge upon our peculiar interest in the obligation to the people of Africa. Thousands of Americans have for years been contributing to the missionary work which has been carried out by the noble men and women who have been sent out in that field by the churches of America."

Germany to the Front

This reveals a real change on the part of prominent statesmen in their attitude on the African question. Then comes another suggestion from Germany, for which Dr. Heinrich Schnee, a former Governor of German East Africa, is author. This German statesman suggests in an interview given out in Berlin, and published in New York, that America takes over the mandatories of Great Britain and France in Africa for the colonization of American Negroes. Speaking on the matter, he says "As regards the attempt to colonize Africa with the surplus American colored population, this would in a long way settle the vexed problem, and under the plan such as Senator France has out-lined, might enable France and Great Britain to discharge their duties to the United States, and simultaneously ease the burden of German reparations which is paralyzing economic life."

With expressions as above quoted from prominent world states-men, and from the demands made by such men as Senators France and MacCullum, it is clear that the question of African nationality is not a far-fetched one, but is as reasonable and feasible as was the idea of an American nationality.

A "Program" at Last

I trust that the Negro peoples of the world are now convinced that the work of the Universal Negro Improvement Association is not a visionary one, but very practical, and that it is not so far fetched, but can be realized in a short while if the entire race will only co-operate and work toward the desired end. Now that the work of our organi-zation has started to bear fruit we find that some of these "doubting Thomases" of three and four years ago are endeavoring to mix them-selves up with the popular idea of rehabilitating Africa in the interest of the Negro. They are now advancing spurious "programs" and in a short while will endeavor to force themselves upon the public as ad-vocates and leaders of the African idea.

It is felt that those who have followed the career of the Universal Negro Improvement Association will not allow themselves to be de-ceived by these Negro opportunists who have always sought to live off the ideas of other people.

The Dream of a Negro Empire

It is only a question of a few more years when Africa will be com-pletely colonized by Negroes, as Europe is by the white race. What we want is an independent African nationality, and if America is to help the Negro peoples of the world establish such a nationality, then we welcome the assistance.

It is hoped that when the time comes for American and West In-dian Negroes to settle in Africa, they will realize their responsibility and their duty. It will not be to go to Africa for the purpose of exer-cising an over-lordship over the natives, but it shall be the purpose of the Universal Negro Improvement Association to have established in Africa that brotherly co-operation which will make the interests of the African native and the American and West Indian Negro one and the same, that is to say, we shall enter into a common partnership to build up Africa in the interests of our race.

Oneness of Interests

Everybody knows that there is absolutely no difference between the native African and the American and West Indian Negroes, in that we are descendants from one common family stock. It is only a matter of accident that we have been divided and kept apart for over three hundred years, but it is felt that when the time has come for us to get back together, we shall do so in the spirit of brotherly love, and any Negro who expects that he will be assisted here, there or anywhere by the Universal Negro Improvement Association to exercise a haughty superiority over the fellows of his own race, makes a tremendous mistake. Such men had better remain where they are and not attempt to become in any way interested in the higher development of Africa.

The Negro has had enough of the vaunted practice of race superiority as inflicted upon him by others, therefore he is not prepared to tolerate a similar assumption on the part of his own people. In America and the West Indies, we have Negroes who believe themselves so much above their fellows as to cause them to think that any readjustment in the affairs of the race should be placed in their hands for them to exercise a kind of an autocratic and despotic control as others have done to us for centuries. Again I say, it would be advisable for such Negroes to take their hands and minds off the now popular idea of colonizing Africa in the interest of the Negro race, because their being identified with this new program will not in any way help us because of the existing feeling among Negroes everywhere not to tolerate the infliction of race or class superiority upon them, as is the desire of the self-appointed and self-created race leadership that we have been having for the last fifty years.

The Basis of an African Aristocracy

The masses of Negroes in America, the West Indies, South and Central America are in sympathetic accord with the aspirations of the native Africans. We desire to help them build up Africa as a Negro Empire, where every black man, whether he was born in Africa or in the

Western world, will have the opportunity to develop on his own lines under the protection of the most favorable democratic institutions.

It will be useless, as before stated, for bombastic Negroes to leave America and the West Indies to go to Africa, thinking that they will have privileged positions to inflict upon the race that bastard aristocracy that they have tried to maintain in this Western world at the expense of the masses. Africa shall develop an aristocracy of its own, but it shall be based upon service and loyalty to race. Let all Negroes work toward that end. I feel that it is only a question of a few more years before our program will be accepted not only by the few statesmen of America who are now interested in it, but by the strong statesmen of the world, as the only solution to the great race problem. There is no other way to avoid the threatening war of the races that is bound to engulf all mankind, which has been prophesied by the world's greatest thinkers; there is no better method than by apportioning every race to its own habitat.

The time has really come for the Asiatics to govern themselves in Asia, as the Europeans are in Europe and the Western world, so also is it wise for the Africans to govern themselves at home, and thereby bring peace and satisfaction to the entire human family.

Speech Delivered at Liberty Hall, August 1921

Four years ago, realizing the oppression and the hardships from which we suffered, we organized ourselves into an organization for the purpose of bettering our condition, and founding a government of our own. The four years of organization have brought good results, in that from an obscure, despised race we have grown into a mighty power, a mighty force whose influence is being felt throughout the length and breadth of the world. The Universal Negro Improvement Association existed but in name four years ago, today it is known as the greatest moving force among Negroes. We have accomplished this through unity of effort and unity of purpose, it is a fair demonstration of what we will be able to accomplish in the very near future, when the millions who are outside the pale of the Universal Negro Improvement Association will have linked themselves up with us.

By our success of the last four years we will be able to estimate the grander success of a free and redeemed Africa. In climbing the heights to where we are today, we have had to surmount difficulties, we have had to climb over obstacles, but the obstacles were stepping stones to the future greatness of this Cause we represent. Day by day we are writing a new history, recording new deeds of valor performed by this race of ours. It is true that the world has not yet valued us at our true worth but we are climbing up so fast and with such force that every day the world is changing its attitude towards us. Wheresoever you turn your eyes today you will find the moving influence of the Universal Negro Improvement Association among Negroes from all corners of the globe. We hear among Negroes the cry of "Africa for the Africans." This cry has become a positive, determined one. It is a cry that is raised simultaneously the world over because of the universal oppression that affects the Negro. You who are congregated here tonight as Delegates representing the hundreds of branches of the Universal Negro Improvement Association in different parts of the world will realize that we in New York are positive in this great desire of a free and redeemed Africa. We have established this Liberty Hall as the center from which we send out the sparks of liberty to the four corners of the globe, and if you have caught the spark in your section, we want you to keep it a-burning for the great Cause we represent.

There is a mad rush among races everywhere towards national independence. Everywhere we hear the cry of liberty, of freedom, and a demand for democracy. In our corner of the world we are raising the cry for liberty, freedom, and democracy. Men who have raised the cry for freedom and liberty in ages past have always made up their minds to die for the realization of the dream. We who are assembled in this Convention as Delegates representing the Negroes of the world give out the same spirit that the fathers of liberty in this country gave out over one hundred years ago. We give out a spirit that knows no compromise, a spirit that refuses to turn back, a spirit that says "Liberty or Death," and in prosecution of this great ideal — the ideal of a free and redeemed Africa, men may scorn, men may spurn us, and may say that we are on the wrong side of life, but let me tell you that way in which you are travelling is just the way all peoples who are free have traveled in the past. If you want Liberty you yourselves must strike the blow. If you must be free you must become so through your own effort, through your own initiative. Those who have discouraged you in the past are those who have enslaved you for

centuries and it is not expected that they will admit that you have a
right to strike out at this late hour for freedom, liberty, and democracy.

At no time in the history of the world, for the last five hundred
years, was there ever a serious attempt made to free Negroes. We
have been camouflaged into believing that we were made free by
Abraham Lincoln. That we were made free by Victoria of England,
but up to now we are still slaves, we are industrial slaves, we are social slaves, we are political slaves, and the new Negro desires a freedom that has no boundary, no limit. We desire a freedom that will
lift us to the common standard of all men, whether they be white men
of Europe or yellow men of Asia, therefore, in our desire to lift ourselves to that standard we shall stop at nothing until there is a free
and redeemed Africa.

I understand that just at this time while we are endeavoring to create public opinion and public sentiment in favor of a free Africa, that
others of our race are being subsidized to turn the attention of the
world toward a different desire on the part of Negroes, but let me tell
you that we who make up this Organization know no turning back,
we have pledged ourselves even unto the last drop of our sacred
blood that Africa must be free. The enemy may argue with you to
show you the impossibility of a free and redeemed Africa, but I want
you to take as your argument the thirteen colonies of America, that
once owned their sovereignty to Great Britain, that sovereignty has
been destroyed to make a United States of America. George Washington was not God Almighty. He was a man like any Negro in this
building, and if he and his associates were able to make a free America, we too can make a free Africa. Hampden, Gladstone, Pitt, and
Disraeli were not the representatives of God in the person of Jesus
Christ. They were but men, but in their time they worked for the expansion of the British Empire, and today they boast of a British Empire upon which "the sun never sets." As Pitt and Gladstone were
able to work for the expansion of the British Empire, so you and I
can work for the expansion of a great African Empire. Voltaire and
Mirabeau were not Jesus Christs, they were but men like ourselves.
They worked and overturned the French Monarchy. They worked for
the Democracy which France now enjoys, and if they were able to do
that, we are able to work for a democracy in Africa. Lenine and
Trotzky were not Jesus Christs, but they were able to overthrow the
despotism of Russia, and today they have given to the world a Social

Republic, the first of its kind. If Lenine and Trotzky were able to do that for Russia, you and I can do that for Africa. Therefore, let no man, let no power on earth, turn you from this sacred cause of liberty. I prefer to die at this moment rather than not to work for the freedom of Africa. If liberty is good for certain sets of humanity it is good for all. Black men, Colored men, Negroes have as much right to be free as any other race that God Almighty ever created, and we desire freedom that is unfettered, freedom that is unlimited, freedom that will give us a chance and opportunity to rise to the fullest of our ambition and that we cannot get in countries where other men rule and dominate.

We have reached the time when every minute, every second must count for something done, something achieved in the cause of Africa. We need the freedom of Africa now, therefore, we desire the kind of leadership that will give it to us as quickly as possible. You will realize that not only individuals, but governments are using their influence against us. But what do we care about the unrighteous influence of any government? Our cause is based upon righteousness. And anything that is not righteous we have no respect for, because God Almighty is our leader and Jesus Christ our standard bearer. We rely on them for that kind of leadership that will make us free, for it is the same God who inspired the Psalmist to write "Princes shall come out of Egypt and Ethiopia shall stretch out her hands unto God." At this moment methinks I see Ethiopia stretching forth her hands unto God and methinks I see the Angel of God taking up the standard of the Red, the Black and the Green, and saying "Men of the Negro Race, Men of Ethiopia, follow me." Tonight we are following. We are following 400,000,000 strong. We are following with a determination that we must be free before the wreck of matter, before the crash of worlds.

It falls to our lot to tear off the shackles that bind Mother Africa. Can you do it? You did it in the Revolutionary War. You did it in the Civil War; You did it at the Battles of the Marne and Verdun; You did it in Mesopotamia. You can do it marching up the battle heights of Africa. Let the world know that 400,000,000 Negroes are prepared to die or live as free men. Despise us as much as you care. Ignore us as much as you care. We are coming 400,000,000 strong. We are coming with our woes behind us, with the memory of suffering behind us — woes and suffering of three hundred years — they shall be our inspiration. My bulwark of strength in the conflict for free-

dom in Africa, will be the three hundred years of persecution and
hardship left behind in this Western Hemisphere. The more I remember the suffering of my fore-fathers, the more I remember the lynch-
ings and burnings in the Southern States of America, the more I will
fight on even though the battle seems doubtful. Tell me that I must
turn back, and I laugh you to scorn. Go on! Go on! Climb ye the
heights of liberty and cease not in well doing until you have planted
the banner of the Red, the Black and the Green on the hilltops of
Africa.

Harry Haywood

The Road to Negro Liberation

Will Herberg

Marxism and the American Negro

Even though the Communist Party never attracted large numbers of African Americans — by the end of the 1930s there were some 650 official members in Harlem and around 6,000 nationally — it nonetheless galvanized blacks politically on a number of issues. From the 1920s through the 1940s, many black political leaders placed their faith in communism because it often seemed the only predominantly white organization willing to fight for racial equality. However, in some cases — such as the party's defense of the young black men charged with raping two white women in the 1932 Scottsboro case, or its activism in the wake of the 1935 Harlem riot, one of two significant historical riots that Ellison drew on for his novel (see p. 220 and p. 226 of this book) — charges that the party was exploiting race issues for its own benefit were frequent. Although the Communist Party went so far as to hold trials to purge itself of "white chauvinism," prejudice remained commonplace. Tactics and ideology were not always well synchronized. On the one hand, for example, the Communist International thought it crucial to eliminate any nationalist-separatist tendencies among the black membership; but on the other hand, the party advocated a separatist state in the Black Belt South, which was counterproductive to the goals of an integrated class struggle.

Perhaps the most conspicuous feature of the Communist Party's appeal to blacks lay in the necessity, and at times the harshness, of its opposition to other leaders or schools of thought, past and present. Eugene Gordon, a black journalist from Boston, accused both Frederick Douglass and Booker T. Washington of losing their vision in "a miasma of opportunism," charging that "entrenched Negro leadership is today totally bankrupt, and the masses are hoarse with clamouring for a figure tall enough to be seen above their heads" (Gordon 139). For his part, James

W. Ford, the party's 1932 vice presidential candidate, premised legitimation of revolutionary force on slave rebellions and the Russian revolution alike, and he condemned the NAACP as representing "the highest expression of the united front of the Negro bourgeoisie with the white imperialist enemies of the Negro masses" (Ford 146–47). In *Path of Negro Liberation* (1947), fellow Harlem political activist Benjamin J. Davis promoted the argument that black Americans, especially in the South, constituted a nation according to "the only scientific definition of nationhood" — that provided by Stalin (Davis 8).

The appeal to a "science" of history that runs throughout Ellison's evisceration of the Brotherhood in *Invisible Man* (e.g., 291–306) — derived from the Marxist theories that explained social and cultural relations strictly in terms of the world's economic structure — is likewise prevalent throughout black communist literature of the era. Doubt that such theories or an antidemocratic government could ultimately address American racism, along with direct experience of the party's internal politics and the initial revelation of atrocities committed under Stalin's rule, led to many blacks' rapid abandonment of the party in the 1930s and early 1940s. After an initial attraction to communist ideology during his friendship with Richard Wright, Ellison was among those blacks who became disenchanted (see p. 16 and pp. 18–19 of this book). Wright, too, became alienated from the party, and accounts of his break with communism can be found in his sequel to *Black Boy*, titled *American Hunger*, and in the well-known essay "I Tried to Be a Communist" (reprinted in a 1949 collection of statements from former communists, *The God That Failed*).

An example of the party's attempt to construct a viable political theory based on a "science" of history appears in the selection from Harry Haywood's *Road to Negro Liberation* (1934) reprinted below. Haywood (1898–1985), a midwesterner who had briefly been a member of the African Blood Brotherhood, was one of the leading black communists in Harlem, an active party member for many years to come, and the author of a later autobiography, *Black Bolshevik* (1978). The second selection below, from the white historian and biblical theologian Will Herberg (1901–1977), appeared in *Negro: An Anthology* (1934). This volume, edited by Nancy Cunard, a British expatriate and enthusiast of African American culture, gathered contemporary essays on black cultural, economic, and social issues, including the essays by James Ford and Eugene Gordon mentioned above. Because it offers an argument less governed by party jargon and grounded more overtly in the history of American racial injustice, Herberg's essay is perhaps a fairer index of the popular appeal of communism to blacks of the 1930s.

FURTHER READING: James S. Allen's *The Negro Question in the United States* (New York: International, 1936); Wilson Record, *Race and Radicalism: The NAACP and the Communist Party in Conflict* (Ithaca: Cornell UP, 1964); Mark Naison, *Communists in Harlem During the Depression* (Urbana: U of Illinois P, 1983); Harvey Klehr, *The Heyday of American Communism: The Depression Decade* (New York: Basic, 1984); Mark I. Solomon, *Red and Black: Communism and Afro-Americans, 1929–1935* (New York: Garland, 1988); Philip S. Foner and Herbert Shapiro, eds., *American Communism and Black Americans: A Documentary History, 1930–1934* (Philadelphia: Temple UP, 1991); Will Herberg, *From Marxism to Judaism: Selected Essays,* ed. David G. Dalin (New York: M. Wiener, 1989).

Harry Haywood
The Road to Negro Liberation

An outstanding characteristic of the present moment is the sharp increase in the activities of the Negro bourgeois reformists and petty bourgeois nationalist leaders among the Negro masses. We find that these activities have not only been intensified, but are assuming more varied and subtle forms. In addition to the official bourgeois reformist organizations and their activities, there has appeared upon the scene in the recent period numerous petty bourgeois nationalist movements. We also witness definite attempts to crystallize "Left" reformist Negro movements.

This phenomenon is directly connected with the sharpening class struggle and growing radicalization of the Negro toilers. Only on this basis can it be explained. We might say that the increased activities of the Negro reformists, their attempts to strengthen nationalism among the masses, take place in direct proportion to the increase of our revolutionary influence among the Negro masses. We see that wherever we begin serious work among the Negroes, wherever our influence is extended among them, we find ourselves confronted sharply with the problem of the struggle against Negro reformism as an immediate obstacle in the revolutionization of the Negro masses, as for example, in

Chicago, in St. Louis, the South, in connection with the Scottsboro campaign and the struggle against lynching. Everywhere, Negro reformists and petty bourgeois nationalist leaders of all shades, under the cover of the most cunning demagogy, are feverishly working.

What is the object of these activities? It is clear that their object is to halt the growing revolutionary drift of the Negro masses, to hinder the growing unity of Negro and white toilers in the struggle against rising fascist reaction, to hold the masses under the influence of bourgeois reformism, petty bourgeois nationalism, which means objectively, to hold them to the shackles of imperialism. It is now becoming clearer than ever that Negro reformism is the main enemy within the ranks of the Negro people, the chief social support of imperialist Jim-Crow reaction among the Negro masses. Therefore, the struggle against and exposure of the Negro reformists and the petty bourgeois nationalist leaders, their isolation from the masses, is a central, most urgent task of our Party and the revolutionary movement at the present time. Involved in this fight for the liberation of the masses from the treacherous influences of the Negro reformists and their organizations, is the whole question of proletarian hegemony and Party leadership in the rising national revolutionary movement of the Negro people. It is a question of who will beat whom. What policy shall prevail? Our proletarian class policy of a revolutionary alliance between the Negro masses and the white working class for the overthrow of American imperialism and the realization of the rights of Negroes or the reformist policy of surrender to imperialism, the policy which substitutes reactionary utopian illusions in place of revolutionary struggle, a policy which can lead only to defeat, and to strengthening the yoke of imperialist oppression upon the masses of Negro toilers and the white toilers as well.

Let us examine some of the activities of the Negro bourgeois reformists, petty bourgeois nationalist organizations in the present situation. Among the Negro reformist organizations we find the chief role is still allotted to the National Association for the Advancement of Colored People. In the leadership of this organization, we find Negro bourgeois reformists of the type of Walter White, Pickens, Schuyler, Du Bois en bloc, with white liberals ("enlightened" imperialist elements) of the type of Spingarn, Mary White Ovington, etc., and even outspoken imperialist politicians such as Senator Capper, Governor General Murphy of the Philippines, etc.; also open Negro reactionaries of the type of Dr. Moton of Tuskegee. It is these imperialist elements that govern the policies of the organization. The composition of the leadership of the N.A.A.C.P. thus gives a clear indication of this policy.

What is this policy?

The guiding theory on which the policy is based is that: The Negro question can be solved within the confines of the present capitalist imperialist social order without revolutionary struggle. That the fate of the Negro masses is bound up with the maintenance of capitalism, or as Kelly Miller, outspoken Negro conservative expresses it: "Capital is the Negro's friend; white labor is his enemy." Therefore, according to this, the winning of Negro rights does not entail a fight against capital, *i.e.*, imperialism; on the contrary, it implies the collaboration with the white imperialist rulers, or in the words of the N.A.A.C.P. leaders, "united front of the 'best' elements of both races." Against whom? Against the rising mass movement of Negro and white toilers, particularly against its leaders — the Communists.

This is the core of Negro bourgeois reformism. From this flows its tactical line of reliance on bourgeois courts, legislative bodies, its treacherous compromises with the white ruling class, its reactionary sabotage of the revolutionary struggles for Negro rights. "The Constitution is the ship, all else is the sea," says Kelly Miller.

In the present period of sharpening class struggles and political awakening of the Negro peoples, this policy implies the active supplementing of the ruling class tactic of split and division in the ranks of the working class; it implies active alliance with all reactionary forces against the rising national liberation movement of the Negro masses, against the revolutionary labor movement, and its leaders, the Communist Party. Negro reformism has become an active agent of the ruling imperialist bourgeoisie in helping to prepare the way for fascism.

The division of the toiling masses along lines of race and nationality, above all, the fostering of friction between black and white workers — this is the very heart of the strategy of rising fascism. This is definitely the meaning of the present campaign of white chauvinism and anti-Negro feeling launched by the bourgeoisie. Its object is to split off the rising struggle of the Negro masses from the revolutionary movement — to deprive the revolutionary working class of one of its main reserves. This is why Negro reformism with its policy of collaboration with the white ruling class oppressors, its anti-labor activities, its doctrines of Jim-Crow nationalism and racial seclusion, complement completely the program of fascism. It is but the reverse side

of the fascist coin. This is why, at the present moment, American imperialism, as it proceeds with its policy of fascization, is consciously
building up Negro reformism as its best agent within the ranks of the
Negro people. It is not accidental, therefore, that just at this moment
the imperialist government in Washington has embarked upon a policy of drawing Negro reformists and bourgeois politicians directly
into the government apparatus and the N.R.A. machinery. This is not
only recognition on the part of imperialism of the services of its
Negro lackeys. This policy of corruption of Negro upper class elements is intended to strengthen the social base of the imperialist
rulers among the Negro middle classes, to use sections of them as an
effective buffer to ward off the gathering mass movement and to
make easier the carrying through of its policy of increased plunder of
the Negro masses. . . .

Against these counter-revolutionary schemes for the solution of
the Negro question, we must put forth our full program on the Negro
question in the U.S.A. as well as in Africa. We must advance and pop-
ularize the revolutionary way out of the crisis for the Negro people,
through an alliance with the revolutionary working class of the imperialist nations, for equal rights and the right of self-determination for
the Negroes in the U.S.A., for complete independence of the Negro
colonies in Africa and the West Indies, through the establishment of
independent native republics. This alone is the only path to real freedom for the oppressed Negro peoples throughout the world.

Any attempt to draw the Negro masses away from struggle, from
coming to grips with the imperialist masters, can lead only to defeat
and to the tightening of the shackles of oppression upon them. In exposing these petty-bourgeois nationalist leaders, it is absolutely necessary to make clear that we Communists not only recognize the aspirations of the Negro toilers in this movement as authentic, but that
the Communists *alone* are the only *true champions of Negro freedom*, that we alone have the correct program by which oppression
can be abolished and these aspirations fulfilled.

In our exposure of these Negro traitors, the chief emphasis must
be placed on the fact that their treachery consists precisely in the fact
that they are betraying the national liberation aspirations of the
Negro people. Our slogan must be: No reactionary utopian dream of
"back to Africa" or a Jim-Crow State in the U.S.A.! These are only
reactionary caricatures of real self-determination. But revolutionary
struggle in alliance with the white toilers and under the leadership of

the Communist Party for the overthrow of American imperialism, for the establishment of equal rights for Negroes all over the country and self-determination for the Negro nation in the Southern Black Belt.

In our agitation an important weapon must be the widest popularization of the solution of the national question in the Soviet Union. We must show how the establishment of the proletarian State through the overthrow of Czarist imperialism permitted for the first time the real establishment of complete equality and self-determination for the formerly oppressed national minorities within the Soviet Union. We must show that only this step made possible the tremendous economic and cultural development of the numerous nationalities once held in slavery by Czarism.

Will Herberg
Marxism and the American Negro

Communism, revolutionary Marxism, bases its program and conclusions not upon vague and indefinable sentiment but upon a scientific analysis and an objective evaluation of social relations and class forces. When Communism approaches the "Negro problem" in the U.S.A. the first question it puts is: "What is the actual status of the Negro in American society, how did this status arise and how is it maintained?"

The American Negro is not free — even in the extremely limited sense in which freedom can be spoken of at all in bourgeois society. In the South, the Negro peasant is practically a serf; in fact his status is substantially no more than a modified form of the slavery of former days. In Northern industry, the hundreds of thousands of Negro proletarians occupy a position of definite inferiority — they have no access to the more desirable situations, they are hindered in their approach to skilled or even semi-skilled jobs, they are forced into the least paid and most menial occupations, they are discriminated against in wages and in working conditions. The black man, concentrated in the South and in about a dozen Northern cities, is segregated by law and custom into veritable ghettos. In a large part of the country he cannot eat where the white man eats; he cannot attend the white man's places of amusement and recreation or else cannot frequent them on an equal basis; he cannot even travel as does the white man. In an even larger part of the country, Negro children cannot attend "white" schools, colleges or libraries and are forced to be content with the most shamefully inadequate facilities. Throughout the entire South the Negro is deprived of every civil and political right. And over all hovers the dark shadow of Judge Lynch. . . .

The Negro in the United States forms a well-defined subject caste, with a distinctly inferior economic, social and political status.

Communism traces the roots of the present subject status of the Negro in America back to the days of slavery, nearly three-quarters of a century ago. Under slavery there was an immediate and obvious basis for the social subjection of the black men — their economically enslaved condition as a race. Had the American Civil War really effected the complete emancipation of the Negro slave, there would indeed have been no ground for the continued existence of the Negro as an inferior caste. But the victorious industrial bourgeoisie of the North adopted a course of action that led to quite other results. It rejected the "Radical" plan of Reconstruction, a plan that envisaged the complete destruction of the economic and political power of the slaveocracy and the real emancipation of the Negro slaves, *i.e.* their transformation into free peasant-proprietors and into free proletarians. On the contrary, the Northern bourgeoisie, after considerable hesitation, threw its support to the "moderate" plan of Reconstruction which aimed to conciliate the old slave-owners by abolishing chattel slavery in name but retaining it in somewhat modified form in fact. The bourgeois-democratic revolution — the historical essence of the Civil War — was thereby stifled and distorted; the emancipation of the Negro was rendered incomplete, even from the consistent bourgeois standpoint. Thus the present economic status of the Negro farmer (and at least 50 per cent of the Negro people are still farmers) is essentially a survival of slavery. And when, in the course of time, the Negro farmer comes to enter industry, he naturally brings with him his caste status. The *specially depressed* economic position of the Negro is the basis upon which the whole system of social, political and cultural subjection is reared.

The caste status of the American Negro is a pre-capitalist survival, a "relic of feudalism." But such pre-capitalist survivals find a welcome place in the decaying structure of capitalism in its final, imperialist-monopolist epoch. The bourgeoisie is no longer, as it was in the great days of its youth, the ruthless destroyer of the reactionary and the obsolete. In its senility, "the decaying bourgeoisie . . . supports everything that is backward, dying and medieval . . ." (Lenin). The British Raj sustains the forces of feudalism and the dark powers of superstition in India; American imperialism carefully fosters everything that tends to keep the colored man in his semi-serf state.

The specially depressed economic status of the Negro peasant and proletarian serves as a valuable source of super-profit for monopoly capital — in a strictly analogous manner to colonial exploitation. At the same time it also serves as a point of support for the class domination of the bourgeoisie ("Divide and conquer!"). For this reason the race oppression of the Negro has become an integral element of the bourgeois-imperialist system in this country. . . .

The whole burden of the Communist analysis goes to prove that, although the deliverance of the Negro people from their caste existence is in its content essentially a democratic task, in all respects similar to the liberation of subject nations or colonies, the "Negro question" today cannot be solved within the framework of the capitalist system and of bourgeois democracy. It is clear that only the elimination of the underlying economic conditions upon which the subjection of the American Negro is predicated, can make possible any real emancipation. The radical eradication of tenancy, share-cropping, "furnishing," and all other forms of semi-slave exploitation, the shattering of the power of the Southern landlords through the nationalisation of the land and its distribution among the cultivators, the elimination of all elements of inferiority in the Negro's position in industry — these are the very basic prerequisites. Obviously enough, these proposals represent merely the demands of consistent democracy; they are in all respects akin to the classical ideals of the bourgeois-democratic revolution, the great French Revolution, for example. Not a single one is a specifically Socialist demand — not one necessarily implies the socialisation of all the means of production, etc. Yet the opposition of capitalism today to such a program is not a whit less bitter for all that. So anti-democratic has the bourgeoisie become in its period of decay, so organically bound up with everything that is outlived, reactionary and decadent, that the realisation of these democratic demands in the present historical period is possible only through the overthrow of capitalist "democracy," through the concentration of political power in the hands of the proletariat. In such dialectical contradiction does history move that only the dictatorship of the proletariat can guarantee democracy to the masses and bring real democracy, for the first time, to the Negro people. Today only a proletarian revolution can accomplish what the American bourgeois revolution that was the Civil War failed to do!

The great Negro migrations during the last two decades, in the course of which scores of thousands of Negro farmers swarmed to the great Northern industrial centers and to the basic industries of the land, really introduced a new stage in the history of the American Negro. They effected a profound social fermentation and a basic realignment of class forces. They really created the modern Negro proletariat. They greatly stimulated the development of the Negro bourgeoisie and petty bourgeoisie and seriously transformed the relations between these classes. Above all they opened a new chapter in the long and painful story of a race striving for deliverance.

The *Negro bourgeoisie* is rather weak numerically, but through it, through the more pliant elements of the petty bourgeoisie, and through the professional "race leaders," the white bourgeoisie exerts tremendous influence over the Negro people. The fundamental standpoint of these conservatives was theoretically formulated by Booker T. Washington in the famous "Atlanta Compromise": the Negro is to be content with the place in the American scheme of things so graciously vouchsafed him by the white man. He is to bend his energies towards becoming an efficient servant of the white master, a hardworking farmer, a skilled artisan, a small business man if possible. Any present aspiration for social and political rights — and above all, any yearning for social equality — is a vain and dangerous delusion. In the South the Negroes are to acquiesce in their complete political disfranchisement; in the North, they are to serve as blind voting cattle for the Republican party. (Lately an infamous flirtation with the Democrats has even been initiated.) Clique squabbles, gross corruption, and shameless patronage mark the "political" activities of these "race leaders" — all at the expense of the life interests of the Negro masses. Of the emancipation of their people they know nothing and care less!

The *Negro petty bourgeoisie*, especially the intellectuals and the professionals, are quite numerous and of considerable consequence. Like the bourgeoisie, this class found a firm basis of existence only with the great Negro migrations and the creation of huge Negro cities in the relatively free atmosphere of the North. In the post-war "renascence," a period of deep-going fermentation and great achievement, the Negro intellectual played a brilliant role, especially in literature and the fine arts. As a significant factor in the life and development of the race, the petty bourgeoisie is second only to the new proletariat.

The social outlook of the *Negro petty bourgeoisie* has always been marked — quite inevitably, as the Communist sees it — by its lack of consistency and resolution, by its grave inner contradictions, by its endless vagaries, by its extravagant oscillations from one extreme to another, by its fantastic utopianism combined with an equally fantastic "practicalism" — but all within the bounds of the basic bourgeois preconceptions. Especially characteristic is its touching faith in the belief that the "Negro question" can be solved within the framework of capitalism, perhaps even with the benevolent aid of the white capitalists themselves — a delusion that no amount of experience or thought, it seems, has as yet been able to dispell. At one time Garveyism, an essentially reactionary philosophy based on an inverted form of the "white supremacy" gospel of the white masters and shot through with the crassest demagogy and the grossest charlatanism, had considerable hold over the lower middle class elements in the large Negro cities. Now Garveyism is happily dead. Today the Negro intellectual and professional are lost in the absurd utopia of creating a self-contained Negro economy through utilising the "organised buying power" of the race, or through some equally efficacious means. The capricious and ever-changing vagaries that dominate the Negro petty bourgeoisie are a certain indication of the gulf that has arisen between it and the masses of the Negro people, the peasants and workers, whose interests are poles apart from the unreal fantasies of the small business man or professional. Their growing estrangement from their own people is unquestionably the greatest inner weakness of the Negro petty bourgeoisie.

Nevertheless, from a general historical viewpoint, this class still has progressive potentialities. Considerable sections of the Negro intellectuals are already definitely moving leftwards. But the actual realisation of its historical potentialities implies an end to reactionary and futile utopian dreaming, an organic approach to the masses, a participation in their interests and aspirations, a close alliance with the advanced sections of the proletariat, black and white.

The wave of Negro migrations and the experiences of the World War had an immense effect upon the great and basic mass of *Negro peasants* in the South. The bleak seclusion, the dreary isolation of decades was broken. A vigorous breath of fresh air swept through the poisonous atmosphere of the Old South. The vision of the Negro peasant was suddenly and immensely enlarged; intimate contacts were established with migrated friends and relatives in the North; an understanding that things must not be always — and are not everywhere — the same, began to dawn. The Negro peasant began to mature as a vital factor in the movement for freedom.

The rise of the *modern Negro proletariat* that came with the migrations drew scores of thousands of black men out of the narrow and stultifying conditions of Southern rural life and threw them into the very whirlpool of modern America — the great industrial centers of the North. The creation of an industrial proletariat on a large scale constituted a change of colossal historical importance, for it gave to the Negro people its natural leadership, a class thrust to the fore of modern society by the immanent processes of capitalist production themselves. The creation of the modern Negro proletariat was the most significant advance in the history of the Negro people since the days of Reconstruction.

The sudden influx of tens of thousands of black workers into Northern industry inevitably aggravated the anti-Negro prejudice of the backward white workers — and the vast majority of the American workers are still backward. At the same time, the narrow and exclusive craft structure and the opportunist philosophy of American trade unionism served from the very beginning as a most serious obstacle in the way of the black workers in industry. The Negro is almost exclusively an unskilled laborer: why should the craft unions of skilled workers "bother" about him? The Negro is thrown into a despised position of caste inferiority by the capitalists: why should the opportunists, who slavishly anticipate the mere thoughts of their masters, whose very fibres are seeped through with the poison of race prejudice, "bother" about him? The conservative trade unions have practically closed their doors to the Negro workers and have all but invited them to throw in their lot with the white capitalists as scabs and strike-breakers — a course incessantly urged by the conservative Negro leaders as well. The darkest page in the history of the American organised labor movement is its shameful record of antipathy and discrimination against the black worker.

But the progress of the class struggle — Communism points out — promises to heal even this ominous breach in the ranks of the American proletariat. The white heat of class war will burn out the corruption of race prejudice. The fraternisation of white and colored workers in the South during recent strikes, however hesitating, uncertain and unstable, is a straw in the wind. The slow but inevitable deepening of the class consciousness of the white proletariat, *i.e.* its growing ideological liberation from the bourgeoisie, will certainly deliver the white workers from the thoroughly bourgeois nightmare of race prejudice.

Avram Landy
Marxism and the Woman Question

When Ellison's protagonist in *Invisible Man* is demoted from his position as a leading Brotherhood speaker on the race question because of insubordination, he is sent downtown to lecture on the "Woman Question." His speech is not reproduced in the novel, but Ellison makes clear that he would likely have been instructed to deliver a programmatic view similar to that found in this selection from *Marxism and the Woman Question* (1943) by Avram Landy, a white communist organizer in New York. Landy's pamphlet is characteristic of arguments delivered in numerous speeches and in a variety of ephemeral texts such as Klara Zetkin's *Lenin on the Woman Question* (1934), many of them published by the leading communist press, International Publishers. The writings of more famous women socialists or communists such as Emma Goldman and Elizabeth Gurley Flynn provide more comprehensive perspectives on women's issues in the party from the early part of the century through World War II. Outside the framework of the party itself, many black women, as well as white, were active in labor struggles in Harlem, among them Nannie Helen Burroughs and Elise McDougald, but Ellison's portrait of the Brotherhood focuses on the rhetorical manipulation of gender issues, as of black issues, by the Communist party.

From the stripper dancing at the men's smoker through Trueblood's act of incest, the prostitutes at the Golden Day, and the protagonist's several encounters with white women who wonder if, as a Brotherhood spokesman, he should not be "a little blacker" (*Invisible Man* 303) or who typecast him as a "black brute" lover (*Invisible Man* 414–16, 516–26), Ellison's novel often treats women as objects of sexual attention or violence. A few early Marxist critics of the novel contended that this was part of the book's own "pathology," and some recent feminist critics have judged that Ellison's treatment of women is one-dimensional (Tate). At the same time, however, *Invisible Man* clearly critiques sexual stereotypes and male sexual aggression as a function of racism, and shows keen awareness that the Communist Party's elimination of white chauvinism brought on sexual complications across the racial line that many members — white men and black women in particular — resented. The crude complaint that the "ass struggle" replaced the "class struggle" was apparently common enough that the protagonist's own use of it is something of a cliché (Naison 136–37, 280–81; Ellison, *Invisible Man* 418).

FURTHER READING: Emma Goldman, *Red Emma Speaks: Selected Writings and Speeches* (New York: Random, 1972); Barbara W. Jancar, *Women Under Communism* (Baltimore: Johns Hopkins UP, 1978); Candace Falk, *Love, Anarchy, and Emma Goldman* (New York: Holt, 1984); Rosalyn Fraad Baxandall, ed., *Words on Fire: The Life and Writings of Elizabeth Gurley Flynn* (New Brunswick: Rutgers UP, 1987); Darlene Clark Hine, ed., *Black Women in United States History* (Brooklyn: Carlson, 1990).

The first question concerns the usefulness of woman's work in the home. Of course the housewife's work is useful. It is useful by virtue of the fact that it satisfies the wants of a group of people, and to the extent that it does that, there can be no question of the usefulness of such work to these people. After all, the housewife performs certain activities which contribute to the functioning of the family under the conditions imposed by capitalism. It is self-evident, therefore, that these activities are useful.

But it is also self-evident that this fact is of no special importance either for the scientific analysis of the housewife's position in society or for the formulation of a program of practical demands, not to speak of its utter uselessness as an argument for socialism. Granted that a housewife's work is useful. So is the labor of a shoemaker who has spent two days making a pair of shoes by hand. Someone can certainly make good use of those shoes, but the fact remains that the labor expended was far from socially necessary in view of the fact that modern industry can make the same pair of shoes in a tiny fraction of the time spent by the handicraft shoemaker.

The real question, therefore, is whether the work performed is socially necessary, and this, not in the sense of whether work in the home or the production of shoes is necessary in society. For, as long as people have homes and wear shoes, it is obvious that shoes will be made and housework will be done in one way or another, and that such work will be of a useful character. The only legitimate question is whether this work is performed in accord with the technical level achieved by the development of the productive forces. And here it must be said that most of the individual drudgery characteristic of housework under capitalism is unnecessary in view of the technical achievements of society.

It is from this fact, and not from the bare and inconsequential statement that housework is useful, that it is possible to draw important conclusions both as regards a program of immediate demands and as regards the need for socialism. The fact that the housewife is condemned to drudgery despite the material possibilities of freeing her from it is only further evidence that capitalism has outlived its usefulness and must be replaced by socialism. Similarly, the difficulties and misery connected with the home under capitalism, and not the usefulness or dignity of the work performed in it, are the ground out of which the immediate issues of struggle grow.

The theoretical significance of this is evident the moment we examine into the nature of the two different approaches involved here. No one, of course, is merely interested in establishing academically whether housework is useful or not. The question is whether by emphasizing this fact and taking it as the point of departure in an approach to the housewives it will be possible to involve millions of housewives in the people's struggles. The answer to this is contained in the very essence of Marxist theory, which teaches us that both the struggle for immediate demands and the socialist reconstruction of society have a common source in the *contradictions* inherent in capitalist society. These contradictions alone are the source of mass struggle and they rest on the solid foundation of the material productive forces of society. Thus to help the millions of women, the majority of whom are housewives, to take part in the struggle for immediate demands and to learn the need for socialism from their own experiences in this struggle, we must base our teachings and activity on the *contradiction* between the material possibilities for their liberation provided by modern industry and the subjection imposed upon them by capitalist production relations. It is only along this road that we will find the answer to the really important question of how to activize the millions of women.

We can see this very concretely. Any program of immediate demands for the millions of housewives would necessarily involve such issues as better housing, cheaper rents, the high cost of living, day nurseries, free lunches for school children, and a host of other issues arising out of the maintenance of the home. All these demands derive their force from the physical needs of the housewives and their families, from the fact that society has the material resources to meet these demands, and from the even more vital fact that the capitalist production relations stand between the toilers and these resources. It is obvious that if, in their struggle to live, there were no need for the mass of the people to overcome certain restrictions imposed upon them by the capital-wage labor relationship, there would be no demands and no struggle. If the millions of housewives, as members of the working class and toiling population, were not circumscribed by the conditions of the capitalist exploitation of labor — in short, if there were no contradictions between their struggle to live and the socio-economic conditions in which this struggle takes place, there would be no need of activizing these millions of women. It is only in this *contradiction* that the struggle for the housewives' demands can be theoretically or even practically grounded. By the same token, however, the very conditions that give rise to the struggle and impress their specific nature on it make it a struggle not to maintain the status of the housewife (in effect the status of a drudge and the "slave of a slave") in bourgeois-imposed conditions of life, but to overcome these conditions as part of the basic proletarian struggle.

Likewise, to convince these millions of housewives of the need for socialism, it is necessary to show them that socialism will liberate them in every respect — from the misery of capitalist life, from the drudgery of housework, from the inequalities and discrimination practiced against them daily. In other words, the argument for socialism must also be based on the irreconcilable antagonism between the millions of housewives and the consequences of the capitalist production relations. It must be based on a *rejection* and not on an affirmation of these relations as materially outmoded and unnecessary. There is no other way of arguing for socialism.

Now it is quite obvious that you cannot ground the need for socialism in the rejection of capitalism and at the same time ground the program of immediate demands in an affirmation of the housewife's usefulness to capitalism. Such a procedure simply throws overboard the scientifically established Marxist principle that there is the closest organic connection between the struggle for immediate demands and the struggle for the ultimate establishment of socialism. The masses can learn the need for socialism out of their own experience only if that experience demonstrates an irreconcilable antagonism and contradiction to capitalism.

But what is the nature of the "usefulness" approach? Where does it lead us? It leads us to look for the source of struggle not in the contradiction but in the *contribution* of the housewife to capitalism. This is necessarily so because the whole point to the argument about the usefulness of housework is that it is useful and necessary to the functioning of capitalist society. How does it help the capitalist system function? *It does this by helping capital to reproduce labor power as wage-labor!* This "useful" contribution may be a source of dignity to the housewife, as some people prefer to believe, although it is hard to see what dignity there is in the role of helping capital to reproduce the laborer as a wage slave; but it is certainly not a source of struggle. If it is anything, it is a source of *reconciliation* with the capitalist system. For it is obvious that in taking the emphasis on the "usefulness" of the housewife as the starting point of our tactics, we necessarily make the housewife's "contribution" the dominant feature of the relationship between herself and the capitalist system and not the *antagonism*, the contradiction and conflict between herself and the capitalist system. If we insist on assuring the housewife that she has a useful, dignified role to play in the capitalist system, what logical obstacle do we put in the way of the housewife's drawing the conclusion that it is desirable to perpetuate this role and of course the system that goes with it? Such an approach merely provides the logical mood and atmosphere of accommodation to the capitalist system, if not to all of its daily conditions. It is certainly not a *revolutionary* approach, to say the least.

Generally, it must be said that the Marxist social and economic theory is a theory of the *exploitation* of *labor* and not of the usefulness of labor to the functioning of the capitalist system. It is quite generally recognized that the labor of the working class is very useful to the capitalists, but no Marxist would ever dream of grounding the struggle between labor and capital in anything but the irreconcilable contradictions between the two classes. Is there any scientific reason for treating the question of women's relations to capitalism in any other way?

The eviction of Harlem tenants was a frequent occurrence during the depression. In *Invisible Man,* one such eviction prompts the protagonist to make an extemporaneous speech on behalf of those evicted, setting in motion his career as a public speaker for the Brotherhood (*Invisible Man* 268–84).

James Weldon Johnson

Negro Americans, What Now?

James Weldon Johnson (1871–1938), a man of diverse talents, was a successful lyricist with his composer-brother J. Rosamond Johnson (among his two hundred or more songs is "Lift Every Voice and Sing," often identified as the unofficial anthem of African America). He also wrote one of the great novels of the early twentieth century, *The Autobiography of an Ex-Colored Man* (1912); an excellent history of modern Harlem, *Black Manhattan* (1930); an autobiography, *Along This Way* (1933); and several volumes of poetry, including *Fifty Years and Other Poems* (1917) and *God's Trombones* (1927). His public service was equally remarkable. After serving as U.S. consul to Venezuela (1906–08) and Nicaragua (1909–12), Johnson worked as the first black secretary of the NAACP from 1920 until 1930, when he accepted a teaching position at Fisk University. The argument of his *Negro Americans, What Now?* (1934) is characteristic of the NAACP's moderate view that the struggle for equality through integration, rather than separatism, emigration, or revolution, is the most certain path to racial justice.

FURTHER READING: Charles Flint Kellogg, *NAACP: A History of the National Association for the Advancement of Colored People* (Baltimore: Johns Hopkins UP, 1967); Bernard Eisenberg, *James Weldon Johnson and the National Association for the Advancement of Colored People, 1916–1934* (n.p., 1968); Eugene Levy, *James Weldon Johnson: Black Leader, Black Voice* (Chicago: U of Chicago P, 1973); Nancy Weiss, *Farewell to the Party of Lincoln: Black Politics in the Age of FDR* (Princeton: Princeton UP, 1983).

Choices

The world today is in a state of semi-chaos. We Negro Americans as a part of the world are affected by that state. We are affected by it still more vitally as a special group. We are not so sanguine about our course and our goal as we were a decade ago. We are floundering. We are casting about for ways of meeting the situation, both as

Americans and as Negroes. In this casting about we have discovered and rediscovered a number of ways to which we have given more or less consideration. Let us see if we cannot by elimination reduce confusion and narrow down the limits of choice to what might be shown to be the one sound and wise line to follow.

Exodus

Exodus has for generations been recurrently suggested as a method for solving the race problem. At the present time there is being fomented by some person or persons in Chicago a plan based on the idea of colonization. The plan calls for the setting aside of a state or territory of the United States exclusively for Negro Americans.

The idea of physical separation of the races as a solution antedates the Revolutionary War. Thomas Jefferson strongly expressed himself in favor of the colonization of the Negroes in some area on the coast of Africa. The first attempt, however, to put colonization into effect was made by Paul Cuffe, a free Negro and a shipowner of New Bedford, Massachusetts, who in 1815 transported at his own expense nine families to Africa. The first attempt on a grand scale was made in 1820, with the American Colonization Society and the United States government behind it — an attempt that culminated in the establishment of Liberia. At the outbreak of the Civil War there was another effort, fostered by a group within the race, and some two thousand colonists sought refuge in Haiti. The latest of the attempts on a large scale was the Garvey Movement. All of these efforts practically failed; that is, they had no effect on the problem and in no degree changed the condition of the race in the United States.

A century and a quarter ago deportation of the free Negroes might have been feasible; a half century later *that* was not a practicable undertaking; today the deportation or exodus of the Negro American population is an utter impossibility. Not within a bounded period could twelve million people be transported; and before that period was over the total number would be well above twelve million. Nor is there any place to which to take them. There are no more "vacant" places on earth; and no government in the world, with the barest possibility of Brazil as the exception, would welcome even one-twelfth the whole number; Liberia would no doubt be as reluctant as any. None of the tribes of colonial Africa would relish sharing their best lands with us merely because we and they are of somewhat the same complexion. The United States government might purchase territory somewhere and deport us. But that would involve a pretty stiff political job and a financial expenditure that would make the figures of the National Recovery program look small.

We may cross out exodus as a possible solution. We and the white people may as well make up our minds definitely that we, the same as they, are in this country to stay. We may be causing white America some annoyance, but we ourselves are not passing the time in undisturbed comfort. White America will simply have to sustain a situation that is of its own making, not ours.

Physical Force

Our history in the United States records a half-dozen major and a score of minor efforts at insurrection during the period of slavery. This, if they heard it, would be news to that big majority of people who believe that we have gone through three centuries of oppression without once thinking in terms of rebellion or lifting a finger in revolt. Even now there come times when we think in terms of physical force.

We must condemn physical force and banish it from our minds. But I do not condemn it on any moral or pacific grounds. The resort to force remains and will doubtless always remain the rightful recourse of oppressed peoples. Our own country was established upon that right. I condemn physical force because I know that in our case it would be futile.

We would be justified in taking up arms or anything we could lay hands on and fighting for the common rights we are entitled to and denied, if we had a chance to win. But I know and we all know there is not a chance. It is, I believe, among the certainties that some day, perhaps not very far off, native blacks of Africa will, by physical force if necessary, compel the whites to yield their extra privileges and immunities. The increasing inability of the great powers to spare the strength and resources necessary for maintaining imperialism will hasten the certainty. The situation of the African natives is, however, on one point at least, the reverse of our own — on the point of comparative numerical strength.

Yet, there is a phase of physical force that we in the United States should consider. When we are confronted by the lawless, pitiless, brutish mob, and we know that life is forfeit, we should not give it

up; we should, if we can, sell it, and at the dearest price we are able
to put on it.

The Revolution

Communism is coming to be regarded as the infallible solution by an
increasing number of us. Those who look to the coming revolution
(and why they should believe it is coming in the United States I see no
good reason; it is obvious that the United States is going through revolutionary economic and social changes, but the changes do not point
to Communism) seem to think it will work some instantaneous and
magical transformation of our condition. It appears to me that this
infinite faith in Communism indicates extreme *naiveté*. Those who
hold this faith point to Soviet Russia as a land in which there is absolutely no prejudice against Negroes. This is an unquestioned fact,
but I can see no grounds on which to attribute it to Communism.
There was no prejudice against Negroes in Tsarist Russia. Tsarist
Russia was the country that could honor a black Hannibal; the country that could make a mulatto Pushkin its national poet; the country
in which university students in St. Petersburg could unhitch the
horses from the carriage of Ira Aldridge, the black American trage-
dian, after his performance of Othello, and themselves draw him
back to his hotel. The simple truth is: the *Russian people* have no
prejudice against Negroes.

In considering Communism with respect to the Negro, the question before us, of course, is not how it works in Russia, but how it
would probably work in the United States. If the United States goes
Communistic, where will the Communists come from? They certainly
will not be imported from Russia. They will be made from the Americans here on hand. We might well pause and consider what variations Communism in the United States might undergo.

I hold no brief against Communism as a theory of government. I
hope that the Soviet experiment will be completely successful. I know
that it is having a strong influence on the principal nations of the
world, including our own. I think it is a high sign of progress that
Negro Americans have reached the point of holding independent
opinions on political and social questions. What I am trying to do is
to sound a warning against childlike trust in the miraculous efficacy
on our racial situation of any economic or social theory of government — Communism or Socialism or Fascism or Nazism or New

Deals. The solving of our situation depends principally upon an evo-
lutionary process along two parallel lines: our own development and
the bringing about of a change in the national attitude toward us.
That outcome will require our persevering effort under whatever
form the government might take on.

It may be argued that although there is not and has not been any
anti-Negro feeling in Russia, it is the country in which anti-Semitism
was stronger than in any other, and that oppression and repression of
the Jews have been greatly abated or entirely wiped out by Communism. Such an argument goes to prove the possibility that Communism in the United States would wipe out oppression and repression
of Negro Americans and give them a status of equality. I grant the
possibility — what though it may not be realized miraculously and
suddenly. I grant that if America should turn truly Communistic (by
which I mean — if it should adopt and practice Communism without
reservations, and not adapt it as it has adapted democracy and Christianity so as to allow every degree of inequality and cruelty to be
practiced under them); that if the capitalistic system should be abolished and the dictatorship of the proletariat established, with the
Negro aligned, as he naturally ought to be, with the proletariat, race
discriminations would be officially banned and the reasons and feelings back of them would finally disappear.

But except to a visionary there are no indications that the present
or prospective strength of Communism is able or will be able to work
such a change, either by persuasion or by military coup. In the situation as it now exists it would be positively foolhardy for us, as a
group, to take up the cause of Communistic revolution and thereby
bring upon ourselves all of the antagonisms that are directed against
it in addition to those we already have to bear. It seems to me that the
wholesale allegiance of the Negro to Communistic revolution would
be second in futility only to his individual resort to physical force.

I have said that there is no apparent probability that the United
States will go over to Communism; but the same cannot be said
about Fascism. Most of us, it is true, have for long years lived in the
Fascist South; so it is hardly possible that we could fare worse under
a national Fascist government. That may not be true as to other minorities. We should oppose with our utmost strength any encroach-
ment of Fascism, for we have both a practical and a moral obligation
to do all we can to defend the rights of other minorities, as well as
our own.

Isolation or Integration?

By this process of elimination we have reduced choices of a way out to two. There remain, on the one hand, the continuation of our efforts to achieve integration and, on the other hand, an acknowledgment of our isolation and the determination to accept and make the best of it.

Throughout our entire intellectual history there has been a division of opinion as to which of these two divergent courses the race should follow. From early times there have been sincere thinkers among us who were brought to the conclusion that our only salvation lies in the making of the race into a self-contained economic, social, and cultural unit; in a word, in the building of an *imperium in imperio*.

All along, however, majority opinion has held that the only salvation worth achieving lies in the making of the race into a component part of the nation, with all the common rights and privileges, as well as duties, of citizenship. This attitude has been basic in the general policy of the race — so far as it has had a general policy — for generations, the policy of striving zealously to gain full admission to citizenship and guarding jealously each single advance made.

But this question of direction, of goal, is not a settled one. There is in us all a stronger tendency toward isolation than we may be aware of. There come times when the most persistent integrationist becomes an isolationist, when he curses the White world and consigns it to hell. This tendency toward isolation is strong because it springs from a deep-seated, natural desire — a desire for respite from the unremitting, grueling struggle; for a place in which refuge might be taken. We are again and again confronted by this question. It is ever present, though often dormant. Recently it was emphatically brought forward by the utterances of so authoritative a voice as that of Dr. Du Bois.

The question is not one to be lightly brushed aside. Those who stand for making the race into a self-sufficient unit point out that after years of effort we are still Jim-Crowed, discriminated against, segregated, and lynched; that we are still shut out from industry, barred from the main avenues of business, and cut off from free participation in national life. They point out that in some sections of the country we have not even secured equal protection of life and property under the laws. They declare that entrance of the Negro into full citizenship is as distant as it was seventy years ago. And they ask: What is the Negro to do? Give himself over to wishful thinking? Stand shooting at the stars with a popgun? Is it not rather a duty and a necessity for him to face the facts of his condition and environment, to acknowledge them as facts, and to make the best use of them that he can? These are questions which the thinkers of the race should strive to sift clearly.

To this writer it seems that one of the first results of clear thinking is a realization of the truth that the making of the race into a self-sustaining unit, the creating of an *imperium in imperio,* does not offer an easier or more feasible task than does the task of achieving full citizenship. Such an *imperium* would have to rest upon a basis of separate group economic independence, and the trend of all present-day forces is against the building of any foundation of that sort.

After thoughtful consideration, I cannot see the slightest possibility of our being able to duplicate the economic and social machinery of the country. I do not believe that any other special group could do it. The isolationists declare that because of imposed segregation we have, to a large degree, already done it. But the situation they point to is more apparent than real. Our separate schools and some of our other race institutions, many of our race enterprises, the greater part of our employment, and most of our fundamental activities are contingent upon our interrelationship with the country as a whole.

Clear thinking reveals that the outcome of voluntary isolation would be a permanent secondary status, so acknowledged by the race. Such a status would, it is true, solve some phases of the race question. It would smooth away a good part of the friction and bring about a certain protection and security. The status of slavery carried some advantages of that sort. But I do not believe we shall ever be willing to pay such a price for security and peace.

If Negro Americans could do what reasonably appears to be impossible, and as a separate unit achieve self-sufficiency built upon group economic independence, does anyone suppose that that would abolish prejudice against them and allay opposition, or that the struggle to maintain their self-sufficiency would be in any degree less bitter than the present struggle to become an integral part of the nation? Taking into account human nature as it is, would not the achievement be more likely to arouse envy and bring on even more violent hatreds and persecutions?

Certainly, the isolationists are stating a truth when they contend that we should not, ostrich-like, hide our heads in the sand, making believe that prejudice is non-existent; but in so doing they are apostles of the obvious. Calling upon the race to realize that prejudice is an actuality is a needless effort; it is placing emphasis on what has never been questioned. The danger for us does not lie in a possible failure to acknowledge prejudice as a reality, but in acknowledging it too fully. We cannot ignore the fact that we are segregated, no matter how much we might wish to do so; and the smallest amount of common sense forces us to extract as much good from the situation as there is in it. Any degree of sagacity forces us at the same time to use all our powers to abolish imposed segregation; for it is an evil *per se* and the negation of equality either of opportunity or of awards. We should by all means make our schools and institutions as excellent as we can possibly make them — and by that very act we reduce the certainty that they will forever remain schools and institutions "for Negroes only." We should make our business enterprises and other strictly group undertakings as successful as we can possibly make them. We should gather all the strength and experience we can from imposed segregation. But any good we are able to derive from the system we should consider as a means, not an end. The strength and experience we gain from it should be applied to the objective of *entering into*, not *staying out of* the body politic.

Clear thinking shows, too, that, as bad as conditions are, they are not as bad as they are declared to be by discouraged and pessimistic isolationists. To say that in the past two generations or more Negro Americans have not advanced a single step toward a fuller share in the commonwealth becomes, in the light of easily ascertainable facts, an absurdity. Only the shortest view of the situation gives color of truth to such a statement; any reasonably long view proves it to be utterly false.

With our choice narrowed down to these two courses, wisdom and far-sightedness and possibility of achievement demand that we follow the line that leads to equal rights for us, based on the common terms and conditions under which they are accorded and guaranteed to the other groups that go into the making up of our national family. It is not necessary for our advancement that such an outcome should suddenly eradicate all prejudices. It would not, of course, have the effect of suddenly doing away with voluntary grouping in religious and secular organizations or of abolishing group enterprises — for example, Negro newspapers. The accordance of full civil and political rights has not in the case of the greater number of groups in the nation had that effect. Nevertheless, it would be an immeasurable step forward, and would place us where we had a fair start with the other American groups. More than that we do not need to ask.

Claude McKay
Harlem Runs Wild

Born in Jamaica, Claude McKay (1890–1948) wrote successfully in a number of genres. His poetry, especially *Harlem Shadows* (1922), and novels such as *Home to Harlem* (1928), *Banjo* (1929), and *Banana Bottom* (1933) made him a key figure of the Harlem Renaissance era even though he spent significant periods of time in France, Germany, North Africa, and Russia, where, after an initial attraction to communism during the early 1920s, he grew disillusioned with its social reality. He published an autobiography, *A Long Way from Home*, in 1937, and a few years later a wide-ranging social history entitled *Harlem: Negro Metropolis* (1940), which includes commentary on the political movements and economic conditions that intersected in depression-era Harlem and the civil disturbance known as the riot of 1935.

The 1935 outbreak of violence and looting was produced in part by the hardships of the depression, which hit urban African Americans with additional force; in part by longstanding employment and service discrimination against blacks (most businesses were white owned, and by one estimate only one hundred of the five thousand store employees concentrated along 125th Street, Harlem's main shopping district, were black); and in part by a random incident. At the W. H. Kress store, where the management had refused to hire any black clerks, a black youth accused of shoplifting was let go, but when rumors spread that he had been beaten to death by police, a crowd of people began to smash store windows and loot merchandise. Although the Communist Party can hardly be said to have caused the riot — a claim made by some at the time and one woven into Ellison's depiction of the riot that engulfs his protagonist — it was among the groups that organized protests against the racist employment practices of white merchants and the insufficient government relief afforded urban blacks; and soon after the crowd gathered, the militant Young Liberators, a communist youth group, distributed leaflets accusing the police of lynching. The violence left several African Americans dead, resulted in close to $2 million in property damage, and crystallized the desperate condition of many in Harlem.

To Alain Locke, the riot exposed the fragility of the relative prosperity
that had led to the Harlem Renaissance and forced him to reassess, in a
new essay titled "Harlem: Dark Weather-Vane," his earlier celebration
of the cultural promise of 1920s Harlem: "No emerging elite — artistic,
professional, or mercantile — can suspend itself in thin air over the abyss
of a mass of unemployed stranded in an over-expensive, disease- and
crime-ridden slum. It is easier to dally over black Bohemia or revel in the
hardy survivals of Negro art and culture than to contemplate this dark
Harlem of semi-starvation, mass exploitation and seething unrest" (457).
The following essay by Claude McKay, which appeared in the April 3,
1935 *Nation,* offers a succinct view of the conditions that made possible
the riot of 1935 and that had not changed dramatically by 1943, the date
of another significant Harlem riot on which Ellison drew in *Invisible
Man* (see p. 226 of this book).

FURTHER READING: Raymond Wolters, *Negroes and the Great Depression: The Problem of Economic Recovery* (Westport, CT: Greenwood, 1970); Harvard Sitkoff, *A New Deal for Blacks: The Emergence
of Civil Rights as an Issue* (New York: Oxford UP, 1978); Cheryl Lynn
Greenberg, *"Or Does It Explode?": Black Harlem in the Great Depression* (New York: Oxford UP, 1991).

Docile Harlem went on a rampage last week, smashing stores
and looting them and piling up destruction of thousands of dollars
worth of goods.

But the mass riot in Harlem was not a race riot. A few whites were
jostled by colored people in the melee, but there was no manifest hostility between colored and white as such. All night until dawn on the
Tuesday of the outbreak white persons, singly and in groups, walked
the streets of Harlem without being molested. The action of the police was commendable in the highest degree. The looting was brazen
and daring, but the police were restrained. In extreme cases, when
they fired, it was into the air. Their restraint saved Harlem from becoming a shambles.

The outbreak was spontaneous. It was directed against the stores
exclusively. One-Hundred-and-Twenty-fifth Street is Harlem's main
street and the theatrical and shopping center of the colored thousands. Anything that starts there will flash through Harlem as quick

as lightning. The alleged beating of a kid caught stealing a trifle in
one of the stores merely served to explode the smoldering discontent
of the colored people against the Harlem merchants.

It would be too sweeping to assert that radicals incited the Harlem
mass to riot and pillage. The Young Liberators seized an opportune
moment, but the explosion on Tuesday was not the result of Communist propaganda. There were, indeed, months of propaganda in it.
But the propagandists are eager to dissociate themselves from Communists. Proudly they declare that they have agitated only in the
American constitutional way for fair play for colored Harlem.

Colored people all over the world are notoriously the most ex-
ploitable material, and colored Harlem is no exception. The population is gullible to an extreme. And apparently the people are exploited so flagrantly because they invite and take it. It is their
gullibility that gives to Harlem so much of its charm, its air of insou-
ciance and gaiety. But the façade of the Harlem masses' happy-go-
lucky and hand-to-mouth existence has been badly broken by the depression. A considerable part of the population can no longer cling
even to the hand-to-mouth margin.

Wherever an ethnologically related group of people is exploited by
others, the exploiters often operate on the principle of granting certain concessions as sops. In Harlem the exploiting group is overwhelmingly white. And it gives no sops. And so for the past two years
colored agitators have exhorted the colored consumers to organize
and demand of the white merchants a new deal: that they should employ Negroes as clerks in the colored community. These agitators are
crude men, theoretically. They have little understanding of and little
interest in the American labor movement, even from the most conservative trade-union angle. They address their audience mainly on the
streets. Their following is not so big as that of the cultists and oc-
cultists. But it is far larger than that of the Communists.

One of the agitators is outstanding and picturesque. He dresses in
turban and gorgeous robe. He has a bigger following than his rivals.
He calls himself Sufi Abdul Hamid. His organization is the Negro Industrial and Clerical Alliance. It was the first to start picketing the
stores of Harlem demanding clerical employment for colored persons.
Sufi Hamid achieved a little success. A few of the smaller Harlem
stores engaged colored clerks. But on 125th Street the merchants
steadfastly refused to employ colored clerical help. The time came
when the Negro Industrial and Clerical Alliance felt strong enough to

picket the big stores on 125th Street. At first the movement got scant sympathy from influential Negroes and the Harlem intelligentsia as a whole. Physically and mentally, Sufi Hamid is a different type. He does not belong. And moreover he used to excoriate the colored newspapers, pointing out that they would not support his demands on the bigger Harlem stores because they were carrying the stores' little ads.

Harlem was excited by the continued picketing and the resultant "incidents." Sufi Hamid won his first big support last spring when one of the most popular young men in Harlem, the Reverend Adam Clayton Powell, Jr., assistant pastor of the Abyssinian Church — the largest in Harlem — went on the picket line on 125th Street. This gesture set all Harlem talking and thinking and made the headlines of the local newspapers. It prompted the formation of a Citizens' League for Fair Play. The league was indorsed and supported by sixty-two organizations, among which were eighteen of the leading churches of Harlem. And at last the local press conceded some support.

One of the big stores capitulated and took on a number of colored clerks. The picketing of other stores was continued. And soon business was not so good as it used to be on 125th Street.

In the midst of the campaign Sufi Hamid was arrested. Some time before his arrest a committee of Jewish Minute Men had visited the Mayor and complained about an anti-Semitic movement among the colored people and the activities of a black Hitler in Harlem. The *Day* and the *Bulletin,* Jewish newspapers, devoted columns to the Harlem Hitler and anti-Semitism among Negroes. The articles were translated and printed in the Harlem newspapers under big headlines denouncing the black Hitler and his work.

On October 13 of last year Sufi Hamid was brought before the courts charged with disorderly conduct and using invective against the Jews. The witnesses against him were the chairman of the Minute Men and other persons more or less connected with the merchants. After hearing the evidence and the defense, the judge decided that the evidence was biased and discharged Sufi Hamid. Meanwhile Sufi Hamid had withdrawn from the Citizens' League for Fair Play. He had to move from his headquarters and his immediate following was greatly diminished. An all-white Harlem Merchants' Association came into existence. Dissension divided the Citizens' League; the prominent members denounced Sufi Hamid and his organization.

In an interview last October Sufi Hamid told me that he had never styled himself the black Hitler. He said that once when he visited a store to ask for the employment of colored clerks, the proprietor remarked, "We are fighting Hitler in Germany." Sufi said that he replied, "There is no Hitler in Harlem." He went on to say that although he was a Moslem he had never entertained any prejudices against Jews as Jews. He was an Egyptian and in Egypt the relations between Moslem and Jew were happier than in any other country. He was opposed to Hitlerism, for he had read Hitler's book, "Mein Kampf," and knew Hitler's attitude and ideas about all colored peoples. Sufi Hamid said that the merchants of Harlem spread the rumor of anti-Semitism among the colored people because they did not want to face the issue of giving them a square deal.

The Citizens' League continued picketing, and some stores capitulated. But the Leaguers began quarreling among themselves as to whether the clerks employed should be light-skinned or dark-skinned. Meanwhile the united white Harlem Merchants' Association was fighting back. In November the picketing committee was enjoined from picketing by Supreme Court Justice Samuel Rosenman. The court ruled that the Citizens' League was not a labor organization. It was the first time that such a case had come before the courts of New York. The chairman of the picketing committee remarked that "the decision would make trouble in Harlem."

One by one the colored clerks who had been employed in 125th Street stores lost their places. When inquiries were made as to the cause, the managements gave the excuse of slack business. The clerks had no organization behind them. Of the grapevine intrigue and treachery that contributed to the débâcle of the movement, who can give the facts? They are as obscure and inscrutable as the composite mind of the Negro race itself. So the masses of Harlem remain disunited and helpless, while their would-be leaders wrangle and scheme and denounce one another to the whites. Each one is ambitious to wear the piebald mantle of Marcus Garvey.

On Tuesday the crowds went crazy like the remnants of a defeated, abandoned, and hungry army. Their rioting was the gesture of despair of a bewildered, baffled, and disillusioned people.

The Harlem riots of 1935 and 1943 were the result of mass public frustration with economic deprivation and racial injustice. The last scenes of *Invisible Man* are set against the backdrop of a Harlem uprising comparable to the one depicted in this 1943 photograph.

Adam Clayton Powell, Sr.

The Harlem Riot of 1943

As in the case of World War I, increased black migration to urban areas, expanded labor opportunities, and expectations of justice as a reward for service to the nation in wartime contributed to heightened racial antagonism on the home front during World War II. The 1943 riots by African Americans in Detroit, where twenty-five blacks were killed, mostly by police, and in Harlem, where injuries were fewer but looting more widespread, were the most visible signs of frustration with discrimination that exploded in various localities. During the same year, for example, Los Angeles was the scene of what were known as the Zoot-Suit Riots, violent clashes caused by white soldiers attacking Mexican Americans, especially those dressed in the flashy styles of the youths, some of them gang members, known as *pachucos*. A number of contemporary commentators pointed to nationwide incidents of racism and violence against black soldiers in particular as one cause of the Harlem riot, which was touched off when a policeman attempting to arrest a black woman shot a black soldier who protested the arrest. As Roy Wilkins wrote in *Crisis*, alluding to a slightly distorted rumor then circulating in New York, the Harlem mob "could not reach the Arkansas cop who fired a full magazine of his revolver into the prone body of a Negro sergeant, or any of the others, so it tore up Harlem" (Wilkins 263). Ellison had already written an essay on the 1863 draft riots in New York City for *The Negro in New York* (see p. 149 of this book), and he composed a journalistic report on the 1943 riot for the *New York Post* (Ellison, "Eyewitness Story of Riot"). According to several contemporary accounts, the riot had taken on a sometimes wild, festive atmosphere, which may have influenced Ellison's conception of the event when he reimagined it in *Invisible Man*.

Adam Clayton Powell, Sr. (1865–1953), was from 1908 to 1937 the pastor of the Abyssinian Baptist Church in New York, which, on its move to Harlem in 1923, became a center for black activism. He was also a founder of the Urban League, a black economic and civil rights organization, and the father of Adam Clayton Powell, Jr., who succeeded

him in the pulpit but was best known as a powerful congressman representing Harlem in the 1940s and 1950s. The selection below is drawn
from the elder Powell's book about Harlem's twentieth-century struggle
for social and economic justice, *Riots and Ruins* (1945).

FURTHER READING: Harold Orlansky, *The Harlem Riot: A Study in
Mass Frustration* (New York: Social Analysis, 1943); Arthur McClung
Lee, *Race Riot* (New York: Dryden, 1943); Dominic J. Capeci, *The
Harlem Riot of 1943* (Philadelphia: Temple UP, 1977).

It is just as impossible to know what one thing starts a race riot as
it is to know the one snowflake in the one hundred trillion flakes that
makes the avalanche go grinding, crushing, and thundering down the
Alps. All the veteran Alpine traveler can say is that that avalanche of
death and destruction was the result of an accumulation of snowflakes
for thousands of years.

To know the cause of race riots you must go back three hundred
and twenty-five years to a ship called *Jesus* which brought a load of
African slaves to Virginia. Half of them died of starvation, neglect,
and brutal treatment before the *Jesus* reached the shores of this country. The most dehumanizing chapter in the history of the world is the
story of American slavery from 1619 to 1865. For this reason no one
has ever written it correctly and no one can.

It ought to be a tradition without bitter memories that the Negroes
could celebrate the anniversary of the Emancipation Proclamation,
January first, like the Jews keep the annual Feast of the Passover but
the white man will not let them.

Those and their descendants who enslaved and brutalized the
Negro for two hundred and fifty years have not left a single stone un-
turned to keep the Negro from enjoying the rights, including the right
to freedom guaranteed by the Thirteenth Amendment to the Constitution of the United States. The Negroes' emancipation celebrations
are not occasions for rejoicing and praise but for hours of petitioning
and protesting. In political campaigns, state and federal legislative
halls, churches, religious conventions, and the homes, Negroes are
fighting for the protection of life, liberty, and property.

The United States Constitution gave all these things to the Negro
more than seventy-five years ago. What a parody on the Constitu-

tion, what a parody on justice, what a parody on the white man's
Christianity that the largest minority group in America has to fight
for its constitutional, human, and divine rights!

One of the largest audiences of Negroes ever seen in America was
at Madison Square Garden June 7, 1943. Every standing space was
occupied and, according to the daily papers, more than ten thousand
were on the outside. The People's Committee with headquarters at
Abyssinian Baptist Church, New York, drew a record-breaking
crowd of more than thirty thousand. Dr. A. Clayton Powell, Jr., pastor of the church and then city councilman is the moving spirit of the
Committee. That huge crowd not only paid an admission fee but it
gave in addition more than five thousand dollars to aid the fight for
freedom. "Freedom's Rally," the meeting was called. Some of the
best speakers from every section of the country were on the program.
The theme of the evening was "Let My People Go."

Why all this money and trouble to secure freedom seventy-nine
years after the death of the Emancipator? It is because the states
which mercilessly robbed the Negro for two hundred and fifty years
are still robbing him by filibustering in the United States Senate, by
extralegal devices to deprive him of the ballot, by shameful inequalities in public school appropriations, by lower wages and limited economic opportunities, by placing discriminatory laws upon the statute
books, and, worst of all, by creating an atmosphere in which he is in-
timidated, browbeaten, and lynched. In a word, they have annihilated
the freedom which Lincoln, the Union soldiers, and the United States
Constitution gave the Negro.

One old Civil War veteran said to me in a trembling voice that
night, "It looks like we fought and died in vain." The thought seemingly retarded his dying feet as they moved falteringly toward home.

So this young Negro in churches, in halls, and homes has to fight
the Civil War over when he should be giving himself whole-heartedly
to winning World War II. That fifty-thousand-dollar Madison Square
Garden meeting should have been in the interest of War Bonds, but
alas! . . .

Of all the riots in the United States since the Civil War, the Harlem
riot beginning Sunday evening, August 1, 1943, is the most puzzling.
It is puzzling because we have tried to view it as a whole instead of
seeing it as two distinct parts, as the remainder of this chapter and
the third chapter will show. While truckloads of window glass were
raining on every avenue from 110th Street to 145th Street, Mayor

LaGuardia was screaming from a sound truck or broadcasting, "This is not a race riot, go home, go to bed!" The enraged and outraged people hissed him, for they knew the Mayor was slandering them. These window-smashers were not looters, they were race rioters expressing their pent-up hatred of the white man's pagan civilization, called Christian. If these rioters smashed a window of a colored man's place of business, it was done ignorantly. If they touched a colored policeman it was because he was meddling in their business.

On Monday every daily paper and the colored weeklies that followed repeated the words of the Mayor. All carried editorials to the effect that we can bless our lucky stars that New York had escaped a race riot. All of those editorials also mentioned just causes for a race riot. Nearly all the accumulated grievances of the Negro from Jamestown to Stuyvesant Town were named. If it was not a race riot, why waste all this printer's ink and paper?

The New York Times, which is usually fair and tolerant in its attitude toward the Negro, had two excellent editorials on the Harlem race riot. One begins by repeating the Mayor's words that it was not a race riot and then ends by giving it all the marks of a race riot:

> Mayor LaGuardia was correct in the literal meaning of his words when he said that the disturbances which began in Harlem Sunday night were "not a race riot."

But read this paragraph:

> No friend of the Negro will defend the Harlem rioters. The overwhelming majority of Harlem's law-abiding people, who are as good and useful citizens as can be found anywhere, do not defend them. We have to ask, as we have to ask in instances of white hoodlumism, what produces such outbreaks. Immediate causes for it can be found in a sense of grievance fanned into flame by sinister agitators, lies deliberately spread, in an ignorance that might be diminished if white people in this city took a more friendly interest in the welfare of the new additions to our Negro population. Some of the ultimate causes have been explored again and again. Bad and costly housing, lack of recreational facilities, the failure to give equal economic opportunities — these things corrupt the weak and unstable among the Negro population just as they do among other varieties of population.

The *Times* recites enough grievances to touch off five race riots.

PM, which Harlemites read more than they do the Bible, carried thirteen pages on the riot in its August 3 issue. This paper, perhaps,

gets closer to the cause of the Harlem riot than any other daily in
New York, as the following paragraphs show:

> The City and Nation would make a grave mistake if they try to shake
> off this incident as just another riot. It is not a race riot in the strictly
> technical sense of physical conflict between two races. But it stems
> from essentially the same sources as created by the bloody outbreaks in
> Mobile, Beaumont and Detroit. In part, it climaxes the mounting ten-
> sions within the Harlem community itself, the piled-up resentments
> against segregation and discrimination, against the pushing around the
> Negro has been getting in civil and military life.
> The solution to this riot, as to the dangerous tensions accumulating
> in hundreds of Harlems throughout this land, must be sought in rea-
> son, not force; in justice, not repression; in understanding, not blind
> hate or fear.

Colored men who know Harlem better were not so easily misled
by Mayor LaGuardia's statement — "It is not a race riot." Roi Ottley, who was born in New York, covered Harlem as a reporter on
The Amsterdam-Star News for seven years, and is the author of *New
World A-Coming*, writes in the issue of *PM* just quoted:

> Harlem's rioting is clearly a protest against the flagrant jim crow pol-
> icy of the U.S. Army.
> Everyone who knows what's rankling in the hearts of Negroes con-
> cedes that their treatment as soldiers is the most inflammatory point on
> a long agenda of injustice.
> Sunday night's incident is only a part of an ominous pattern. The
> facts fit together neatly, almost prosaically — and indeed have an all
> too familiar ring.

Roy Wilkins, assistant secretary of the N.A.A.C.P., is one of the
brainiest young men in the race. He is locally and nationally known.
He knows the Negro in Harlem and the soul of the Negro in America. For years he has been a newspaper columnist and the editor of
The Crisis, the most sanely radical magazine in America. In the Sep-
tember 1943 issue of that monthly the leading editorial is on the
Harlem riot. Regardless of the opinion of Mayor LaGuardia or any
city newspaper, Mr. Wilkins treats it as a race riot motivated by the
venomous recollection of the way the Negro soldiers have been mis-
treated in all parts of the "land of the free and the home of the
brave." Here is an excerpt which tells the brief story and gives his
opinion of the riot:

A soldier in uniform was shot by a policeman in Harlem. The question of who was right and who wrong at the moment did not interest the mob. Mobs, white or black, don't reason. The white Beaumont mob did not reason. A white woman had not been raped, but you could not tell them that — not that night. So, in Harlem the wildfire story was of the shooting of a Negro soldier in uniform by a civilian policeman.

Negro soldiers have been shot down by civilian police in Alexandria, La., in Little Rock, Ark., in Baltimore, Md., in Beaumont, Texas, and in a half dozen other places. They have been humiliated, manhandled, and beaten in countless instances.

The Harlem mob knew all this. It hated all this. It could not reach the Arkansas cop who fired a full magazine of his revolver into the prone body of a Negro sergeant, or any of the others, so it tore up Harlem.

Here is the plain truth, stripped of all those false and slanderous trappings, of what happened. On Sunday evening, August 1, 1943, when forty thousand people were being dismissed from Harlem churches with the Benediction "grace, mercy, and peace," and were on their way home, they passed through the hottest hell ever created in Harlem. Let us see if Mr. Wilkins is correct in calling this a race riot.

That evening about 7:30 o'clock a white policeman, James Collins, was called to the Hotel Braddock on West 126 Street to arrest a colored woman on a charge of disorderly conduct. While performing his duty, Pvt. Robert Bandy, a colored MP from New Jersey, twisted the nightstick from the white cop's hand and struck him over the head with it and ran. Collins shot Bandy, inflicting a slight wound. The news was flashed to every section of Harlem that a white policeman had shot a colored soldier. Some said he was dead or dying in the hospital. Thousands stormed the precinct on West 123rd Street and Sydenham Hospital.

On reaching home I was informed by one of our church workers that six carloads of soldiers had left a given point to wreak vengeance on a white policeman for killing one of their comrades. I phoned the 28th Precinct, to which a number of my friends are attached, that the soldiers were on their way there with blood in their eyes. I offered my services to the officer at the desk, saying — "I have been in Harlem thirty-six years, helped to feed, clothe and to find work for its citizens during the long years of depression. Perhaps they will hear me." But it was too late, the hurricane had broken loose. Within ninety min-

utes there were few glass windows and iron gratings left in any of the
white business places on Lenox, Seventh, and Eighth avenues and in
most of the main crosstown streets. The Germans and Japanese could
not have played more havoc.

Bandy and ninety-five per cent of these window-smashers were not
looters, burglars, and thieves; most of them were honest citizens.
When Bandy hit Collins over the head with that club, he was not mad
with him only for arresting a colored woman, but he was mad with
every white policeman throughout the United States who had constantly beaten, wounded, and often killed colored men and women
without provocation. Those window-smashers were not mad with the
windows, they were mad with all the white men living or dead who
had heaped every insult and indignity upon them for centuries. When
they were smashing windows they thought they were breaking the
skulls of Ben Tillman, Cole Blease, Cotton Ed Smith, Dixon of Alabama, and Bilbo, Rankin, and the whole Mississippi tribe of race-
haters and race-baiters. They were wrong, terribly wrong, but they
were mad and mad men are always abnormal.

Moses was mad when he beat the rocks. The rocks had not done
anything to Moses. The Israelites had treated him outrageously so he
tried to get even with them by giving the rocks the worst lashing they
ever had.

The Beaumont white people were mad when they burned the
homes of Negroes. The white men of Detroit were crazy mad when
they drove around in cars looking for innocent Negroes to shoot.

The white mobs who during my lifetime have lynched five thousand Negroes, in many cases burning their bodies chained to stakes,
selling their fingers, slices of liver, and sex organs for souvenirs, were
disgracefully mad. In the face of all the examples given him by the
white man, who will be the first to throw a stone at the Negro for
being as mad as hell and beating Harlem property until its screams
were heard from Central Park to Sugar Hill?

If the first wave on that Sunday night was not a race riot, then we
have never had one in the United States.

Ralph Ellison

The Negro and the Second World War

Even though African Americans made significant gains in civil rights and economic opportunity during World War II, they did so primarily through effective leadership and organizing. In a 1943 editorial from *Negro Quarterly* reprinted below, Ralph Ellison (1914–1994) wrote his fullest essay on the war. In it he makes clear that the war provided an arena in which blacks could fight on two fronts at once. The campaign for the "Double V" — victory abroad in the military, and victory at home against racism and discrimination — was a common political slogan and the occasion for many important books and essays aimed at the destruction of Jim Crow. In *Marching Blacks* (1945) Adam Clayton Powell, Jr., who succeeded his father (author of the preceding selection) as Harlem's leading minister before going on to a long political career as its congressional representative, described African American participation in the "white man's war" in a telling way: "On December 7, 1941, America for the first time in its history entered upon two wars simultaneously. One was a world war and the other a civil war. One was to be a bloody fight for the preservation and extension of democracy on a world basis — the other a bloodless revolution within these shores against a bastard democracy" (Powell, *Marching Blacks* 125). Among the important documents produced by the crisis at home was a collection of essays titled *What the Negro Wants* (1944), edited by Rayford W. Logan and containing essays on the state of black cultural and social life by prominent black figures such as Sterling Brown, Mary McLeod Bethune, A. Philip Randolph, and George Schuyler. Randolph's contribution, for instance, was one of his many statements advocating a massive march on Washington to demand black rights — an event finally realized in 1963 in the national gathering that culminated in Martin Luther King, Jr.'s famous "I Have a Dream" address. In addition to writing about school segregation and zoot suit youth, the black psychologist Kenneth Clark contributed an essay on African Americans to a 1942 volume on civilian morale (Clark, "Morale Among Negroes").

Taking its title from a jazz classic recorded by Lionel Hampton and others, one of Ellison's earliest and best short stories, "Flying Home"

(1944), combines reflections on the segregated training of black Air
Force pilots at Tuskegee during World War II with elements of black
folklore about the ability of African Americans to fly. The story is a brilliant comic counterpart to the more somber arguments of the essay
below, which was featured in the same issue of *Negro Quarterly* that carried the black communist Angelo Herndon's essay about Frederick Douglass as an African American leader whose qualities might well be emu-
lated in the 1940s. Ellison's essay is important, in part, for its clear
enunciation of an underlying motive for the cultural rebellion signaled in
the rise of a hipster youth culture, whose zoot suits, dark glasses, and
conked hair gave style a political dimension (see p. 136 of this book). Between the essays of Herndon and Ellison, one can find two important
strands of the search for leadership that the novel's protagonist engages
in as he weighs the liabilities of black participation in the Communist
Party (see pp. 18–20 of this book).

FURTHER READING: Mary Penick Motley, ed., *The Invisible Soldier:
The Experience of the Black Soldier, World War II* (Detroit: Wayne
State UP, 1975); Neil A. Wynn, *The Afro-American and the Second
World War* (New York: Holmes and Meier, 1976); John Morton Blum,
V Was for Victory: Politics and American Culture during World War II
(San Diego: Harcourt, 1976); C. L. R. James, et al., *Fighting Racism in
World War II* (New York: Monad, 1980).

By way of group self-examination it might be profitable to list a
few of the general attitudes held by Negroes toward their war-time
experiences.

First might be listed the attitude of unqualified acceptance of the
limited opportunity for Negro participation in the conflict: whether
in the war industries or in the armed forces. Along with this is found
an acceptance of the violence and discrimination which so contradicts
a war for the Four Freedoms. This attitude is justified by the theory
that for Negroes to speak out in their own interest would be to follow a "narrow Negro approach" and to disrupt war-unity. This attitude (sometimes honestly held) arises, on one hand, out of a lack of
group self-consciousness which precludes any confidence in the
Negro people's own judgment, or in its potentialities for realizing its
own will. Others who voice this attitude, however, are simply expressing what they are paid to express. Still others suffer from what

might be termed a "disintegration of the sense of group personality." For these the struggle has been too difficult: in order to survive they feel that Negroes must resort to the most vicious forms of the uncle-tomism. Its most extreme expression, to date, has been Warren Brown's plaint — in the face of the United States' glaring jimciuw system — that most of the Negro press desires to be "Negro first and American second." While another striking instance of it is seen among those Negro actors who continue to accept Hollywood's anti-Negro roles.

Back of this attitude lies a fear and uncertainty that is almost psychopathic. It results in the most disgusting forms of self-abasement. The decadent Negro counterpart of American rugged individualism, it would willingly have the Negro people accept the depths of degradation rather than risk offending white men by lifting a hand in its own defense. Men who hold this attitude are comfortable only when taking orders: they are happy only when being kicked. It is this basic attitude that produces the spy, the stool pigeon, and the agent provocateur — all of which types are found today among those who call themselves Negro leaders.

A second attitude encountered is that of *unqualified rejection:* of the war; of the Allies' statement of their war aims; and of the role which Negroes have been elected to play in any of its phases. Arising out of a type of Negro nationalism which, in a sense, is admirable, it would settle all problems on the simple principle that Negroes deserve equal treatment with all other free human beings. It is this which motivates those Negroes who go to jail rather than endure the Jim Crow conditions in the Armed forces. It is the basis of Negro cynicism and it views every situation which requires Negroes to struggle against fascist forces within our own country as evidence that the United States is fighting a "white man's" war.

But this is the attitude of one who, driven into a corner, sees no way of asserting his manhood except to choose his own manner of dying. And during the folk period, before the Negro masses became politically conscious, such an attitude created folk heroes and gave birth to legend and folksong. For Negroes admire men who die rather than compromise their principles. But on the day John Henry's great heart was burst in his struggle against the machine, this attitude became impractical. Today we live in a political world and such an attitude is inadequate to deal with its complex problems. Not that the courageous display of manhood no longer has a place in our lives, but that when asserted blindly it results only in empty, individualistic action — or worse, admiration for the ruthless and violent *action* of fascism. Feeling that so much experienced by Negroes in the U.S. is tinged with fascism, some Negroes went so far as to join the pro-Japanese Pacific Movement.

Superficially, this attitude seems the direct opposite of the first; and in basic human terms it is. Yet, when expressed in action in the present political situation it is revealed as a mere *inversion* of the first. For in its blind rejection it falls over backwards into an even blinder acceptance. Unconsciously it regards all acts of aggression against Negroes as inevitable, the forces behind these acts as invincible. Being blind it does not recognize that Negroes *have their own stake in the defeat of fascism* — which would be true even if white Americans were still practising isolationism. It conceives of positive action for the Negro people only in terms of death — or passivity, which is another form of death. Individuals who hold this attitude become conscious of themselves *as Negroes* only in terms of dying; they visualize themselves only as followers, never as leaders. Deep down they see no possibility of an Allied victory being a victory for Negroes as well as for others. Refusing to see the *peoples* aspect of the war, they conceive of victory as the triumph of "good white men" over "bad white men"; never as the triumph of the common peoples of the world over those who foster decayed political forms and systems. Should "good white men" triumph they will, perhaps, *give* Negroes a few more opportunities. Should "bad white men" win, then things will continue as before, perhaps a little worse. And since during the course of the war the sincerity of even good white men frequently appears doubtful, the Negro can expect but little in any case.

This is a political form of self-pity, and an attitude of political children. Actually it holds no desire for Negroes to assume an adult role in government. And perhaps its most naive expression is found among those who, frustrated and impotent before the complex problems of the Negro situation, would resort to a primitive form of magic and solve the whole problem by simply abolishing the word *Negro* from the American language. It never occurs to them that no matter what name they give themselves that name will mean no more than they can *make* it mean. Nor do they understand that in the process of fighting for a free American and a free world, Negro Americans (insofar as they approach it consciously) are also creating themselves as a free people and as a nation.

Fortunately there is a third attitude. Also a manifestation of Negro nationalism, it is neither an attitude of blind acceptance, nor one of unqualified rejection. It is broader and more human than the first two attitudes; and it is scientific enough to make use of both by transforming them into strategies of struggle. It is committed to life and it holds that the main task of the Negro people is to work unceasingly toward creating those democratic conditions in which it can live and re-create itself. It believes the historical role of Negroes to be that of integrating the larger American nation and compelling it untiringly toward true freedom. And while it will have none of the slavishness of the first attitude, it is imaginative and flexible enough, to die if dying is forced upon it.

This is an attitude of critical participation, based upon a sharp sense of the Negro people's group personality. Which is the basis of its self-confidence and morale in this period of confusion. Thus, while affirming the justice of the Allies' cause, it never loses sight of the Negro peoples' stake in the struggle. This for them is the point of departure, a basic guide to theory and action which allows for objectivity and guards against both the fearful acceptance of the first and the sullen rejection of the second. It regards men unsentimentally; their virtues are evaluated and cherished, their weakness anticipated and guarded against. This attitude holds that any action which is advantageous to the United Nations must also be advantageous for the Negro and colonial peoples. Programs which would sacrifice the Negro or any other people are considered dangerous for the United Nations; and the only honorable course for Negroes to take is first to protest and then to fight against them. And while willing to give and take in the interest of national unity, it rejects that old pattern of American thought that regards any Negro demand for justice as treasonable, or any Negro act of self-defense as an assault against the state. It believes that to fail to protest the wrongs done Negroes as we fight this war is to participate in a crime, not only against Negroes, but against all true anti-Fascists. To fight against defects in our prosecution of the war is regarded as a responsibility. To remain silent simply because friends commit these wrongs is no less dangerous than if Negroes should actively aid the enemy.

Recently this attitude has led Negroes to employ the contradictory tactic of withdrawal for the purpose of closer unity. It motivated Judge William H. Hastie's resignation from the War Department, where it was expected of him to remain silent while the window-dressing air school at Tuskegee was palmed off on the American people as the real thing. For Hastie this might have been an act of courage which lost him prestige among Fascist-minded whites, but it has made his name meaningful among thousands of Negroes, bringing eligibility for that support which is the basis of true leadership. One wonders when the other members of the so-called "Black Cabinet" will learn this basic truth? As yet, however, this attitude is found implied in the sentiments of the Negro masses, rather than in the articulated programs of those who would lead them. Hastie's action is the first by a public figure.

The existence of the attitude, however, emphasizes more than ever before the need for representative Negroes to come to terms with their own group through a consideration of the major problems of our revolutionary times. First in terms of the problem of the centralization of political power. They must (1) see the Negro people realistically as a political and economic force which has, since the Civil War, figured vitally in the great contest for power between the two large economic groups within the country; that (2) despite the very real class divisions within the Negro group itself during periods of crisis — especially during periods of war — these divisions are partially suspended by outside pressures, making for a kind of group unity in which great potential political power becomes centralized — even though Negro leadership ignores its existence, or are too timid to seize and give it form and direction; that (3) although logically and historically the Negro's interests are one with those of Labor, this power is an objective force which might be channelized for Fascist ends as well as for democratic ones; and (4) that they as leaders have a responsibility in seeing to it that this vital force does not work for Fascism — either native or foreign. To the extent that Negro leadership ignores the power potential of the group, to that extent will the Negro people be exploited by others: either for the good ends of democratic groups or for the bad ends of Fascist groups. And they have the Civil War to teach them that no revolutionary situation in the United States will be carried any farther toward fullfilling the needs of Negroes than Negroes themselves are able, through a strategic application of their own power to make it go. As long as Negroes fail to centralize their power they will always play the role of a sacrificial goat, they will always be "expendable." Freedom, after all, cannot be imported or acquired through an act of philanthropy, it must be won.

In order to plan the direction of power, Negro leaders must obey the impetus toward Negro self-evaluation which the war has made a necessity. They must integrate themselves with the Negro masses; they must be constantly alert to new concepts, new techniques, and new trends among other peoples and nations with an eye toward appropriating those which are valid when tested against the reality of Negro life. By the same test they must be just as alert to reject the faulty programs of their friends. When needed concepts, techniques, or theories do not exist they must create them. Many new concepts will evolve when the people are closely studied in action. And it will be out of this process that true Negro leadership will come; fortunately, the era of subsidized Negro leadership is fast passing. Even the mild protest of a William Pickens has become too radical for those who for years have pulled the strings of Negro middle class leadership.

A second problem for Negro leadership to master is that of accurately defining the relation between the increasing innovations in technology and the Negro peoples' political and economic survival and advancement. During the war the mastery of hitherto unavailable techniques by Negroes is equivalent to the winning of a major military objective; after the war they will be politically effective to the extent that they are able to give leadership to the working class; and that leadership always rests with those workers who are most skilled.

A third major problem, and one that is indispensible to the centralization and direction of power, is that of learning the meaning of the myths and symbols which abound among the Negro masses. For without this knowledge, leadership, no matter how correct its program, will fail. Much in Negro life remains a mystery; perhaps the zoot suit conceals profound political meaning; perhaps the symmetrical frenzy of the Lindy-hop conceals clues to great potential power — if only Negro leaders would solve this riddle. On this knowledge depends the effectiveness of any slogan or tactic. For instance, it is obvious that Negro resentment over their treatment at the hands of their allies is justified. This naturally makes for a resistance to our stated war aims, even though these aims are essentially correct; and they will be accepted by the Negro masses only to the extent that they are helped to see the bright star of their own hopes through the fog of their daily experiences. The problem is psychological; it will be solved only by a Negro leadership that is aware of the psychological attitudes and incipient forms of action which the black masses reveal in their emotion-charged myths, symbols, and wartime folklore. Only

through a skillful and wise manipulation of these centers of repressed
social energy will Negro resentment, self-pity, and indignation be
channelized to cut through temporary issues and become transformed
into positive action. This is not to make the problem simply one of
words, but to recognize (as does the O.W.I. with its fumbling *Negroes and the War* pamphlet) that words have their own vital importance.

Negro participation in other groups is valuable only to the extent
that it is objectively aggressive and aware of this problem of self-
knowledge. For no matter how sincere their intentions, misunder-
standings between Negroes and whites are inevitable at this period of
our history. And unless these leaders are objective and aggressive they
have absolutely no possibility of leading the black masses — who are
thoroughly experienced with leaders who, in all crucial situations, ca-
pitulate to whites — in any direction. Thus instead of participating
along with labor and other progressive groups as equals with the
adult responsibility of seeing to it that all policies are formulated and
coordinated with full consideration of the complexities of the Negro
situation, they will have in effect, chosen simply to be subsidized by
Labor rather than by Capital.

Finally, the attitudes listed above must be watched, whether dis-
played by individuals or organizations. They take many forms; the
first two being exploited by those who like the Negro best when he is
unthinking or passive. The second will help only Fascism. The third
contains the hope of the Negro people and is spreading; but these
hopes can be used by the charlatan and agent provocateur as well as
by the true leader. In this time of confusion many wild and aggressive-
sounding programs will be expounded by Negroes who, seeking personal power, would lead the people along paths *away* from any creative action. Thus all programs must be measured coldly against
reality. Both leaders and organizations must be measured not by their
words, but by their actions.

Ralph Ellison
Harlem Is Nowhere

Ellison's essay on the Lafargue Psychiatric Clinic, the selection that follows, is the occasion for his meditation on the surrealism produced by the collision of deprivation and creativity in Harlem. The essay, written in 1948, isolates features of ghetto life at the historical moment of the 1930s and 1940s when Ellison himself, like other New York black intellectuals, found Harlem to offer a plenitude of cultural stimulation predicated in part on its separation from the rest of the city, its being "the shining transcendence of a national negative [that] took its fullest meaning from that which it was not" (Ellison, "An Extravagance of Laughter" 157). In providing an answer of "Oh, man, I'm *nowhere*" to the question of "Who am I, What am I, Why am I, and Where," the essay also links the protagonist's experience in the Liberty Paints episode and on the streets of Harlem to the book's overarching theme of the elusiveness of self-discovery. "Outside the Brotherhood we were outside history," his protagonist muses, "but inside of it they didn't see us. It was a hell of a state of affairs, we were nowhere" (*Invisible Man* 499–500).

FURTHER READING: John Henrik Clarke, ed., *Harlem, U.S.A.* (rev. ed., New York: Collier, 1971); James De Jongh, *Vicious Modernism: Black Harlem and the Literary Imagination* (New York: Cambridge UP, 1990).

One must descend to the basement and move along a confusing mazelike hall to reach it. Twice the passage seems to lead against a blank wall; then at last one enters the brightly lighted auditorium. And here, finally, are the social workers at the reception desks; and there, waiting upon the benches rowed beneath the pipes carrying warmth and water to the floors above, are the patients. One sees white-jacketed psychiatrists carrying charts appear and vanish behind screens that form the improvised interviewing cubicles. All is an atmosphere of hurried efficiency; and the concerned faces of the pa-

tients are brightened by the friendly smiles and low-pitched voices of
the expert workers. One has entered the Lafargue Psychiatric Clinic.

This clinic (whose staff receives no salary and whose fee is only
twenty-five cents — to those who can afford it) is perhaps the most
successful attempt in the nation to provide psychotherapy for the underprivileged. Certainly it has become in two years one of Harlem's
most important institutions. Not only is it the sole mental clinic in the
section, it is the only center in the city wherein both Negroes and
whites may receive extended psychiatric care. Thus its importance
transcends even its great value as a center for psychotherapy: it represents an underground extension of democracy.

As one of the few institutions dedicated to recognizing the total
implication of Negro life in the United States, the Lafargue Clinic rejects all stereotypes, and may be said to concern itself with any possible variations between the three basic social factors shaping an American Negro's personality: he is viewed as a member of a racial and
cultural minority; as an American citizen caught in certain political
and economic relationships; and as a modern man living in a revolutionary world. Accordingly, each patient, whether white or black, is
approached dynamically as a being possessing a cultural and biological past who seeks to make his way toward the future in a world
wherein each discovery about himself must be made in the here and
now at the expense of hope, pain, and fear — a being who in re-
sponding to the complex forces of America has become confused.

Leaving the Lafargue Clinic for a while, what are some of the
forces which generate this confusion? Who is this total Negro whom
the clinic seeks to know; what is the psychological character of the
scene in which he dwells; how describe the past which he drags into
this scene, and what is the future toward which he stumbles and becomes confused? Let us begin with the scene: Harlem.

To live in Harlem is to dwell in the very bowels of the city; it is to
pass a labyrinthine existence among streets that explode monoto-
nously skyward with the spires and crosses of churches and clutter
under foot with garbage and decay. Harlem is a ruin — many of its
ordinary aspects (its crimes, its casual violence, its crumbling buildings with littered areaways, ill-smelling halls, and vermin-invaded
rooms) are indistinguishable from the distorted images that appear in
dreams, and which, like muggers haunting a lonely hall, quiver in the
waking mind with hidden and threatening significance. Yet this is no
dream but the reality of well over four hundred thousand Americans;
a reality which for many defines and colors the world. Overcrowded

and exploited politically and economically, Harlem is the scene and symbol of the Negro's perpetual alienation in the land of his birth.

But much has been written about the social and economic aspects of Harlem; we are here interested in its psychological character — a character that arises from the impact between urban slum conditions and folk sensibilities. Historically, American Negroes are caught in a vast process of change that has swept them from slavery to the condition of industrial man in a space of time so telescoped (a bare eighty-five years) that it is possible literally for them to step from feudalism into the vortex of industrialism simply by moving across the Mason-Dixon line.

This abruptness of change and the resulting clash of cultural factors within Negro personality account for some of the extreme contrasts found in Harlem, for both its negative and its positive characteristics. For if Harlem is the scene of the folk-Negro's death agony, it is also the setting of his transcendence. Here it is possible for talented youths to leap through the development of decades in a brief twenty years, while beside them white-haired adults crawl in the feudal darkness of their childhood. Here a former cotton picker develops the sensitive hands of a surgeon, and men whose grandparents still believe in magic prepare optimistically to become atomic scientists. Here the grandchildren of those who possessed no written literature examine their lives through the eyes of Freud and Marx, Kierkegaard and Kafka, Malraux and Sartre. It explains the nature of a world so fluid and shifting that often within the mind the real and the unreal merge, and the marvelous beckons from behind the same sordid reality that denies its existence.

Hence the most surreal fantasies are acted out upon the streets of Harlem; a man ducks in and out of traffic shouting and throwing imaginary grenades that actually exploded during World War I; a boy participates in the rape-robbery of his mother; a man beating his wife in a park uses boxing "science" and observes Marquess of Queensberry rules (no rabbit punching, no blows beneath the belt); two men hold a third while a lesbian slashes him to death with a razor blade; boy gangsters wielding homemade pistols (which in the South of their origin are but toy symbols of adolescent yearning for manhood) shoot down their young rivals. Life becomes a masquerade, exotic costumes are worn every day. Those who cannot afford to hire a horse wear riding habits; others who could not afford a hunting trip or who seldom attend sporting events carry shooting sticks.

For this is a world in which the major energy of the imagination

goes not into creating works of art, but to overcome the frustrations
of social discrimination. Not quite citizens and yet Americans, full of
the tensions of modern man but regarded as primitives, Negro Americans are in desperate search for an identity. Rejecting the second-class
status assigned them, they feel alienated and their whole lives have
become a search for answers to the questions: Who am I, What am I,
Why am I, and Where? Significantly, in Harlem the reply to the greet-
ing, "How are you?" is very often, "Oh, man, I'm *nowhere*" — a
phrase revealing an attitude so common that it has been reduced to a
gesture, a seemingly trivial word. Indeed, Negroes are not unaware
that the conditions of their lives demand new definitions of terms like
primitive and *modern, ethical* and *unethical, moral* and *immoral, patriotism* and *treason, tragedy* and *comedy, sanity* and *insanity.*

But for a long time now — despite songs like the "Blow Top
Blues" and the eruption of expressions like *frantic, buggy,* and *mad*
into Harlem's popular speech, doubtless a word-magic against the
states they name — calm in face of the unreality of Negro life becomes increasingly difficult. And while some seek relief in strange
hysterical forms of religion, in alcohol and drugs, and others learn to
analyze the causes for their predicament and join with others to correct them, an increasing number have found their way to the Lafargue Psychiatric Clinic.

In relation to their Southern background, the cultural history of
Negroes in the North reads like the legend of some tragic people out
of mythology, a people which aspired to escape from its own un-
happy homeland to the apparent peace of a distant mountain; but
which, in migrating, made some fatal error of judgment and fell into
a great chasm of mazelike passages that promise ever to lead to the
mountain but end ever against a wall. Not that a Negro is worse off
in the North than in the South, but that in the North he surrenders
and does not replace certain important supports to his personality.
He leaves a relatively static social order in which, having experienced
its brutality for hundreds of years — indeed, having been formed
within it and by it — he has developed those techniques of survival to
which Faulkner refers as "endurance," and an ease of movement
within explosive situations which makes Hemingway's definition of
courage, "grace under pressure," appear mere swagger. He surrenders the protection of his peasant cynicism — his refusal to hope for
the fulfillment of hopeless hopes — and his sense of being "at home
in the world" gained from confronting and accepting (for day-to-day

living, at least) the obscene absurdity of his predicament. Further, he leaves a still authoritative religion which gives his life a semblance of metaphysical wholeness; a family structure which is relatively stable; and a body of folklore — tested in life-and-death terms against his daily experience with nature and the Southern white man — that serves him as a guide to action.

These are the supports of Southern Negro rationality (and, to an extent, of the internal peace of the United States); humble, but of inestimable psychological value, they allow Southern Negroes to maintain their almost mystical hope for a future of full democracy — a hope accompanied by an irrepressible belief in some Mecca of equality, located in the North and identified by the magic place names New York, Chicago, Detroit. A belief sustained (as all myth is sustained by ritual) by identifying themselves ritually with the successes of Negro celebrities, by reciting their exploits and enumerating their dollars, and by recounting the swiftness with which they spiral from humble birth to headline fame. And doubtless the blasting of this dream is as damaging to Negro personality as the slum scenes of filth, disorder, and crumbling masonry in which it flies apart.

When Negroes are barred from participating in the main institutional life of society they lose far more than economic privileges or the satisfaction of saluting the flag with unmixed emotions. They lose one of the bulwarks which men place between themselves and the constant threat of chaos. For whatever the assigned function of social institutions, their psychological function is to protect the citizen against the irrational, incalculable forces that hover about the edges of human life like cosmic destruction lurking within an atomic stockpile.

And it is precisely the denial of this support through segregation and discrimination that leaves the most balanced Negro open to anxiety.

Though caught not only in the tensions arising from his own swift history, but in those conflicts created in modern man by a revolutionary world, he cannot participate fully in the therapy which the white American achieves through patriotic ceremonies and by identifying himself with American wealth and power. Instead, he is thrown back upon his own "slum-shocked" institutions.

But these, like his folk personality, are caught in a process of chaotic change. His family disintegrates, his church splinters; his folk wisdom is discarded in the mistaken notion that it in no way applies

to urban living; and his formal education (never really his own) provides him with neither scientific description nor rounded philosophical interpretation of the profound forces that are transforming his
total being. Yet even his art is transformed; the lyrical ritual elements
of folk jazz — that artistic projection of the only real individuality
possible for him in the South, that embodiment of a superior democracy in which each individual cultivated his uniqueness and yet did
not clash with his neighbors — have given way to the near-themeless
technical virtuosity of bebop, a further triumph of technology over
humanism. His speech hardens; his movements are geared to the time
clock; his diet changes; his sensibilities quicken and his intelligence
expands. But without institutions to give him direction, and lacking a
clear explanation of his predicament — the religious ones being inadequate, and those offered by political and labor leaders obviously incomplete and opportunistic — the individual feels that his world and
his personality are out of key. The phrase "I'm nowhere" expresses
the feeling borne in upon many Negroes that they have no stable, recognized place in society. One's identity drifts in a capricious reality in
which even the most commonly held assumptions are questionable.
One "is" literally, but one is nowhere; one wanders dazed in a ghetto
maze, a "displaced person" of American democracy.

   And as though all this were not enough of a strain on a people's
sense of the rational, the conditions under which it lives are seized
upon as proof of its inferiority. Thus the frustrations of Negro life
(many of them the frustrations of *all* life during this historical moment) permeate the atmosphere of Harlem with what Dr. Frederick
Wertham, Director of the Lafargue Clinic, terms "free-floating hostility," a hostility that bombards the individual from so many directions
that he is often unable to identify it with any specific object. Some
feel it the punishment of some racial or personal guilt and pray to
God; others (called "evil Negroes" in Harlem) become enraged with
the world. Sometimes it provokes dramatic mass responses, and the
results are the spontaneous outbreaks called the "Harlem riots" of
1935 and 1943.

   And why have these explosive matters — which are now a problem of our foreign policy — been ignored? Because there is an argument in progress between black men and white men as to the true nature of American reality. Following their own interests, whites
impose interpretations upon Negro experience that are not only false
but, in effect, a denial of Negro humanity (witness the shock when A.

Philip Randolph questions, on the basis of Negro experience, the meaning of *treason*). Too weak to shout down these interpretations, Negroes live nevertheless as they have to live, and the concrete conditions of their lives are more real than white men's arguments.

And it is here exactly that lies the importance of the Lafargue Psychiatric Clinic — both as a scientific laboratory and as an expression of forthright democratic action in its scientific willingness to dispense with preconceived notions and accept the realities of Negro, i.e., *American* life. It recognizes that the personality damage that brought it into being represents not the disintegration of a people's fiber, but the failure of a way of life. For not only is it an antidote to this failure, it represents a victory over another of its aspects.

For ten years, while heading various psychiatric institutions, Dr. Wertham had fought for a psychiatric center in which Negroes could receive treatment. But whether he approached politicians, city agencies, or philanthropists, all gave excuses for not acting. The agencies were complacent, the politicians accused him of harboring political rather than humanitarian motives; certain liberal middlemen, who stand between Negroes and philanthropic dollars, accused him of trying to establish a segregated institution. Finally it was decided to establish the clinic without money or official recognition. The results were electric. When his fellow psychiatrists were asked to contribute their services, Dr. Wertham was overwhelmed with offers. These physicians, all of whom hold jobs in institutions which discriminate against Negroes, were eager to overcome this frustration to their science; and like some Southern Negroes who consider that part of themselves best which they hide beneath their servility, they consider their most important work that which is carried out in a Harlem basement.

Here, in the basement, a frustrated science goes to find its true object: the confused of mind who seek reality. Both find the source of their frustrations in the sickness of the social order. As such, and in spite of the very fine work it is doing, a thousand Lafargue clinics could not dispel the sense of unreality that haunts Harlem. Knowing this, Dr. Wertham and his interracial staff seek a modest achievement: to give each bewildered patient an insight into the relation between his problems and his environment, and out of this understanding to reforge the will to endure in a hostile world.

Bibliography

Further readings relevant to individual topics in this volume are listed after the headnote to each selection. The following bibliography contains works quoted in the Introduction and headnotes, as well as selected key volumes or collections of essays devoted to Ralph Ellison.

Allen, William Francis. *Slave Songs of the United States.* 1867. Rpt. New York: Arno, 1971.
Anderson, Jervis. *This Was Harlem, 1900–1950.* New York: Farrar, 1982.
Baldwin, James. "Many Thousands Gone." *Notes of a Native Son.* Boston: Beacon, 1955. 18–36.
Banks, Ann, ed. *First-Person America.* New York: Knopf, 1980.
Benston, Kimberly W., ed. *Speaking for You: The Vision of Ralph Ellison.* Washington, DC: Howard UP, 1987.
Black World 20 (Dec. 1970). Special issue devoted to Ellison.
Bloom, Harold, ed. *Modern Critical Views: Ralph Ellison.* New York: Chelsea, 1986.
Botkin, B. A. *New York City Folklore.* New York: Random, 1956.
Busby, Mark. *Ralph Ellison.* Boston: Twayne, 1991.
Callahan, John F. "Chaos, Complexity, and Possibility: The Historical Frequencies of Ralph Waldo Ellison." Benston 125–43.
Carleton Miscellany 18 (Winter 1980). Special issue devoted to Ellison.

CLA Journal 13 (Mar. 1970). Special issue devoted to Ellison.

Clark, Kenneth. "Morale Among Negroes." Civilian Morale. Ed. Goodwin Watson. Boston: Houghton, 1942. 228–48.

———. "The Zoot Effect in Personality." *Journal of Abnormal Psychology* 40 (Apr. 1945): 143–48.

Cole, Herbert M. *Icons: Ideals and Power in the Art of Africa.* Washington, DC: Smithsonian, 1989.

Cosgrove, Stuart. "The Zoot Suit and Style Warfare." *History Workshop* 18 (Autumn 1984): 77–91.

Couch, W. T., ed. *These Are Our Lives.* By Couch. Chapel Hill: U of North Carolina P, 1939.

Courlander, Harold. *Negro Folk Music, U.S.A.* New York: Columbia UP, 1963.

Covo, Jacqueline. *The Blinking Eye: Ralph Waldo Ellison and His American, French, German, and Italian Critics, 1952–1971.* Metuchen, NJ: Scarecrow, 1974.

Cruse, Harold. *The Crisis of the Negro Intellectual: A Historical Analysis of the Failure of Black Leadership.* 1967. Rpt. New York: Quill, 1984.

Cunard, Nancy, ed. *Negro: An Anthology.* Abridged ed. Hugh Ford. 1934. Rpt. New York: Frederick Ungar, 1970.

Daniel, Pete. "Black Power in the 1920s: The Case of Tuskegee Veterans Hospital." *Journal of Southern History* 36 (1970): 368–88.

Davis, Benjamin J. *Path of Negro Liberation.* New York: New Century, 1947.

Dietze, Rudolf F. *Ralph Ellison: The Genesis of an Artist.* Nürnberg: Verlag, 1982.

Du Bois, W. E. B. *Dusk of Dawn: An Essay Toward an Autobiography of a Race Concept.* 1940. Rpt. New York: Schocken, 1968.

———. "Returning Soldiers." *Crisis* 18 (May 1919): 13–14.

Dunjee, Roscoe. ["The Negro and Communism."] Oklahoma *Black Dispatch.* n.d. *A Documentary History of the Negro People in the United States.* Ed. Herbert Aptheker. 4 vols. Secaucus, NJ: Citadel, 1973. III, 712–14.

Ellison, Ralph. "An American Dilemma: A Review." *Shadow and Act* 303–17.

———."The Art of Fiction." *Shadow and Act* 167–83.

———."The Art of Romare Bearden." *Going to the Territory* 227–38.

——."Change the Joke and Slip the Yoke." *Shadow and Act* 45–59.

——."The Charlie Christian Story." *Shadow and Act* 233–40.

——."An Extravagance of Laughter." *Going to the Territory* 145–97.

——."Eyewitness Story of Riot." *New York Post* 2 Aug. 1943: 4.

——.*Going to the Territory.* New York: Random, 1986.

——."The Golden Age, Time Past." *Shadow and Act* 199–212.

——."The Great Migration." *New Masses* 41 (Dec. 2, 1941): 23–24.

——."Hidden Name and Complex Fate." *Shadow and Act* 144–66.

——.*Invisible Man.* 1952. Rpt. New York: Vintage, 1982.

——."New World A-Coming." *Tomorrow* 3 (Sept. 1943): 67–68.

——."On Bird, Bird-Watching, and Jazz." *Shadow and Act* 221–32.

——."On Initiation Rites and Power." *Going to the Territory* 39–63.

——."Out of the Hospital and Under the Bar." *Soon One Morning: New Writing by American Negroes, 1940–1962.* Ed. Herbert Hill. New York: Knopf, 1963. 242–90.

——."Perspective of Literature." *Going to the Territory* 321–38.

——."Remembering Richard Wright." *Going to the Territory* 198–216.

——. *Shadow and Act.* New York: Random, 1964.

——."That Same Pain, That Same Pleasure." *Shadow and Act* 3–23.

——."Transition: Review of *Blood on the Forge*." *Negro Quarterly* 1 (Spring 1942): 87–92.

——."A Very Stern Discipline." *Going to the Territory* 275–307.

——."The World and the Jug." *Shadow and Act* 107–43.

Fabre, Michel. "From *Native Son* to *Invisible Man*: Some Notes on Ralph Ellison's Evolution in the 1950s." Benston 199–216.

Firestone, Harold. "Cats, Kicks, and Color." *Social Problems* 5 (1957): 3–13.

Ford, James W. "Communism and the Negro." Cunard 146–52.

Forrest, Leon. "Luminosity from the Lower Frequencies." Benston 308–21.

Fullinwider, S. P. *The Mind and Mood of Black America.* Homewood, IL: Dorsey, 1969.

Gordon, Eugene. "Blacks Turn Red." Cunard 138–43.

Granger, Lester B. "The Negro — Friend or Foe of Organized Labor?" *Opportunity* 12 (May 1935): 234–39.

Hayes, Roland. *My Songs: Aframerican Religious Folk Songs.* Boston: Little, Brown, 1948.

Haynes, George Edmund. "Negroes Move North." *Survey* 40 (4 May 1918): 115–22; (4 Jan. 1919): 455–61.

Henry, Charles P. *Culture and African American Politics.* Bloomington: Indiana UP, 1990.

Herndon, Angelo. "Frederick Douglass: Negro Leadership and War." *Negro Quarterly* 1 (Winter-Spring 1943): 303–29.

Hersey, John, ed. *Ralph Ellison: A Collection of Critical Essays.* Englewood Cliffs, NJ: Prentice, 1974.

Howe, Irving. "Black Boys and Native Sons." *Dissent* 10 (Autumn 1963): 353–68.

Huggins, Nathan. *Harlem Renaissance.* New York: Oxford UP, 1971.

Hughes, Langston, and Arna Bontemps. *Book of Negro Folklore.* New York: Dodd, 1957.

Isaacs, Harold. "Five Writers and Their African Ancestors." *Phylon* 21 (1960): 317–36.

Johnson, Charles S. "Black Workers and the City." *Survey Graphic* 6 (Mar. 1925): 641–43, 718–21.

Johnson, James Weldon. *Black Manhattan.* 1930. Rpt. New York: Atheneum, 1968.

Kelley, William Melvin. "The Ivy-League Negro." *Esquire* Aug. 1963: 54–56, 108–09.

Kennedy, Louise Venable. *The Negro Peasant Turns Cityward: Effects of Recent Migrations to Northern Cities.* New York: Columbia UP, 1930.

Killens, John Oliver. Review of *Invisible Man. Freedom* (June 1952). Cruse 235.

Kluger, Richard. *Simple Justice: The History of Brown v. Board of Education and Black America's Struggle for Equality.* New York: Random, 1975.

Lewis, David Levering. *When Harlem Was in Vogue.* New York: Knopf, 1981.

Locke, Alain. "Harlem: Dark Weather-Vane." *Survey Graphic* 35 (Aug. 1936): 457–62, 493–95.

————, ed. *The New Negro: Voices of the Harlem Renaissance.* 1925. Rpt. New York: Atheneum, 1992.

Logan, Rayford, ed. *What the Negro Wants.* Chapel Hill: U of North Carolina P, 1944.

Lomax, Alan. *Mr. Jelly Roll: The Fortunes of Jelly Roll Morton, New Orleans Creole, and "Inventor" of Jazz.* Berkeley: U of California P, 1950.

Lott, Eric. "Double V, Double-Time: Bebop's Politics of Style." *Callaloo* 11 (1988): 597–605.

Martin, Tony, ed. *African Fundamentalism: A Literary and Cultural Anthology of Garvey's Harlem Renaissance.* Dover, MA: Majority, 1991.

McKay, Claude. *Harlem: Negro Metropolis.* New York: Dutton, 1940.

McPherson, James Alan. "Indivisible Man." Interview with Ralph Ellison. Benston 15–29.

Mezzrow, Mezz, and Bernard Wolfe. *Really the Blues.* 1946. Rpt. New York: Citadel, 1990.

Miller, Kelly. *Radicals and Conservatives and Other Essays on the Negro in America.* 1908: Rpt. New York: Schocken, 1968.

Moses, Wilson J. "*Invisible Man* and the American Way of Intellectual History." Parr and Savery 58–64.

Moton, Robert Russo. *Finding a Way Out: An Autobiography.* Garden City, NY: Doubleday, 1921.

Murray, Albert. *South to a Very Old Place.* New York: McGraw, 1971.

————. *Stomping the Blues.* New York: Da Capo, 1976.

Naison, Mark. *Communists in Harlem during the Great Depression.* Urbana: U of Illinois P, 1983.

Neal, Larry. "Ellison's Zoot Suit." Benston 105–24.

Neal, Larry, and LeRoi Jones, eds. *Black Fire: An Anthology of Afro-American Writing.* New York: Morrow, 1968.

Oakley, Giles. *The Devil's Music: A History of the Blues.* New York: Taplinger, 1977.

Odum, Howard, and Guy B. Johnson. *The Negro and His Songs: A Study of Typical Negro Songs of the South.* Chapel Hill: U of North Carolina P, 1925.

————. *Negro Workaday Songs.* Chapel Hill: U of North Carolina P, 1926.

Oliver, Paul. *Blues off the Record: Thirty Years of Blues Commentary.* New York: Da Capo, 1984.

————. *Screening the Blues: Aspects of the Blues Tradition.* New York: Da Capo, 1968.

————. *Songsters and Saints: Vocal Traditions on Race Records.* New York: Cambridge UP, 1984.

O'Meally, Robert. *The Craft of Ralph Ellison.* Cambridge, MA: Harvard UP, 1980.

————, ed. *New Essays on Invisible Man.* New York: Cambridge UP, 1988.

Osofsky, Gilbert. *Harlem: The Making of a Ghetto: Negro New York, 1890–1930.* 2nd ed. New York: Harper, 1971.

Ottley, Roi. *New World A-Coming: Inside Black America.* Boston: Houghton, 1943.

Ottley, Roi, and William J. Weatherby. *The Negro in New York: An Informal Social History.* New York: New York Public Library, 1967.

Parr, Susan Resneck, and Pancho Savery, eds. *Approaches to Teaching Ellison's Invisible Man.* New York: MLA, 1989.

Powell, Adam Clayton, Jr. *Marching Blacks: An Interpretive History of the Rise of the Black Common Man.* New York: Dial, 1945.

Puckett, Newbell Niles. *Folk Beliefs of the Southern Negro.* 1926: Rpt. Montclair, NJ: Patterson Smith, 1968.

Redding, J. Saunders. *No Day of Triumph.* New York: Harper, 1942.

Redl, Fritz. "Zoot Suits: An Interpretation." *Survey Midmonthly* 79 (Oct. 1943): 259–62.

Reilly, John M., ed. *Twentieth-Century Interpretations of Invisible Man: A Collection of Essays.* Englewood Cliffs, NJ: Prentice, 1970.

Remnick, David. "Visible Man." *The New Yorker* 14 Mar. 1994: 34–38.

Rogers, J. A. "Who Is the New Negro, and Why?" *Messenger* 9 (Mar. 1927): 4–6.

Savery, Pancho. "'Not like an arrow, but a boomerang': Ellison's Existential Blues." Parr and Savery 65–74.

Scarborough, Dorothy. *On the Trail of Negro Folk-Songs.* Cambridge, MA: Harvard UP, 1925.

Singer, Barry. *Black and Blue: The Life and Lyrics of Andy Razaf.* New York: Schirmer, 1992.

Siskind, Aaron. *Harlem Photographs, 1932–1940*. Washington, DC: Smithsonian, 1990.

Spero, Sterling, and Abram L. Harris. *The Black Worker: The Negro and the Labor Movement*. New York: Columbia UP, 1931.

Stepto, Robert B. *From Behind the Veil: A Study of Afro American Narrative*. Urbana: U of Illinois P, 1979.

Talley, Thomas W. *Negro Folk Rhymes*. New York: Macmillan, 1922.

Tate, Claudia. "Notes on the Invisible Women in Ralph Ellison's *Invisible Man*." Benston, 163–72.

Trimmer, Joseph F. *A Casebook on Ralph Ellison's Invisible Man*. New York: Crowell, 1972.

Tyler, Bruce M. "Black Jive and White Repression." *Journal of Ethnic Studies* 16 (1989): 31–66.

Walker, Anne Kendrick. *Tuskegee and the Black Belt: Portrait of a Race*. Richmond, VA: Dietz, 1944.

Watts, Jerry G. *Heroism and the Black Intellectual: Ralph Ellison, Politics, and Afro-American Intellectual Life*. Chapel Hill: U of North Carolina P, 1994.

Wilkins, Roy. "The Harlem Riot." *Crisis* 50 (Sept. 1943): 263.

Wright, Richard. "Blueprint for Negro Writing." *Richard Wright Reader*. Eds. Ellen Wright and Michel Fabre. New York: Harper, 1978.

———. "I Tried to Be a Communist." *The God that Failed*. Ed. Richard Crossman. New York: Harper, 1949. 115–62.

———. *12 Million Black Voices*. 1941. Rpt. New York: Thunder's Mouth, 1988.

Yardley, Jonathan. "30 Years on the 'Raft of Hope.'" *Washington Post* 16 Apr. 1982: B6.

Acknowledgments (continued from page iv)

W. E. B. Du Bois, "Of Our Spiritual Strivings" and "Of Mr. Booker T. Washington." From Du Bois, W. E. B., *The Souls of Black Folk: Essays and Sketches.* Chicago: A. C. McClurg & Co., 1953, pp. 1–4, 41–43, 50–52, and 55–59. Reprint, Millwood, N. Y.: Kraus-Thomson Organization Limited, 1973. Reproduced with permission of Kraus International Publications.

Ralph Ellison, "Harlem Is Nowhere." From *Shadow and Act* by Ralph Ellison. Copyright © 1953, 1964 and renewed 1981, 1992 by Ralph Ellison. Reprinted by permission. Reprinted in the British Commonwealth by permission of the William Morris Agency, Inc., on behalf of the Author. Copyright © 1943 by Ralph Ellison.

Ralph Ellison, "The Negro and the Second World War." From *Negro Quarterly,* vol. 1, no. 4 (Winter–Spring, 1943). Reprinted by permission of the William Morris Agency, Inc., on behalf of the Author.

Federal Writers' Project, "Portrait of Harlem." From *New York Panorama* by Federal Writers' Project. Copyright © 1938 by The Guild's Committee for Federal Writers' Publications, Inc. Reprinted by permission of Pantheon Books, a division of Random House, Inc.

Marcus Garvey, "Africa for the Africans" and "Speech Delivered at Liberty Hall N.Y.C. During Second International Convention of Negroes." Reprinted with the permission of Atheneum Publishers, an imprint of Macmillan Publishing Company, from *Philosophy and Opinions of Marcus Garvey* by Amy Jacques-Garvey, editor. Copyright © 1923, 1925 by Amy Jacques-Garvey.

Leo Gurley, "Sweet-the-Monkey," originally untitled. From *First-Person America,* edited by Ann Banks. Copyright © 1980 by Alfred A. Knopf. Reprinted 1991 by W. W. Norton. Reprinted by permission of Ann Banks.

Bernice Kelly Harris, from "Tore Up and a-Movin'." Reprinted from *These Are Our Lives* by the Federal Writers' Project Regional Staff. Copyright © 1939 by The University of North Carolina Press. Used by permission of the publisher.

Harry Haywood, from *The Road to Negro Liberation.* Copyright © 1934 by Workers Library Publishers. Reprinted with permission.

Will Herberg, "Marxism and the American Negro." From *Negro: An Anthology* edited by Nancy Cunard (1934; reprint Frederick Ungar, 1970). Reprinted with permission.

Langston Hughes, "Cowards from the Colleges." From *Good Morning Revolution: Uncollected Writings of Social Protest by Langston Hughes* edited by Faith Berry. Copyright © 1992, 1973 by Faith Berry. Published by arrangement with Carol Publishing Group. A Citadel Press Book.

"Jack the Rabbit! Jack the Bear!" originally untitled, from *American Negro Folk-Songs* by Newman White. Copyright © 1928 by Harvard University Press. Reprinted by permission.

Charles S. Johnson, from *Shadow of the Plantation* by Charles S. Johnson. Copyright © 1934 by University of Chicago Press. Reprinted with permission of University of Chicago Press.

James Weldon Johnson, from *Negro Americans, What Now?* Copyright © 1934 by Viking. Reprinted by permission of Ollie Jewel Sims Okala.

Avram Landy, from "Marxism and the Woman Question." Copyright © 1943 Workers Library Publishers. Reprinted by permission.

Alain Locke, from *The New Negro*. Reprinted with the permission of Atheneum Publishers, an imprint of Macmillan Publishing Company, from *The New Negro: Voices of the Harlem Renaissance* by Alain Locke, editor. Copyright 1925 by Albert & Charles Boni, Inc.

Claude McKay, "Harlem Runs Wild." From the April 3, 1935, issue of *The Nation*. Reprinted with permission from *The Nation* magazine. © The Nation Company, Inc.

Mezz Mezzrow and Bernard Wolfe, from *Really the Blues* by Milton "Mezz" Mezzrow and Bernard Wolfe. Copyright © 1946 by Mezz Mezzrow and Bernard Wolfe. Published by arrangement with Carol Publishing Group. A Citadel Underground Book.

Gunnar Myrdal, from *An American Dilemma: The Negro Problem and Modern Democracy* by Gunnar Myrdal. Copyright © 1944, 1962 by Harper & Row, Publishers, Inc. Reprinted by permission of HarperCollins Publishers, Inc.

Adam Clayton Powell, Sr., from *Riots and Ruins*. Copyright © 1945 by Richard R. Smith. Reprinted by permission of Ayer Publishers.

Andy Razaf, *(What Did I Do to Be So) Black and Blue*. Words are by Andy Razaf. Music by Thomas "Fats" Waller and Harry Brooks. Copyright © 1929 (Renewed 1957) and assigned to Razaf Music Co., care of The Songwriters' Guild of America, Chappell and Co., Inc. (Intersong Music Publisher) and EMI Mills Music, Inc. All rights reserved. Used by permission.

"Run, Nigger, Run," originally untitled, from *American Ballads and Folk Songs* (Macmillan, 1934). Collected, adapted and arranged by John A. Lomax and Alan Lomax TRO - © Copyright 1934 (Renewed) Ludlow Music, Inc., New York, N.Y. Used by permission.

Sterling Spero and Abram L. Harris, from *The Black Worker: The Negro and the Labor Movement* by Sterling Spero and Abram L. Harris. © 1931 Columbia University Press, New York. Reprinted with permission of the publisher.

Anson Phelps Stokes, from *Tuskegee Institute: The First Fifty Years*. Copyright © 1931 by Tuskegee Institute Press. Reprinted with permission of Tuskegee University Archives.

Peetie Wheatstraw, "The Devil's Son-in-Law." From "Folk Songs of Chicago Negroes" by Muriel Davis Longini. Reproduced by permission of the American Folklore Society from *Journal of American Folklore 52:203, 1939*. Not for further reproduction.

"Why Mr. Dog Runs Brer Rabbit," from "Tales of the Rabbit from Georgia Negroes" by Emma M. Backus. Reproduced by permission of the American Folklore Society from *Journal of American Folklore 12:45, 1899*. Not for further reproduction.

Richard Wright, from the book, *12 Million Black Voices* by Richard Wright.

Photo Credits

Interior photographs: Statue of Booker T. Washington, Tuskegee Institute Campus, Eric J. Sundquist, 1994. Louis Armstrong, Michael Ochs Archives, Venice, CA. Three Sharecroppers, Dorothea Lange/Library of Congress. Jim Crow Bank, photograph courtesy of Jan Lindenberger. Leg Shackles on Southern Convicts, copyright © Margaret Bourke White. Courtesy of the Jane Corkin Gallery, Toronto. Sid Grossman, *Harlem Street Scene, 1939* (detail). Federal Arts Program, the Museum of the City of New York. Harlem, *125th Street, 1938–39*, Street Mass Meeting, Morgan & Marvin Smith. Photographs and Prints Division, Schomburg Center/NY Public Library, Astor Lenox Tilden Foundations. *Eviction,* Harlem Street Scenes, Morgan & Marvin Smith. Photographs and Prints Division, Schomburg Center/NY Public Library, Astor Lenox Tilden Foundations. *Harlem Riot,* 1943. Bettman Archives, NY.